Ethnic Pride, American Patriotism

Slovaks and Other New Immigrants in the Interwar Era

JUNE GRANATIR ALEXANDER

TEMPLE UNIVERSITY PRESS
Philadelphia

Temple University Press
1601 North Broad Street
Philadelphia PA 19122
www.temple.edu/tempress

Copyright © 2004 by Temple University
All rights reserved
Published 2004
Printed in the United States of America

Library of Congress Cataloging-in-Publication Data

Alexander, June Granatir, 1948–
    Ethnic pride, American patriotism : Slovaks and other new immigrants
in the interwar era / June Granatir Alexander.
        p.   cm.
    Includes bibliographical references and index.
    ISBN 1-59213-251-0 (cl.) — ISBN 1-59213-252-9 (pbk.)
        1. Slovak Americans—Politics and government.   2. Slovak Americans—
Ethnic identity.   3. East European Americans—Politics and government.
4. East European Americans—Ethnic identity.   5. United States—Emigration
and immigration—History—20th century.   I. Title.

E184.S64A415 2004
973'.049187–dc22   2003064568

2   4   6   8   9   7   5   3   1

For John
with love and gratitude

Contents

Preface and Acknowledgments

HISTORY TAKES ODD TWISTS and turns and so, too, does the writing of history. This project started more than a decade ago as a comparative investigation of ethnic groups during the Great Depression, an era that, fifteen years ago, studies of immigration and ethnicity had generally neglected. Initial attempts to conceptualize the resultant research compelled me to admit that, rather than exploring the past, I had been dictating to it. The questions I was asking reflected the then current state of scholarly studies and, instead of letting history speak to me, I was superimposing contemporary fascinations as well as my own interests on immigrants and their children who lived through the interwar era. As a result, I shifted my approach to focus on group-generated activities and broadened the chronological time frame. The growing scholarship on U.S. and ethnic history has helped sharpen my inquiry, but the burgeoning research on "whiteness" was the only scholarship that unavoidably forced its way into my reevaluation.

My reassessment also stemmed in part from a growing—if reluctant—willingness to admit that my own life experience was not only a valid influence on my interpretation of the past, it offered insight. Raised in a family with parents of ethnically different backgrounds (one of eastern European ancestry; the other of mixed northern European heritage), inculcating an ethnic identity was not part of my or my siblings' upbringing. Yet looking back on those years, it is patently obvious that ethnicity was evident everywhere. It was there in the various holiday traditions upheld by nuclear and extended families. It was apparent in life-cycle events when weddings, funerals, and religious rituals invariably included people who spoke English laden with heavy accents and who reminisced about the land where they had been born and what life "in America" had been like.

On a community-wide scale, ethnicity was visible in the nationality schools, which in the 1950s still existed in this industrial region stretching along the banks of the Ohio River. Many, albeit not all, second-generation parents enrolled their offspring in these nationality institutions, where admission was based on ethnic background. These were adults who, if theorists were right, had purportedly tried to forget their "new immigrant" roots. Although parents from the older immigrant groups sent their children to multiethnic schools, there were discernible patterns in their choices as well. In the centralized high school, boys and girls who had attended the various elementary institutions were finally brought together in a setting where, into the mid-1960s, at least, ethnic consciousness remained a felt sense. Genuine interethnic friendships were common, and it would be reprehensible to suggest otherwise. Ethnicity, however, was at times more relevant than at others, especially when some parents pressured their children to date people of their own ancestral background. These were adults who had participated in the "great common experience" of World War II, including serving in multiethnic military units. This was an experience that, if observers were right, had diluted ethnic particularities, expanded horizons, and hastened second-generation assimilation. Why should these parents care about the ethnic background of people with whom their children socialized? So, although not raised in an ethnically conscious family, I certainly grew up in an ethnic world that some second-generation individuals were trying to hand down to the third and, in the case of northern Europeans, to the fourth and fifth generations and beyond. As a social historian, it is hard to ignore the implications of one's own life experience.

In the mid-1990s, my father inadvertently drove home the ongoing impact that the American-born generations could have on ethnic life in communities. He expressed amazement over his church's highly successful fund-raising effort during Lent. In just a few years what had started with the take-out sale of pierogi, which, despite the Polish spelling organizers used, is a dish belonging to several Slavic groups, and haluška, which is Slovak, had expanded into a lucrative undertaking. Between 1993 and 2000, volunteers had made nearly 323,000 pierogi, and the "Pierogi and Lenten Food Project" was realizing annual net profits of $28,000. Nostalgia no doubt partially explains the popularity of these ethnic foods; the menu, however, had expanded to include an Italian item as well. The Slavic cuisine represented one tradition in the parish; the Italian represented another. Various ethnic groups in the congregation, then, helped turn this affair into a multiethnic undertaking that had the positive effect of benefiting their mutually supported church. What, my father asked, would happen when these "old-timers" passed away? "Old-timers"? Was this not the term historically applied to *immigrants* who reminisced about the Old Country and, by now, had surely passed away? No, he was talking about second-generation persons who had developed a pride in ancestry and, when the opportunity arose, were sufficiently committed to roll up their sleeves to make sure that their group enjoyed a presence in community or multiethnic undertakings. My father was not one of these ethnic activists, but he knew who they were. They were not "leaders" who had any economic or social stake in promoting ethnicity. They were dedicated people who, under certain conditions, would try to prick the sentiments of others who shared the same ancestral heritage.

It impressed me at the time that this local spurt of ethnicity, which brought people together in support of their church, was taking place in a period when some critics, especially scholars, were moaning that diversity, now dubbed multiculturalism, was "disuniting America." Others were heaving a sigh of relief that the "ethnic revival" seemed to be on the wane. From the view of outsiders, it would seem that they were correct. Certainly, the rhetoric that had characterized the emergence of the new ethnicity in the 1960s had died down. Few seemed to notice, though, that the fall of the iron curtain had stirred renewed interest in what—since most first-generation pre–World War I immigrants had passed away—were truly ancestral homelands.

While organizers were planning local ethnic events and volunteers were busily producing ethnic fare for Lenten sales, in the early 1990s the country was also just getting over one of its perennial spasms of indignant nationalism. To be more specific, an obsession about preventing "desecration" of the American flag had caused a resurgence of flag veneration in the late 1980s. There was revived fervor for the Pledge of Allegiance. This fixation with manifestations of patriotism intrigued me. Given the issues the country was facing, it was puzzling that visits to flag factories could be sanctioned as relevant or even seemly to a serious presidential campaign. Many in the country, though, reveled in such superficial expressions of patriotism. Scholars have pointed to societal tensions, whipped-up media coverage, and political opportunism as nurturing renewed obsessions about flag desecration. But the question remains: why is it that proponents of public exhibitions of patriotism can find such a receptive audience? What is it in this country's history that makes people so prone to equating patriotism with allegiant displays, especially playing public homage to the flag? My research told me that part of the answer could be found in the decades stretching from the first to the second world wars.

In the course of this research it also became evident that while historians and social scientists have focused on flare-ups of nativism and nationalism, the country has also experienced periodic spurts of ethnicity. Yes, some scholars have casually noted this phenomenon, but what they have not done is recognize that these eruptions represented the surfacing of sentiments that had gone out of the public eye but continued to flow constant, especially in local communities. The church-related ethnic undertaking that I described earlier and the patriotic fervor that surged forth into the early 1990s took place independently. There is no evidence that they were connected. But the fact that ethnically grounded activities and nationalist surges occur separately obscures the fact that, at times, they have been concurrent. Exploring the waxing and waning manifestations of patriotism and ethnicity during the crucial decades spanning the two world wars became *one* objective of my research. I should clarify that the text of this volume was completed before September 11, 2001. Thus, the outburst of patriotism and ubiquitous flag-waving spawned in the aftermath of that event had no impact on the thinking that went into this work. A major objective of my research was, in fact, to focus on the "quiet periods" when public expressions of patriotism and ethnicity were not so readily evident.

What follows is not a "celebratory" history or a "celebration" of ethnicity. All too often captious observers have applied these descriptions to the scholarly studies of ethnic groups that appeared in the last decades of the twentieth century. Unfortunately, polemics surrounding the "ethnic revival" have overshadowed the phenomenon's factual side. No amount of denigration or rationalization can erase the fact that appeals to ethnicity worked. In short, there were ethnic sentiments there to rouse.

My investigation of the interwar experience of Slovaks and other new immigrants thus attempts to explore, in one historian's words, "the drama of a multiethnic people."[1] A major conviction underlying this work is that to understand this drama of a multiethnic people, who have embraced a larger American identity, investigators need to look at contemporary society from the perspective of ethnic groups. This is not, however, history from the bottom up, but history that looks at the top and the bottom echelons of an ethnic group. It is concerned as much with ordinary people as with those who held prominent positions in national organizations. Too often, especially in the recent past, scholars have tried to speak for immigrants and their children without giving them a voice. My intent is to let them speak for themselves as clearly as I can.

GIVEN MY ORIGINAL PLAN to fashion a comparative study of ethnic organizations, research conducted during that early stage included examining collections deposited at the Archives of Industrial Society (University of Pittsburgh) and the Balch Institute for Ethnic Studies in Philadelphia. Although their holdings informed this study far less than originally anticipated, and the specific individuals who kindly helped me have moved on, I still wish to acknowledge the assistance and benefits I derived from consulting materials at these repositories. I am particularly grateful to the staff of the Immigration History Research Center (IHRC) at the University of Minnesota, where much of the research for this book was conducted. While I believe the IHRC staff members are by nature dedicated individuals, the professionalism that characterizes the center nevertheless reflects the leadership of Joel Wurl, the center's curator and assistant director. Joel is an exemplary model as he cheerfully shares his own expertise and personally assists researchers on site; after they leave, he does not forget them. Whether requesting photocopies, seeking to purchase microfilm, or asking for the expeditious preparation of illustrations, he is ever accommodating. As a "keeper of history," Joel marvelously blends the instincts of archivist and scholar and, in so doing, contributes mightily to the advancement of scholarship. Early research for this project was supported by an IHRC grant-in-aid. By giving me various Slovak-language materials, George T. Halischak, a friend of my parents, has served as a small treasure trove of hard-to-find publications and stray issues of newspapers. I thank him.

I cannot publicly thank each person who has supported my work, but I must acknowledge that, along the way, this project has benefited from the advice of many friends, colleagues, and scholars. I thank them, too. A few people made substantive contributions. With his usual perceptiveness, Rudy Vecoli asked probing questions at the crucial point when I was grappling with the difficult decision to reconceptualize the work. At the same time, participants in a session at the IHRC served as a sounding board and offered welcome comments. I profited from private discussions with Ivan Čizmič and from his remarks during sessions at a 1994 international conference in Maribor, Slovenia, where I presented the paper "Ethnic Fraternalism and Working-Class Activism: The

Expanding Role of Slovak Fraternal Organizations in the United States during the Interwar Years," which was subsequently published by the University of Maribor in the proceedings of the conference. Aspects of that paper were incorporated into Chapter 7 of this work. I also benefited from comments by David Reimers and the audience at the "Conference on World War II and Ethnic America," sponsored by New York University in 1997, where I presented "War and Ethnicity: Slovak Americans and National Identity during World War II," which was also integrated into this book. I am immensely grateful to Tom Dublin for his extraordinarily careful, thoughtful reading of the manuscript. His incisive comments helped sharpen a vital argument. An anonymous reader for Temple University Press also made keen observations. My long tenure as secretary of the Immigration and Ethnic History Society (IEHS) regularly brought me in contact with scholars who share my interest in immigration and ethnic history. Attending annual conventions, meeting with numerous IEHS members, and participating in lively discussions helped create the scholarly and friendly atmosphere so important to seeing a major project through to completion. I especially treasure time that my husband, John, and I spent with Ronald Bayor and his late wife, Leslie. I look forward to Ron's ongoing friendship; I will forever miss Leslie's warmth, wit, and engaging conversation.

And then there is John K. Alexander. I am not sure I could ever find the words adequately to describe what he has meant to this project and, indeed, to all my scholarly undertakings. For thirty years, John has stood by my side and encouraged me. Alas, for these reasons, I am repeating the same thanks I have so gratefully expressed before. Serving as my first reader, John carefully read numerous versions of the manuscript and offered constructive criticism and advice. I am fortunate that, although he is my most devoted supporter, John never allows his desire to be supportive to outweigh the need to be critical. The work, therefore, substantially benefited from the keen analytical skills of this amazingly perceptive, knowledgeable historian. John also lovingly helped in any other way he could, which meant serving as an editor and at times research assistant. He is a first-rate "production manager" and technical adviser. Writing this book relied so much on his support that it is with love and gratitude that I dedicate it to him.

Ethnic Pride, American Patriotism

*Slovaks and Other New Immigrants
in the Interwar Era*

Introduction

Getting a Perspective on "New Immigrant" America

THIS WORK OPENS with World War I and closes with World War II. A major part of the discussion, though, is devoted to the interlude between these two dramatic events. The purpose is to examine a period when, because immigration faded from the national agenda and the Great Depression dominated American life, it has been assumed that immigrants and their children gave little thought to ethnicity. By focusing on Slovaks, this book attempts to view the era from the standpoint of the "new immigrants" and give them a chance to tell the story from their perspective. Since the United States used restrictive laws to curtail the addition of more foreign-born inhabitants, the demographic characteristics of the new immigrant population in 1920 furnish an essential profile of the first- and second-generation people who would live through the interwar era. To explore the interim from their perspective, it is necessary to keep in mind some distinguishing features about America's new immigrants from Europe.

By the early twentieth century, conducting America's decennial censuses involved more than merely counting the number of inhabitants; it entailed scrutinizing the results and their implications for American society. The 1920 census sustained that tradition. It confirmed what some Americans had been dreading since the turn of the century. With slightly more than half (51.4%) of its 105,710,620 inhabitants residing in incorporated places exceeding 2,500 persons, the United States had become an urban country.[1] The 1920 enumeration reinforced a reality already evident in the census ten years earlier: since the turn of the century, America's population had grown increasingly ethnically diverse. The tabulations listed forty specific "countries of origin" and thirty-one different mother tongues.[2] The fourteenth census showed that more than one-half of America's 13,920,692 foreign-born persons had emigrated from new immigrant homelands. Eastern and southern Europeans represented nearly two-thirds (65.3%) of the contingent that had originated from non-English-speaking countries.[3]

While new immigrants were dispersed throughout the country, the preponderance of them and their children lived in urban areas located in what the census designated the Middle Atlantic and East North Central states. The presence of diverse ethnic groups made Americans associate "cities" with the "foreign born." But, while calculations based on the census showed that at least 85 percent of the individual groups from eastern and southern Europe were residing in officially designated urban areas, a significant number actually lived in medium-sized towns.[4] When these immigrants looked out their windows, they saw smokestacks or coal cars, not bustling city streets. Moreover, in industrial and mining towns, new immigrants could make up a larger percentage of the population than in some of America's cities. Hence, the inhabitants of some small towns felt the presence of the foreign born and could be more acutely aware of ethnic diversity than big-city residents.

In 1920, immigrants were much older than the general population. The median age for Americans identified as "native white of native parentage" was 22.7 years; it was 40 for foreign-born whites. Immigrants accounted for less than 2 percent of white children under fifteen years old but represented nearly 28 percent of America's elderly white population over fifty-nine.[5] Migration patterns, however, had skewed this demographic profile. The foreign-born population from northern and western European countries claimed far more elderly than did the new immigrants. Not only had northern Europeans arrived earlier; the economic motivations that had nurtured the more recent migration from eastern and southern Europe meant that working-age people, normally fifteen years and older, had emigrated. As a result, in 1920 new immigrants were usually younger middle-aged people. Children typically made up less than 5 percent and the elderly less than 7 percent of an individual new immigrant group.[6]

New immigrant America was also decidedly more male than the general population. Although the proportion varied among the nationality groups, the average sex ratio was 118.4 males to 100 females. The excess of younger foreign-born males would have a long-term impact on new immigrant America. Although some single men still intended to send to their homelands for brides, in all likelihood in the 1920s immigrants who wanted to marry would have to find a spouse in the United States. The census provided little data for determining whether "mixed marriages"—the unions between foreign-born immigrants and native-born individuals—were ethnically endogamous. Statistics identified the immigrants' nationalities but listed their partners simply as "native born." However, even investigators who adopted the philosophy that marriages between immigrants and native-born Americans were indices of assimilation noted that the data, albeit sparse, suggested that immigrants were marrying second-generation persons of their own nationality. In essence, these marriages were likely intergenerational, intraethnic unions.[7]

The demographic characteristics that overarched new immigrant America in 1920 mirrored the complex differences that prevailed *within* each individual group. For despite their shared "immigrant" classification, significant distinctions existed among newcomers of the same nationality. Varying arrival times and ages represented two of these meaningful differences. Some foreign-born persons had been in the United States for three decades or more; others had lived in the country for less than a decade; another small contingent had come after the war. The immigrant generation, therefore, was made up of people who had achieved different levels of acculturation. The foreign-born population also included the generation and a half, meaning individuals who had been brought to the United States as infants or young children and had thus spent their formative years in the New World. Although they were technically immigrants, their experience more closely resembled that of native-born people.[8] In addition, despite its large middle-aged composition, the first generation contained a broad range of ages and included people at different stages in their family cycle. By 1920, some newcomers had completed their families and had young, adolescent, and even adult offspring; at the same time, a large segment of married couples were just starting their families. Age differences and varying degrees of acculturation among immigrants could be as pronounced as the significant distinctions between them and the native born.

Within the second generation, there were even more subtle diversities. It, too, encompassed a wide age range. In reality, the "second generation" comprised infants in their cradles and children in elementary school as well as young and older adults laboring in mills, factories, and coal mines. Depending on time between births, siblings could experience significantly dissimilar childhoods. The offspring of mixed-marriage couples would grow up in a different family environment from that of youths with two foreign-born parents. Intergenerational unions created familial situations in which one parent was fluent in English and one probably was not. Thus, their children were more likely to speak English from early childhood than those whose parents were immigrants. Whether children of mixed or foreign-born parentage, the more than 6.3 million children of new immigrants could typically expect to be part of a large household. With an average of four or more children, new immigrant families had slightly higher birthrates than the rest of America's population.[9]

Second-generation children of the 1920s could anticipate a different childhood from that of those who had matured before World War I. In postwar America, youths could expect to attend school through the primary grades, and only a few would be gainfully employed before they attained at least fifteen years of age. Child-labor and school-attendance legislation, primarily in northern states, meant that by 1920 more children spent their early ages studying in school instead of drudging at menial jobs. In 1920, parents of 94.1 percent of all the country's second-generation youths told census takers that their children, ages seven to thirteen years, went to school. The figures, of course, belie a reality of new immigrant America: some parents provided false information concerning their children. In addition, part-time or seasonal employment might have been excluded. Still, for the second generation, by 1920 the trend was toward more elementary education and less gainful employment at early ages.[10]

The nearly 7 million eastern and southern Europeans living in the United States at the time of the 1920 census became the mainstay of America's new immigrant population for the next two decades. As a result of restrictive laws, the number of newly arrived immigrants from eastern and southern Europe fell to fewer than 1.2 million persons for the entire decade of the 1920s. With deaths, the obvious net effect was to reduce the foreign-born portion of that population. The increase of native-born children meant that the second generation would ultimately become the major component of what the census termed "foreign white stock." Like other children of the day, second-generation new immigrants would force their parents to endure the rebellions historically associated with the maturation process from adolescence to adulthood. For them, though, challenges to conventional norms included defying parental traditions grounded in foreign cultures. Equally important, both aging immigrants and second-generation people of all ages had been stigmatized by the Immigration Act of 1924 as "undesirables" or "inferior" peoples. During the interwar era, they would have to cope with this reality as well as with the catastrophes and turmoil that characterized the period.

While no single nationality embodied the "new immigration," Slovaks, the second-largest Slavic group to emigrate to the United States, were representative of Americans whose native or ancestral roots were in eastern Europe. Data gleaned from census tables show that, in terms of demographic makeup, Slovaks typified the new immigrant pattern. The foreign-born population, which was recorded as 274,948 persons in 1920, represented 44.3 percent of the Slovak "stock"; the American-born contingent totaled 344,918 (55.6%). Children of mixed native and foreign parentage made up about 7.5 percent of the native-born total. The ratio of men to women, which characterized America's Slavic populations in general, suggested that the number of Slovak children of mixed parentage would increase over the next two decades. Their migration and settlement patterns had taken most Slovaks to the country's industrial north. The socioeconomic makeup of the Slovak populace also resembled that of other new immigrants. Each nationality group did boast a contingent of self-employed people, professionals, and small shopkeepers, but the majority of eastern Europeans toiled in America's mines, manufacturing plants, and mills. Women were engaged in domestic service or held unskilled jobs in factories.[11] Despite social stratification within ethnic communities, most Slovak immigrants remained industrial workers throughout their lifetimes.

Of course, shared demographic characteristics and socioeconomic patterns, which highlight similarities, cannot erase differences that distinguished the various nationalities. Each ethnic group was unique; it would be a distortion to claim otherwise. At the same time, in the early decades of the twentieth century, America's new immigrants from Europe faced similar circumstances. Thus, while groups were distinct, there is a common story to be told. For this reason, I determined that my investigation could be anchored to one immigrant group, the Slovaks who emigrated from northern Hungary. The work, however, is not tethered to that group. This book is about "new immigrants" and their children, not just Slovaks.

As a research strategy, focusing on a single group had decided advantages. Instead of being constrictive, this approach allowed me to broaden my investigation to explore diverse aspects of the first- and second-generation experience over a significant time period. It let me probe deeply into the nettlesome issues of cultural maintenance and intergenerational relations. I was able to examine an array of ethnic activities carried out in local communities nationwide and also to scrutinize the extensive discourse about a range of issues that captured the attention of new immigrant Americans. Moreover, Slovaks of the era themselves would not let the story be narrowly cast. They forced me—and, I hope, my readers in turn—to listen to the more inclusive story they were telling and to consider the wider context of their experience. While it is no surprise that ethnically oriented activities could be shaped by the world around them, this focus on Slovaks uncovered a more complex picture. In addition to anti-foreign sentiments, new immigrants were acutely aware of what they commonly referred to as "other nationalities," a collective term for non-Slovak ethnic groups. Slovak activities were, in part, molded by an awareness of "other nationalities" and what they were doing. Thus, Slovaks function as a lens through which we can not only view America's new immigrant communities but also get their perspective on the crucial decades spanning the twentieth century's two world wars. This study of the Slovak experience, together with its underlying emphasis on "other nationalities," will, I hope, serve as a challenge for future investigations to discern both similarities and differences among the various ethnic groups.

Perhaps most important, this approach permitted in-depth analyses that helped me give voice to thoughts otherwise unheard. For example, it was possible to find out what immigrants meant by "Americanization" and why many actually embraced particular aspects of the idea. I was able to give second-generation individuals a platform to speak for themselves. While one historian lamented that she "wanted to know what working people of the era actually said about their ethnic benefit societies" but could not, by relying on group-generated documents, I was able to learn what they said and to hear it in a way that provides a vivid, yet complex, picture.[12]

Finally, this focused approach helps counter an unsettling trend in recent historical scholarship. The stress on cultural history, together with investigations that fall into the category of "whiteness" studies, seems to be sliding backward, away from the late-twentieth-century attempt to investigate issues from inside ethnic communities. In essence, researchers are slighting materials produced by ethnic groups in favor of suppositions about how first- and second-generation Americans perceived their world. Unfortunately, more and more, commentators are returning to the traditional inclination of speaking for immigrants and their children without giving them a voice. The investigation offered here rests on the premise that it is essential to focus on how immigrants and their offspring interpreted issues, and, in light of their experiences, what battles *they* felt were worth fighting and how *they* waged them.

This work is a conscious attempt to look at the contemporary world from within ethnic communities and thus can be characterized as history from the inside out.

Given the burgeoning scholarship on "race," any discussion aimed at providing a perspective on new immigrant America must give some attention to terminology. Scholars have perceptively demonstrated that modern-day understandings of "ethnicity" are inadequate for fully depicting the history of the new immigrant experience. Perceptions, and especially rankings, of white new immigrants, they remind us, were racial.[13] Nevertheless, this study employs the terms "ethnic," "ethnic group," and "ethnicity" because, despite the objections some scholars have been raising, from the vantage point of the turn-of-the-century new immigrants and their offspring, these terms are appropriate.[14] "New immigrant" is also used because it was *the* term that contemporaries regularly used to identify individuals from southern and eastern Europe; it was universally employed to differentiate between them and the earlier immigrant groups from northern and western Europe. By convention, the descriptions "old" and "new" applied to Europeans and excluded those from Asia, Mexico, and elsewhere. It would be ahistorical not to employ terms that contemporaries used and understood.[15]

Ethnic activism is a focal point of this analysis. As used here, ethnic activism denotes two types of activities. First, it means actions undertaken by individuals to forward their own group's interests; second, it includes collective actions—undertaken as *an ethnic body*—by members of a group for purposes that could promote but also transcend the particular interests of their own nationality. As happened with nativism, ethnic activism could recede from the national scene, become an undercurrent in American society, and under certain circumstances boil to the surface again.[16] This activism was fueled in part by persons committed to preserving separate ethnic identities but was dependent on stirring ethnic sentiments within the larger community.

The beginning and ending points for this work were determined by the fact that both world wars were high points of ethnic activism. Each apex was marked by rhetoric, a frenzy of coordinated activities, and agendas that went beyond the parochial concerns of ordinary immigrants and their offspring. The substantive analysis falls into three chronological periods, but the story is told in two parts. Part I, "The Transatlantic Years," which includes Chapters 1 through 3, examines the period spanning World War I to the Immigration Act of 1924. During this early transatlantic phase, Old World issues captured the interest of ethnic activists and inspired wartime activities. For Slovaks, homeland politics continued to exert an influence as they tried to fashion a distinct identity. The twin effects of the 1924 immigration law, which stigmatized eastern and southern Europeans and effectively stopped immigration from their native lands, accelerated an already detectable shift from an emphasis on homeland matters to a concern with the American scene.

Part II, "Turning Inward," covers the two decades after 1924 and carries the story into World War II. Chapters 4 through 7 explore the mid-1920s to the late 1930s. During these years, in what can be described as a quiescent period, ethnic activism lost its national–international political focus and turned inward to address nagging problems of group survival and achieving respectability in a heterogeneous society. There was a heightened stress on the ideological components of an American identity. Nevertheless, in this period activism receded into an undertow of community activities and nationally based campaigns to sustain an ethnic consciousness. With input by the second generation, the period saw a reassessment of what made up an ethnic identity and a shifting emphasis from language retention to pride in ancestry. In the 1930s, hardships engendered by the Great Depression, especially the intensely personal impact at the community level and on local fraternal lodges, nurtured an ethnic activism that reached across generational lines as well as beyond nationality. While scholars have typically focused on ethnic involvement in the labor movement, this work investigates collective actions to get federal social-insurance legislation for the elderly and America's laboring classes enacted. In essence, class and ethnic interests converged to spark ethnic activism on behalf of the larger society.

Finally, Chapter 8 shows how ethnic activism in the United States surged forth in the 1940s as part of the unified campaign behind America's war effort. Homeland issues actually generated this resurgence on the eve of World War II. Wartime unity campaigns, which acknowledged but coincidentally downplayed ethnicity in favor of stressing a national identity, were nevertheless beholden to the country's persistent ethnic diversity and to the ongoing relevance of ethnicity for both the foreign and native born.

The methodology for this investigation was shaped in part by a recognition that America's ethnic populations had two levels: a national and a local. Ethnic organizations and newspapers, which reached out to a dispersed public and were run by people dedicated to the group's broader political, economic, or social interests, made up the national level. The local plane, which consisted of small towns as well as big cities where ordinary immigrants and their offspring lived, was more demographically and socially diversified.

Since this work postulates that, when analyzing the dynamics behind manifestations of ethnicity, it is more accurate to speak of "activists" than "leaders," a brief comment about ethnic leadership is imperative. Although intensive studies of ethnic leadership have been few, the historical literature is replete with wide-ranging generalizations.[17] The tendency has been to equate articulate individuals with leaders. Consequently, newspaper editors and the elite, often educated individuals, have been assigned leadership status. Those who became organizational officers have been similarly anointed. Typically, however, their rise to the top echelons of an organization was the result of career decisions to align themselves with ethnic organizations rather than a popularly based rise through the ranks. An emphasis on articulate, visible personalities slights committed individuals at the local level who were responsible for taking the lead in promoting ethnic causes. This work thus joins company with the conclusion that "some men and women who were perceived as ethnic leaders by the surrounding society might be viewed much more ambivalently *within* the ethnic community."[18] An underlying premise is that, within the framework of defining leaders as individuals who "exercise decisive influence over others within a context of obligation or common interest," many national officers were not leaders even though they could reach a nationwide audience via the ethnic press.[19] It is therefore more accurate to speak of activists than of leaders. Such an approach transcends class, occupation, generation, gender, and locale.

Persons who held a national office in ethnic organizations, though, were individuals in the business of thinking about ethnicity. During the interwar era, these activists worked to ensure group survival as well as to promote broadly based political issues. Theorizing about their group's national identity, these articulate activists set down the terms of discourse and provided the intellectual leavening for ethnic activism. In this study, they are the national activists.

At the same time, in immigrant enclaves there were ethnically committed men and women who did not necessarily fit conventionally accepted notions of "leaders." In the local arena, these people tried to ensure an enduring group presence in communities characterized by ethnic diversity. One way they attempted to achieve their goal was by holding annual nationality days. To get immigrants and their children to attend these yearly manifestations of ethnicity, enthusiasts had to develop publicity that would resonate with the larger populace. Thus, trying to influence ordinary Slovaks, committed activists created a body of literature that, when carefully scrutinized, becomes a basis for discovering rank-and-file perspectives. This publicity as well as the programs for Slovak Days, which became commonplace in American communities during the 1930s, reveals how ordinary immigrants and their children were coping with life in a heterogeneous society. They show how local activists developed a strategy of using American popular culture to perpetuate an interest in ethnic affairs. To impress Slovak youths as well as "other nationalities," including "Americans," they also routinely incorporated America's national symbols into ethnic undertakings.

Taking a closer look at intergenerational relationships sheds new light on old arguments about alleged conflicts between parents and their American-oriented offspring. By and large, scholars have remained captivated by—and, indeed, captive to—what Marcus Lee Hansen called the second-generation "problem." Historians in general have laid too much emphasis on the notion of parents wishing to remember and children wanting to forget.[20] An underlying point emerging from this study is that parental attitudes were influenced by premigration culture, their American experience, and realities of the society where they now lived. As a consequence, not all parents were equally dedicated to cultural preservation.

It was likewise true that the second generation was monolithic in neither its demographic composition nor its attitudes about ancestral roots. Letting youths express their views about the language-based criteria of ethnicity leads to a more refined understanding of the second generation. Slovak as well as other new immigrant youths did, by and large, become Americanized. This study considers, however, those "Americanized" youths who did not reject their ancestral heritage and instead joined ethnic organizations or participated in ethnically defined undertakings, including organized leisure-time activities. It contends that these young men and women ultimately became part of a core of activists willing, when circumstances moved them, to promote ethnic causes.

It would be an exercise in excess to discuss all the secondary literature informing this investigation. Still, to clarify the perspective this study offers, some general comments about historiographical trends, particularly in the recent past, are in order. Since the latter part of the twentieth century, scholars have engaged in penetrating, often animated discussions about "ethnicity." Disputation has centered on the genuineness and relevance of ethnicity. For example, was the ethnic revival of the 1960s and 1970s a bona fide reawakening or a forced resuscitation? Theories about ethnicity have ranged from averring its authenticity to dismissing it as symbolic, a matter of expedient choice, or a contrived imperative grounded in a chauvinistic self-deception.[21] Trying to explain its persistence, scholars have argued that the flexibility of ethnic groups has allowed ethnicity to endure in invented forms.[22] The debate has also included passing judgment on the effects as well as the desirability of ethnic persistence in America. Some commentators have expressed concern about the potentially adverse impact that emphasizing cultural particularities can have on national unity.[23] In a similar vein, scholars of immigration have grappled with whether group studies were fragmenting historical scholarship.[24]

Useful as these debates were—and remain—in compelling society at large and students of American history to engage in meaningful discourse, the purpose here is to avoid wading into the quagmire of ethnic theory.[25] Instead of trying to answer the ever elusive question of how deeply persons have internalized their ethnic identity, this analysis looks at collective expressions of ethnicity. It is therefore not an intellectual foray into what constituted ethnicity or into the legitimacy or authenticity of its expressions. One intent here is to identify what helped ignite periodic manifestations of ethnicity and, moreover, to assess why in the first part of the twentieth century ethnic activism surfaced in times of patriotic ardor.

The relationship between ethnicity and the imperative of national unity has not gone unnoticed by scholars. Indeed, discussions that investigate the thorny issue of America's national identity and the civic ideals embellishing it have produced insightful as well as provocative works. Explorations from the perspective of intellectual history in particular have enriched our understanding of America's national identity and some of the popular thinking about it.[26] Following methodology similar to intellectual histories, analysts have also examined rhetoric and public discourse to demonstrate how the political language of Americanism contributed to the transformation of immigrant generations into "Americans."[27] Trying to explain the significant impact that democratic ideology has had in forging an American identity, scholars have tended to downplay ethnicity as a significant force in times of national crises, and especially during World War II.[28] When it comes to assessing the connection between ethnicity and national identity, however, intellectual histories and studies of public discourse provide only a limited dimension of a complicated story. To achieve completeness, we must also consider the viewpoint of ordinary people. Exploring the interwar era from the perspective of new immigrants and their offspring reveals a dynamic link between the embracing of democratic ideology and the shaping of ethnic identities, between "being American" and becoming Americans proud of their ancestry.

A complex interplay of factors fed the ethnic impulse that flowed through the decades spanning the two world wars. Examining the content of national and locally generated rhetoric from the early 1920s through the 1930s, however, shows that Slovaks, like other new immigrants, were haunted by the stigma of inferiority inflicted by American society. Community-based efforts such as sponsoring nationality days and athletic teams thus were often promoted by using the rationale of impressing "others." This preoccupation with making an impression on "others" also meant creating an image that the second generation— the Americanized "younger element"—could identify with.

The emphasis on "others" bears on a wide range of issues, including the pertinency of "whiteness" or becoming Caucasian in the minds of ordinary immigrants. Implicit in the recent scholarship known as "whiteness" studies is the supposition that immigrants and the second generation were somehow aware of and moved by a desire to overcome an ascribed status as not-yet-white. It has even been asserted that "new immigrants and their children had to claw their way into the white race."[29] This is an outsider's view. Turning around to look at the situation from *within* ethnic communities, which comprised males and females of all ages and different generations, suggests that becoming white or Caucasian was not part of their aspirations during the interwar era. Their quest was far more complicated. Historical experiences and contemporary circumstances caused new immigrants and their children to view the world through the kaleidoscope of ethnic diversity, not through a lens of multihued whites. That they strove to manifest their whiteness is indeed an onlooker's interpretation. Let us now turn to take a look at the interwar world from a "new immigrant" perspective.

I. THE TRANSATLANTIC YEARS: WORLD WAR I TO 1924

1 Hyphenates and Patriots

An Ethnic Perspective on the Great War

On Sunday, July 8, 1917, in Whiting, Indiana, Slovak immigrants and their children celebrated Slovak Day. Speeches, singing, dancing, and feasting punctuated that year's activities in much the same way they had during previous Slovak celebrations in this small industrial town. Participants commemorated Cyril and Methodius, the apostles credited with bringing Christianity to the Slavic world in the ninth century. Because of their tremendous success in ancient Slovak lands, Slovaks laid claim to these august personages. In their publicity, local promoters called for establishing July 5, the feast of Saints Cyril and Methodius, as an annual nationwide event. Other nationalities, especially the Irish, had a national day, and so, too, should Slovaks, the notice proclaimed. Such fervor leavened with pride was spawned by the prospect that the Slovak homeland would emerge from the war a nation, no longer just a hazy fragment of the Austro-Hungarian Empire. This July day was dedicated to furthering the struggle for a liberated Slovakia. Speakers called on Slovaks to assist efforts to extricate their homeland from Hungarian control, and zealous individuals solicited financial support for people in the Old Country.[1]

This was, nevertheless, wartime America, a time to demonstrate unflinching loyalty to the United States. One commentator unabashedly combined Old World ties to new-land patriotism by urging Slovaks to demonstrate their love for America, whose help he said was necessary to secure the liberation of Slovaks in Europe. At least one non-Slovak took the opportunity to remind these Slavic immigrants of their patriotic duty and simultaneously to garner financial support for the war effort. A representative of the Red Cross told revelers that contributing to that organization was the best way to show their loyalty to America. The day's activities, which began with the celebration of the Roman Catholic mass, ended with a choir's rendition of "The Star-Spangled Banner" followed by the collective singing of "Hej Slováci," the unofficial Slovak anthem. Participants then turned to an evening of traditional folk dancing. For some people, attending the festivities had a small price tag. Passing the hat grossed nearly $54. Slightly more than half went to the "million dollar fund," a collection the Slovak League of America had established toward a "free Slovakia." The remainder was given to the Red Cross.[2] Throughout the summer, Slovaks elsewhere organized similar ethnic affairs. A year later, people who had attended these 1917 nationality events would probably join in "Loyalty Day," a countrywide observance on July 4, 1918. As part of that year's Fourth of July activities, Americans, especially the foreign born, were called upon to exhibit their patriotism.[3] Linking exhibitions of patriotism and displays of ethnicity was a leitmotif of wartime America.

In an abnormal time, these Slovaks probably represented the typical. Despite all the anti-hyphenate oratory, open expressions of interest in the Old World were sanctioned and even nurtured by U.S. foreign policy and Wilsonian rhetoric. In addition, all the patriotically charged bravado and mounting pressure for immigrants to manifest their "Americanism" actually required nationality groups to highlight their ethnicity. It became a paradox of the wartime era that ethnic activities, both individual and group, were used as measures of allegiance to America. The Great War, therefore, gave rise to an aggressive activism among America's ethnic populations.

It is within the context of both the widespread hostility toward the foreign born and the idealism that characterized wartime rhetoric, especially America's foreign policies, that an ethnic perspective on the war emerges. Moving step by step from efforts promoted by ethnic activists at the national level to community-based undertakings provides an especially illuminating picture of wartime America. Through their actions, Slovaks revealed an interest in the homeland, demonstrated a loyalty to America, and reflected a concern about how others viewed them. Their experience shows that, after anti-hyphenism evolved into 100 percent Americanism, people could still be both hyphenates and patriots.

EVEN BEFORE THE ONSET of the Great War, nettlesome European politics aroused anxiety in America about "hyphenates," persons defined as having divided loyalties. They stood accused of putting the interests of other countries before those of the United States. Indeed, as early as May 1914, Woodrow Wilson pinpointed the "hyphen" as an undesirable element of American life and politics. In a speech dedicating a statue of Commodore John Barry, a native of Ireland who had fought in the American Revolution, the president disdainfully asserted that "some Americans need hyphens in their names, because only part of them has come over." Wilson maintained that when the "whole" person in "heart and thought" comes to America, "the hyphen drops." An irritation with Irish Americans who were agitating in favor of home rule for Ireland no doubt prompted Wilson to take his first potshot at the "hyphen." The president shared with his audience his own "infallible test of a genuine American." Only a person who "when he votes or when he acts or when he fights his heart and his thought are nowhere but in the center of the emotions and the purposes and the policies of the United States" could pass. After war broke out in Europe, Wilson apparently believed that fewer people could fare well on the exam. In December 1915, alleging that some citizens "born under other flags" were pouring the "poison of disloyalty into the very arteries of our national life," he urged Congress to enact repressive legislation.[4] His call both reflected the contemporary temper and reinforced the chilling fact that the times were growing increasingly intolerant of the foreign born.

It was Theodore Roosevelt, however, who served as the era's leading popularizer of anti-hyphenism. Even though he spewed much venom toward German Americans, Roosevelt's anti-hyphenate assaults took aim at all nationalities.[5] And when it came to hyphenates, Roosevelt did not speak softly. By the summer of 1915, he had openly targeted "the hyphenated American" as "a danger to the country."[6] Later that same year, the former president ranted that people "who do not become Americans and nothing else are hyphenated Americans; and there ought to be no room for them in this country." Among the people for whom America most particularly had no room in 1914–1915 were those who attempted to influence American foreign policy and, more specifically, advocated measures at odds with the official position. Roosevelt, not one to shy away from bombast, accused "hyphenated Americans who terrorize American politicians by threats of the foreign vote" of engaging "in treason."[7] During the 1916 presidential campaign, candidate Wilson sounded the same theme when he tagged the followers of an Irish American, who headed an organization supporting home rule for Ireland, as "disloyal Americans" and rejected their support.[8] Seeking national solidarity and unqualified endorsement of American policies, Wilson, Roosevelt, and many others continually tried to equate "hyphenism" with "disloyalty." All this rhetoric reflected the basic reality that, given the country's heterogeneous population, an ocean of distance could not protect the United States from turmoil in Europe.

During the interim of declared neutrality, then, being disloyal was not limited to overt or even covert acts of treason. From the standpoint of those insisting on national unity, disloyalty could merely entail trying to influence American foreign policy or taking positions that diverged from the official line. Implicit in the attack on hyphenism was the demand that "the foreign-born population ... in word and deed ... must show that in very fact it has renounced allegiance to every ... foreign government."[9] As the United States ambled from neutrality to war, Americans would give the foreign born abundant opportunity to show this very fact, especially as anti-hyphenism gave way to 100 percent Americanism.

Wilson and Roosevelt coupled their assaults on hyphenism with short discourses on "Americanism," a nebulous mixture of hazy principles and duties. Wilson postulated that "Americanism consists in utterly believing in the principles of America and putting them first, as above anything that might ... come into competition." Calling "Americanism ... a matter of the spirit and of the soul," Roosevelt shared that view.[10] Constructed at best out of vague notions, Americanism nevertheless contained features that could captivate the high-minded and the sincerely patriotic. For despite the increasing fascination with eugenics and the touted biological roots of cultural traits, "being American" was intrinsically linked to adherence to principles. Throughout the war years, as more people jumped onto the Americanization bandwagon, the concept of Americanism would prove its elasticity as it stretched to meet the needs of both the chauvinistic and the sincere. Despite the high-pitched rhetoric, though, during the early years of the Great War, achieving 100 percent Americanism did not become the articulated national aim. Squelching hyphenated Americanism commanded the agenda.[11]

The constant attacks on hyphenism reflected a popular animosity toward the persistence of ethnic enclaves and institutions in the United States. Speaking to newly naturalized citizens in the spring of 1915, Wilson proclaimed that "America does not consist of groups."[12] In reality, however, he knew that it did. That was the root of the problem. As war engulfed Europe, many of America's immigrants turned their attention to events in their homelands. This interest stirred fears that the country's foreign inhabitants had not only a sentimental attachment but, perhaps, a loyalty to their native lands. The concern immigrants displayed about happenings in Europe bothered many Americans. Consequently, in addition to denouncing hyphenism, a new emphasis was laid on "Americanizing" the foreign born, on turning immigrants into "Americans." The president's address acted as a catalyst to patriotically inspired Americans who were becoming increasingly distraught about the continued existence of "foreign colonies," as contemporaries called them. Their commitment to Americanizing immigrants and drawing native-born Americans into this effort led to "Americanization Day" in 1915. A nationwide event scheduled for the Fourth of July, the day would honor naturalized Americans and those who had declared their intention to become citizens. Promoters envisioned it as a time when both the native and foreign born could jointly and "fittingly express . . . their patriotism and loyalty to America."[13] More and more, Americans were equating patriotism with visible manifestations, and they wanted immigrants to accommodate this caprice. People were increasingly craving naturalization ceremonies imbued with symbols that would impress the country's foreign born with the meaning of citizenship. Americanization Day contributed to the growing national mania for what Frances Kellor called "cooperative patriotism," public avowals of loyalty.[14]

The National Americanization Day Committee, headed by Kellor, launched a massive campaign to publicize the event, especially among the foreign born. Posters were plastered in railway stations throughout the country. More than 7,600 placards were displayed in companies employing immigrants, and nearly 6,500 were given to cities for their festivities. Although nationally orchestrated, for participants Americanization Day was a local event. Demonstrations took place in 107 cities, towns, and communities scattered throughout the forty-eight states. Kellor raved that in many places people engaged in the activities as members of nationality groups; immigrants displayed their "national colors" and sang their songs. Such displays of ethnicity did not disturb national organizers. On the contrary, paying tribute to the country's ethnic diversity, under the slogan "Many Peoples, But One Nation," the events ostensibly aimed to promote better understanding between immigrants and native-born Americans. Above all, though, these were inflated shows of patriotism. In graphic posters and multi-ethnic parades, the flag, America's sacred emblem, figured prominently. Admonishing "Americans" for their indifference to immigrants and to the significance of Independence Day, Kellor pointed out that "it was symbolic . . . that in some localities, Americans forgot to decorate their homes with the Stars and Stripes, but from the shacks of nearby laborers they floated triumphantly."[15] To her mind, displaying the American flag was the mark of a true patriot.

National Americanization Day 1915 helped reinforce the criteria for assessing patriotism. Foreign-born persons could demonstrate their

Americanism and simultaneously confirm the collective loyalty of their nationality by participating in patriotic exercises as members of a specific ethnic group. Giving homage to the American flag by waving it in parades, hanging it from one's abode, or wearing a reproduction on a pin were declarations of patriotism. Although the United States was not yet at war in 1915, the foundation for how the foreign born could prove loyalty was being laid. Attacks on hyphenism notwithstanding and growing pressure to Americanize notwithstanding, links between American patriotism and ethnic identity were being forged. As nationality groups paraded through the streets, Americans were watching pageantry spawned by a combination of patriotic fervor and ethnic diversity.

While the national coordinators patted themselves on the back, proclaimed the endeavor a huge success, and surged forward with their Americanization campaign, the whole event underscored the significance of local activities. Following the countrywide Fourth of July activities, local Americanization efforts exploded. The number and variety of agencies involved in Americanizing immigrants immediately mushroomed and continued to expand in communities throughout the United States.[16] The National Americanization Committee touted an array of programs—citizenship and English-language classes, surveys, lectures, teacher training at institutions of higher education—as "by-products" of the Fourth of July extravaganza. Snippets about local efforts sprinkled the "Record of Progress" sections of the committee's official organ.[17] Attempting to encourage naturalization, which they were convinced would create a united citizenry, Americanizers directed particular energy toward teaching English and instilling the principles of Americanism and citizenship. Taking its message directly to the foreign born, the National Americanization Committee exerted subtle pressure as it tried to cajole immigrants by appealing to their pragmatism. The committee's "America First" poster pointed to the practical reasons for learning English, attending night school, and becoming a citizen. This would mean "a better opportunity and better home in America . . . a better job . . . a better chance for your children."[18] Some enthusiasts, focusing on the workplace, took a potentially intimidating approach. The Detroit Board of Commerce launched a campaign to get its members to persuade their immigrant workers to learn English and become citizens.[19]

Exaggerated exuberance by the committee notwithstanding, the range of activities initiated in cities and towns throughout the country suggests that foreign-born people could not avoid encountering an Americanization agency of one ilk or another.[20] Even if they could not read English, the Americanization Committee's pictorial propaganda—such as its "Many Peoples, One Nation" poster with the flag majestically waving—surely caught the eyes of some immigrants. Whether the poster's banner really inspired individuals is a question with an elusive answer, but placards with the Stars and Stripes prominently depicted did contribute to the age's patriotic ardor and reinforced the significance of displaying this national symbol.

While Americanizers labored at the street level, national spokespersons continued to assault "hyphenated Americanism." Amid his anti-hyphenism oratory, though, President Wilson sent conflicting messages—or, at least, messages that ethnic activists could interpret to suit their respective purposes. Wilson's pronouncements in the spring of 1916 that "every people has a right to choose the sovereignty under which they shall live" actually buoyed the spirits of ethnic nationalists who were already viewing the European war as an opportunity to gain independence for their homelands.[21] Before the United States entered the hostilities, however, the signals were at no time more contradictory than during the 1916 presidential campaign. The Democratic Party platform dealt with hyphenism by not mentioning the specific term. Instead, it included a plank on "Americanism" and denounced people who, in seeking to advance the welfare of a "foreign power," disregarded or conspired against America's interests.

Despite the fact that candidate Wilson exploited the hyphenism issue and took swipes at individuals who were allegedly putting concern for their homeland ahead of the welfare of the United States, he also enunciated sympathy for the aspirations of subject peoples. In October, he shared with a Cincinnati audience how he was emotionally affected by individuals who came to his office with appeals to help "those unorganized people who have no political standing in Europe."[22] Although this speech specifically mentioned Armenians and the people of Poland, to ardent nationalists Wilson's comments could be taken as implicitly embracing other peoples as well. In 1916, the president also proclaimed Lithuanian, Armenian, and Syrian days. Intended as occasions for soliciting contributions from the general public for overseas relief, these days nonetheless were ethnic events that vitalized the respective immigrant communities. Designating special days and receiving envoys for nationalist causes into the White House emboldened ethnic groups.[23] Whether election-year ploys or not—and despite the anti-hyphen fervor—candidate Wilson espoused ideals that could not help but give heart to nationalist yearnings.

As the 1916 election faded into history, Wilson increasingly became the recognized proponent of the principle of self-determination. In January 1917, his vision for "peace without victory" embodied this fundamental idea. From his standpoint, a peace with no victors would still be one that achieved the restoration of Poland. The special treatment afforded Poland, together with Wilson's idealistic rhetoric, motivated America's other ethnic groups to organize efforts aimed at persuading the administration to expand self-determination to include eastern Europe's other subject nationalities.[24] In the final analysis, the president's actual intent was less important than how ethnic activists chose to construe his words. Hence, despite all the anti-hyphen hyperbole, Wilson's oratory had the effect of encouraging partisans to work on behalf of their motherlands, to be hyphenates.[25]

Turning to look more closely at America's "foreign colonies" and how they were responding to the war in Europe explains why government policies, together with rhetoric grounded in democratic ideals, helped make people both hyphenates and patriots. Moreover, a view from inside new immigrant America confirms that, for all its chauvinism, the language of anti-hyphenism was rooted to a degree in reality. Americanizers were right: immigrants had been forming their own ethnic enclaves and institutions; foreign-born persons did maintain attachments to their homelands. Indeed, well before the United States became involved in April 1917, the Great War was animating ethnic America. In fact, even before the assassin fired the fatal bullet at Sarajevo, happenings in Europe were already fanning flames of nationalism that during previous decades had smoldered in confined segments of America's ethnic populations.

While Wilson was scolding Irish Americans in the spring of 1914, former residents of central and eastern Europe were similarly engrossed in their homelands. This interest in Old World politics was blatantly expressed when Count Michael Károlyi, a Hungarian nationalist and leader of the political party advocating independence from Austria, visited the United States. His two tours stirred internal friction but also avid enthusiasm among Hungarian immigrants. They expressed this fervor in parades and public displays featuring Hungarian folk costumes, flags, and banners.[26] As Hungarians were setting aside differences in order to advance a united front behind Károlyi's nationalist program, his presence was injecting vigor into what had been a feeble Slovak nationalism in the United States. Activities sponsored in his honor ignited spirited public protests by Slovaks and generated efforts on behalf of the Slovak people in Hungary. Between May and September, Slovak activists held several meetings at which they hammered out a new political program for their homeland. Announced in September 1914, this plan, the "Memorandum of the Slovak League of America, issued in the name of the American Slovaks in behalf of the Slovaks in Hungary," called for Slovak administrative and cultural autonomy in Hungary. Steeped in democratic principles, it demanded that Slovaks be accorded unfettered political, social, educational, and religious rights.[27]

The outbreak of war stoked the tinder of homeland attachments into a blazing nationalism. While the Entente powers did not believe the war should result in the dissolution of Austria-Hungary, the empire's multinational minorities thought differently. In Europe, émigrés formed councils that sought recognition as revolutionary governments. Individual groups in America established contacts with the provisional council whose political program for their homelands coincided with their own. The émigré councils, realizing that immigrant support could be used to buttress their own claims to legitimacy, dispatched emissaries to the United States. By the summer of 1915, sundry immigrant organizations and newspapers in the United States had come out in support of breaking up Austria-Hungary's multinational empire and were proposing constitutional frameworks for their respective motherlands. Thus, despite Wilson's appeal for neutrality, from the onset of the Great War immigrant nationalists in the United States demonstrated that they were not "impartial in thought." As time passed, their actions continually revealed they had clear preferences among the European combatants.[28]

Dawning the mantle of spokespersons, immigrants in America claimed to represent their European compatriots stifled by the war. The possibility that the Habsburg Empire would crumble fostered cooperation among its former nationals. For example, the dream of separating Slovakia from Hungary caused Slovak religious groups to project a unified front. Equally important, Czechs and Slovaks, two Slavic peoples with separate histories and cultures, joined forces to work on behalf of their respective homelands. In October 1915, the Slovak League of America and the Bohemian National Alliance drafted the Cleveland Agreement that, if realized, would draw together the Czechs of Austria and the Slovaks of Hungary into a federated state.[29] Following a similar course, Serbs, Croatians, and Slovenians advocating the formation of a joint Yugoslav state glossed over historical differences. At the same time, however, calls to unify these "South Slavs," as they were collectively called, exposed deeply rooted divisions within the individual ethnic groups.[30] In some cases, homeland interests meant that adversaries within a nationality group sympathized with different sides of the European conflict. Ukrainian nationalists disliked Habsburg control of lands that they claimed for Ukraine, but these nationalists so hated Russia that they hoped it would lose the war. The fact that a Russian defeat would most likely come at the hands of a German victory seemed not to bother these Ukrainians. A Russian loss might pave the way to an independent Ukraine. Out of ethnic America, then, came a dissonant chorus of voices, all clamoring to be heard.[31]

Despite official U.S. neutrality, activists, both foreign and native born, worked hard to advance their programs. The immigrant press was filled with commentary about homelands. Slovak newspapers, for instance, regularly editorialized in favor of the independence movement. Seeking to win over public opinion, nationality groups organized rallies and parades.[32] They held conventions, passed resolutions, and sent memoranda to Wilson. They inundated the president, government officials, and congressional representatives with telegrams. Wilson's 1917 "peace without victory" speech, which supported reunifying Poland and restoring it as an independent nation, clearly inspired Slovak nationalists. In a memorandum, which stands as a stark illustration of hyphenism and patriotism combined, the Slovak League of America simply expanded the president's oratory to include the Slovak people. On behalf of "American citizens of Slovak descent," it praised Wilson for "becoming a champion of the cause of their oppressed brethren in their distant home-land." The president's "welcome words are to the oppressed nations of the world as a shining star of hope," the manifesto declared. And, it stated, "American citizens of Slovak descent would consider themselves lacking in patriotism and in loyalty to their adopted country, if they did not . . . express their heartfelt thanks . . . for the stand you took in behalf of their brethren, and if they would not, in these days of crisis, solemnly reaffirm their oath of allegiance to the United States of America."[33] The league's memorandum slid over the fact that Wilson had not taken a stand advocating the severance of Slovakia from Hungary. Instead, league spokesmen read Wilson's words through the lens of their own political agenda for their homeland.

When the United States finally declared war on Germany in April 1917, former Austro-Hungarian subjects saw an opportunity to further their homeland agendas. Nationalists in both Europe and the United States were dismayed, though, when Wilson reaffirmed his opposition to dismembering the Austro-Hungarian Empire. In addition, since the United States remained at peace with Austria-Hungary, the nationalist aspirations of Czechs, Slovaks, "South Slavs," and other groups in central and eastern Europe ran counter to American policy. Nevertheless, at least for anti-Habsburg immigrants, America's declaration of war on Germany raised the possibility that the United States would ultimately wage war against Austria-Hungary. They believed that that would sound the death knell for the Austro-Hungarian Empire. Thus, despite the atmosphere of anti-hyphenism and mounting 100 percent Americanism, ethnic groups still bombarded the president, government officials, and congressional representatives with telegrams, memoranda, and resolutions. Immigrant newspapers kept editorializing in favor of liberating their homelands. European émigré councils also continued to rely on immigrants to convince the United States to recognize them as provisional governments and, in short, persuade Wilson to alter his position on the Austro-Hungarian Empire. These objectives clearly ran counter to American policy, but that did not dissuade articulate nationalists. Moreover, the repressive environment did not stop spokespersons from trying to attract ordinary Slovaks to the homeland cause. Just three weeks after war was declared, the Slovak Evangelical Union, a Lutheran mutual aid society, called on its members to seek new recruits for the organization because increased numbers would enhance its ability to work for Slovakia's freedom and demonstrate loyalty to the United States.[34]

Activities on behalf of the Old Country characteristically included declarations of loyalty to their "adopted country" and to President Wilson as well. As they sought to impress the administration with their numbers, and maybe create some political muscle, ethnic activists consistently sought to reaffirm that partisanship in European politics did not dilute their allegiance to the United States.

During the eight months before the Wilson administration concluded that Austria-Hungary, too, was an enemy, a host of ethnic organizations hoped for a declaration of war against the Habsburg Empire. When it finally came in early December 1917, the proclamation rang hollow for self-determination. To the dismay of ethnic nationalists, Wilson reconfirmed America's commitment to preserving the integrity of the empire. One month later, announcing his fourteen-point plan to make the postwar world "fit and safe to live in," the president reiterated his position that Poland should be restored. For Austria-Hungary's nationalities, though, Wilson's vision of a fit and safe world was one that merely "accorded the freest opportunity of autonomous development." His conditions for peace thus widened the door for organized lobbying by ethnic partisans. Further energized by the fact that the hated Habsburgs were now counted among America's enemies, ethnic organizations worked vigorously to convince Wilson to redefine "autonomous development" to mean independence.[35] Calling for the dissolution of Austria-Hungary smacked of hyphenism, especially as people put their hopes for their homeland ahead of official American policies.

The desire to influence U.S. policy regarding postwar Europe kept fueling flurries of activity in America's "foreign colonies." Amid militant campaigns for loyalty, ethnic groups not only lobbied for their motherlands, but, to further their causes, they organized public demonstrations. Slovaks and Czechs were among the most zealous. In May 1918, Thomas Masaryk, president of the Czechoslovak National Council, arrived in the United States, and during the next few months he traveled to areas with large concentrations of Slovaks and Czechs. In Chicago, Cleveland, Pittsburgh, and Baltimore, boisterous crowds greeted him, and huge public meetings were held. In some areas, Slovak and Czech groups arranged massive parades; Slovak, Czech, and American flags waved all over and bedecked buildings. Masaryk hoped that large numbers of main-street supporters would impress Wilson and convince the president to recognize Slovak and Czech aspirations to join together in an independent state. By spring 1918, though, Wilson had not changed his mind about letting the Austro-Hungarian Empire remain intact. Still sending mixed signals to former nationals, however, the administration authorized the recruitment of eligible Slovak and Czech men in America for a Czechoslovak unit of the French Army, a division that symbolized a desire to fight for Czech and Slovak independence.[36]

Masaryk continued to rally support among immigrants in America. In May 1918, at a meeting with representatives of Czech and Slovak immigrant organizations, he signed the Pittsburgh Agreement, which outlined a political framework for Czechoslovakia and was destined to become one of the most significant and controversial documents in that country's history. Using criteria earlier enunciated by both Wilson and Roosevelt, the "American" signers of foreign birth certainly could have been accused of being "hyphenates."[37] By late June 1918, Wilson had shifted his position and accepted the idea that, following the war, Austria-Hungary would be dismembered. In September 1918, the United States recognized the Czechoslovak National Council as the provisional government of a future independent Czech–Slovak state. For

Slovak and Czech nationalists, this meant that their objectives were finally in tandem with U.S. policy. For other nationalities promoting homeland interests, Wilson's actions offered a ray of hope.[38]

Throughout the war, nationality groups had striven to persuade Wilson to support their vision of what could be chiseled from the rubble of the Austro-Hungarian Empire. Historical scholarship suggests that, overall, immigrant activities probably had little significant influence on the president.[39] But ineffectiveness can neither expunge history of the aggressive actions taken by the country's foreign-born denizens in the hope that American officials might be swayed nor negate their belief that their efforts had indeed paid off.

All the activities on behalf of homelands were illustrations of hyphenism, pure and simple. As Americans fidgety about divided loyalties witnessed such overt devotion to ancestral lands, they believed they had cause for consternation. Even if only segments of each ethnic group participated, the efforts by these activists contributed to the impression of hyphenism run rampant. Thus, while enthusiasts were pushing homeland agendas, clement Americanization was giving way to a militant nationalism nurtured by fears that immigrants harbored divided loyalties. The declaration of war by the United States on Germany agitated the already heightening anxieties and anti-foreign sentiment in the country. Once the United States became a combatant, the government and self-proclaimed patriots launched a massive campaign to create unwavering support for the war effort and for President Wilson.[40]

When anti-hyphenism gave way to 100 percent Americanism, the Committee on Public Information, under the stewardship of George Creel, led the charge into the battle for national solidarity. The committee's aggressive campaign for unity, though, relied in part on mobilizing America's foreign born. As this octopus of government propaganda extended its tentacles deep into American society, it tapped into energy that ethnic colonies had been generating since hostilities had broken out in Europe. Specifically, it relied on preexisting networks of ethnic institutions, organizations, and communities in the United States. To carry out activities among immigrants, the committee created the "Division of Work among the Foreign Born." The scheme included forming nationality bureaus to direct activities among former European nationals. Hoping to create "loyalty leagues" within ethnic communities, the committee's strategy was to identify "group leaders" willing to conduct "virtual evangelization" among their own nationalities. These local go-betweens could channel wide-ranging official information and propaganda into their respective "foreign colonies."[41] The aim was to manufacture open support for the war.

The committee's activities included sponsoring patriotic exercises nationwide. Loyalty Day 1918 epitomized this approach. Reminiscent of Americanization Day three years earlier, this wartime extravaganza scheduled for the Fourth of July was envisioned "as a day for the foreign born to manifest, by special celebrations, . . . loyalty to this country and to the cause for which we fight."[42] Responding to a petition requesting that July 4 be set aside as Loyalty Day, Wilson voiced appreciation for this "expression of loyalty and good will." The president praised foreign-born citizens for having "shown where you stand not only by your frequent professions of loyalty to the cause for which we fight, but by your eager response to calls to patriotic service." Wilson thus encouraged the continuation of what he had helped initiate in the spring of 1915: multiethnic manifestations of American patriotism. After Wilson's approval, a slew of state and local proclamations declaring local Loyalty Days followed.[43] America then went on parade to celebrate the Fourth of July in 1918. A burst of activity by the Committee on Public Information resulted in demonstrations in cities, towns, and communities throughout the nation. In nationally orchestrated events such as Loyalty Day 1918, 100-percenters in particular were treated to the displays of patriotism they so eagerly demanded. At the same time, parading in separate ethnic units, immigrants were given an occasion publicly to show their patriotism.

Growing intolerance toward the foreign born notwithstanding, an irony of wartime America was that the aspirations of ethnic nationalists and the programs of militant Americanizers could at times dovetail. Demands that Americans, especially those of foreign birth, show their collective loyalty provided opportunities for ethnic groups to make political statements and simultaneously strut their aggregate strength. While coordinators showered themselves with plaudits, for ethnic groups this nationwide demonstration of patriotism had international, national, and local significance. In fact, Loyalty Day and the sundry expressions of patriotism so prevalent during World War I could be viewed from various—not necessarily contradictory—perspectives. The view from inside ethnic America reveals that a web of interrelated reasons motivated nationality groups such as the Slovaks to participate in Loyalty Day 1918 and in other civic rituals. To gain a more complete picture of the wartime world, it is necessary, while using them as a backdrop, to turn away from international events and nationwide happenings and turn inward to look more closely at what was taking place within America's "foreign colonies."

When the United States declared war on Austria-Hungary in December 1917, Wilson's proclamation classified the empire's nonnaturalized nationals as enemy aliens but did not impose the same severe restrictions on them that the April proclamation had on noncitizen Germans.[44] Nevertheless, from the onset of American involvement in the war, ethnic activists recognized the necessity of declaring their loyalty to the United States.[45] Knowing that their actions reflected on the entire ethnic group, editors and organizations producing foreign-language publications exuded patriotism. Immediately after the American declaration of war, nationality newspapers, whose graphics did not already include the American flag, reproduced this hallowed emblem on their mastheads or editorial pages. Beginning in April, one newspaper, *Slovenský hlásnik,* added a front-page blurb in both Slovak and English averring unqualified allegiance by Slovaks to the United States. Other ethnic newspapers carried similar pronouncements.[46]

National organizations were acutely aware that they could be monitored. Official organs constantly alluded to the many "citizens" their membership rolls boasted; the more citizens an organization could claim, the more patriotic it appeared. As early as August 1916, the First Catholic Slovak Union made it clear that it would strictly enforce the long-standing bylaw requiring delegates to its annual convention to prove they were American citizens. Pointedly referring to the times, the Slovak Evangelical Union also published reminders that representatives to its 1918 convention must be American citizens. Officials of this Lutheran fraternal society went to extremes to enforce its citizenship requirement. If a lodge could not designate a citizen to represent its members, it must choose a member who had taken out first papers. In the event that a lodge could find no one who fit one of these requirements, its members would have to choose an eligible individual from another lodge to serve as their delegate.[47]

Ethnic organizations realized that the spoken word could be as damning as the written. In an English-language letter, which vigorously asserted Slovak patriotism, the General Counsel of the First Catholic Slovak Union admonished delegates to the upcoming 1918 convention to be careful about what they said so that this "may go down in the history of our nation as one of the most loyal and patriotic conventions ever held by a grateful people living under the protection of the Stars and Stripes."[48] Although scholars have typically emphasized immigrants as victims of the vigilante temper that swept over wartime America, some foreign-born spokespersons contributed to the repressive mentality. For instance, while cautioning its convention participants to weigh carefully their own words, the First Catholic Slovak Union counsel simultaneously urged Slovaks to inform the authorities about people who made seditious comments. The editor of one Slovak Catholic newspaper sent a telegram to Wilson informing the president that he "heartily approve[s] your patriotic stand on the question of censorship legislation." Gustave Kosik believed a law was "mandatory for the welfare and safety of our country, especially as it relates to the foreign press."[49]

Persons of foreign birth naturally worried that they might be subjected to the same opprobrious treatment German Americans were enduring. Warning that this might happen, Slovak activists urged aliens to declare their intention to become American citizens so they would then "be considered a friend and supporter of this country."[50] Advising people to demonstrate a committed loyalty to the United States became the admonition of the day. In March 1917, the Slovak Evangelical Union exhorted Slovaks "not to delay, act quickly" lest they "suffer misfortune or unpleasantness." Slovaks had to "show that they are worthy of freedom and know how to honor the stars and stripes—the American flag." Foreign-language publications carried warnings that Congress had adopted "very sharp measures against aliens of the enemy nations."[51]

Public assertions alone were not sufficient to soothe the concerns of Americans suspicious about immigrant loyalty. Ethnic activists recognized that, when it came to assessing their group's loyalty, collective actions mattered. They also understood that mass involvement in public events provided opportunities to create a positive image. Savvy Slovaks at both the national and local levels therefore strove to have their compatriots participate in patriotic events, especially the multinational affairs. They were part of the effort that subsequently let Creel boast about the widespread cooperation the Committee on Public Information had enjoyed from America's nationality groups, the foreign-language press, and ethnic organizations for Loyalty Day 1918. When it announced the event, *Jednota*, the official organ of the First Catholic Slovak Union, called on every Slovak man and woman in the United States to take part in this "public expression." As America prepared to go on parade, the paper admonished Slovaks not to organize separate affairs but, instead, to represent Slovaks in the all-nationality events in their respective communities. *Jednota* published procedures for letting mayors' committees know that Slovaks would be present and what floats they would enter. The announcement also appealed to local organizers to "insist" that their planned involvement be reported in the local English-language newspapers together with "expressions of loyalty" that would "challenge" Slovaks to participate. Finally, Slovaks were pointedly told that publicity about their involvement would ultimately help their compatriots in Europe. Slovaks were not the only ethnic group to link the fate of their homeland to participation in Loyalty Day 1918.[52]

As a patriotic and ethnic exhibition, Loyalty Day was a success. In communities nationwide, columns of separate nationalities wearing folk costumes, carrying national banners, and waving American flags presented majestic sights for onlookers to behold. If reports were right, children were visibly present and extensively involved in the pageantry. Ethnic groups constructed elaborate floats with themes reflecting the motifs of the day: Americanism, patriotism, and Old World histories. Red, white, and blue were everywhere evident. In New York, where reportedly more than forty nationalities participated, floats depicted the historical and tenacious struggle in the immigrants' homelands for freedom based on democratic principles, which in the modern world they identified as "American." The *New York Times* described the parade as a "kaleidoscopic pageant," which thousands of spectators saw in that city. For onlookers, the 70,000 to 75,000 persons marching on Fifth Avenue presented a "wonderful demonstration of loyalty" and, in the minds of many, graphically depicted their conception of America: "a land of many bloods but one ideal." Depending on their migratory history, groups dramatized their ancestors' contributions to advancing freedom in the United States; others portrayed America as a refuge from oppression in their homelands. Representatives of several nationalities traveled to the nation's capital, where they held pageants at various government buildings. Then, in full ethnic regalia, carrying national banners and waving the Stars and Stripes, they marched in a parade reviewed by Wilson. At the same time that ethnic groups were filing through the streets of big-city and small-town America, the Committee on Public Information organized a pilgrimage of nationalities to Mount Vernon, where participants displayed their loyalty by paying homage to George Washington.[53]

Assessing the day's activities, Creel gushed that "never was there such an outpouring of the Nation's millions of new citizens and citizens to be."[54] There was, however, irony in these patriotic exhibitions, which touted cohesion over diversity. To demonstrate the country's unity, its heterogeneity had to be highlighted. Group patriotism was measured by ethnically segregated participation in multinational activities. And immigrants knew it. This was evident in a telegram from Slovaks in Byesville, Ohio, to the committee. Claiming to speak for the 6,000 Slovaks and Czechs living in the area, Slovak promoters of the parade expressed the hope that their participation would confirm their loyalty and, moreover, that they stood behind President Wilson.[55] These exercises nurtured a competitive mentality as enthusiasts toiled to make sure their respective groups were properly represented and not outdone by other nationalities.

For all the patriotic bravado, the day was a graphic demonstration of hyphenism and patriotism at work. As floats tried to forge links between "American" principles and a people's historical struggle for freedom and democracy, national banners carried alongside the American flag symbolized dual interests. In New York, Carpatho-Rusins sported a banner appealing for "American Assistance to Russia." A sign displayed by the Romanian unit proclaimed "Rumania's Ideal—To Be United." Announcing that a "United Greece" would fight for democracy, a Greek contingent revealed its preference in the bitter political struggle at home by carrying a picture of the anti-royalist, pro-Ally leader Eleutherios Venizelos. No doubt, Albanian marchers had their tiny nation in mind when they lettered a sign affirming support for Wilson, "The Protector of Small Nationalities." Relying on less subtlety, the Lithuanian banner proclaimed: "Allied Victory and Independent Lithuania." Serbs, Croats, and Slovenes used images to get their point across. Their float reportedly depicted Columbia as "The Hope of Jugoslavs." Slovaks and Czechs did not enter a float but did march together in a massive display of unity. Described as the parade's "first big division," the combined Czech and Slovak section took nearly a half-hour to pass in front of the reviewing stand. Czech and Slovak servicemen dressed in military uniform were followed by local branches of national gymnastic societies known as sokols. The sokolists came attired in their distinctive colors. Large numbers of marchers, especially women, wearing their Czech or Slovak national costumes enhanced this already impressive show of patriotism and cultural pride.[56]

Thus, while many Americans reveled in this nationwide display, from the ethnic activists' perspective, participating in a massive demonstration of loyalty could help advance homeland causes. *Jednota*'s appeal for Slovaks to take part in Loyalty Day had said as much. It had suggested that a widespread affirmation of loyalty, simultaneously combined with an exhibition of numerical strength, might put pressure on American policymakers. Hence, even as they badgered fellow immigrants to manifest allegiance to their "adopted country," committed nationalists kept a close eye on developments affecting their native lands. As it happened, at the same time preparations were under way for the 1918 Independence Day extravaganza, Secretary of State Robert Lansing prematurely divulged Wilson's altered position about dismantling postwar Austria-Hungary.[57] The constant hope that Wilson would change his mind had been fueling activities among the empire's former nationals.

Public activities on behalf of the homeland were tolerated, but making immigrants demonstrate loyalty to the United States remained the all-out objective in wartime America. Nowhere was the pressure applied more than in the Liberty Loan drives. These massive campaigns to finance the war without raising taxes consciously tapped into the country's highly charged patriotism. From coast to coast, the country was coated with specially commissioned posters.[58] The placards subtly queried what one poster blatantly asked: "Are You 100% American? Prove it! Buy U.S. Government Bonds." While the campaign was aimed at all Americans, the foreign born received special attention. Eye-catching posters and pithy slogans reminded immigrants of what America had done for them and, therefore, of the debt they owed the country. A Second Liberty Loan poster depicting immigrant men, women, and children on a ship passing the Statue of Liberty conjured up memories of arriving in the land of freedom. It told immigrants: "Remember Your First Thrill of AMERICAN LIBERTY" and thus "YOUR DUTY—Buy United States Government Bonds." Another portrayed Slavic immigrants with the American flag waving behind them and admonished: "REMEMBER! The Flag of Liberty! Support It!" The placard indicated that they could do this by purchasing government bonds.[59]

The bond drives pointedly linked ethnicity and patriotism. Not only did the drives target nationality groups, but organizers calculated sales by ethnic categories. Aggregate purchases became gauges of group support for the war and correspondingly of collective patriotism. As one *Jednota* ad tellingly put it, "Your loyalty to our adopted country will be measured by the number of Liberty Bonds you buy."[60] This was evident in efforts of the Committee on Public Information, which used its ethnically structured Division for Work among the Foreign Born to solicit funds from individual nationality groups. These particular government-sponsored bond campaigns were nationally coordinated undertakings that, similar to Americanization and Loyalty days, focused on foreign-born people. They also relied on a strategy that drew on local ethnic resources. Regional directors labored to ensure that campaign committees included representatives of each nationality in the area. "Leaders" recruited from each group worked through established ethnic institutions. Rallies and parades identified participants by nationality; organizers even provided pictorial evidence documenting the ethnic bond drives in their regions. Detailing activities among "Our New Americans," one committee chairperson reproduced a photograph from an ethnic rally that showed participants garbed in native costumes and each holding a small American flag.[61] Once again, demonstrating patriotism and highlighting nationality seemed not only acceptable but inextricably connected.

For their part, Slovak organizations devoted tremendous energy to rousing rank-and-file involvement. Throughout the war, Slovak newspapers, like the rest of the immigrant press, implored the foreign born to buy bonds. Slovak promotions outlined the financial reasons for purchasing them. Acquiring Liberty Bonds "is only a loan, you will get the money back with interest," ads pitched. Others carefully delineated the financial benefits. Reaping monetary profits, though, was clearly secondary. Reproducing the poster exhorting Slavic immigrants to remember the flag of liberty and support it, *Jednota* urged Slovaks to "perform their patriotic duty" (Illustration 1). Readers were told to purchase at least one bond so they could show "that Slovaks are loyal not only in words but in their hearts."[62] Wanting to prove that its members were "loyal" and "grateful citizens," the Slovak Evangelical Union called on everyone who had some money saved to invest in Liberty Bonds. Other organizations took the same tack.[63] Appeals to subscribe could also be laced with both subtle and overt warnings that at times employed language worthy of the 100-percenters. During the Third Liberty Loan drive, one Slovak paper printed an assertion that those who did not buy bonds were demonstrating that they were "not good citizens," did not deserve the freedom they enjoyed in America, and "desire[d] to be German Slaves."[64]

How many Slovaks responded to ethnic appeals and how much money they invested in war bonds are questions with elusive answers. Statistics by nationality are vague. Individual Slovak organizations claimed that their members, together with Slovaks in general, provided generous support. A contemporary report boasted that, during the first three bond drives, the First Catholic Slovak Ladies Union's efforts had resulted in sales of $250,000. This announcement came with ten days left in the third campaign. But for the most part, sources offer only estimates

ILLUSTRATION 1.
Poster by anony-
mous artist, 1918.
Courtesy of Meehan
Military Posters.

or after-the-fact assertions. Thirty-two years after the war, the National
Slovak Society reported that 453 of its local assemblies had invested more
than $64,000 and individual members more than $1.7 million in war
bonds and savings stamps.[65] In addition, Slovaks, like other nationalities, bought bonds at work as well as at other outlets. In terms of their
wartime experience, though, how much Slovaks and other ethnic groups
contributed is not as important as the rhetoric and the contemporary influences motivating them. Certainly, sincere patriotic sentiments moved
many to support the American war effort. Still, to the country's foreign
born, the bond drives conveyed the message that a person could essentially purchase the right to be called a loyal American.

   The immigrant press never stopped emphasizing the litmus-test reasons for why nationalities had to support America's mobilization effort.

But as the war dragged on, homeland interests filtered into bond-drive rhetoric. Following the announcement of the Fourth Liberty Loan in September 1918, for example, activists again urged Slovaks to show their loyalty to the United States by acquiring a bond. For this campaign, however, people were also told that, by listing "Czecho-Slovak" on the subscription form, they were expressing support for the plan to separate their homeland from Hungary and establish a joint Czech–Slovak state. This would also ensure that Hungarians would not get the credit for bonds purchased by Slovaks.[66] By now, Wilson had accepted the idea of creating Czecho-Slovakia, but advocates realized that it would not become a reality until approved in peace negotiations after the war. And they knew that Hungary would oppose losing its northern territory. So from the perspective of ethnic activists, increasing the number of "Czecho-Slovaks" could enhance their political clout and simultaneously reinforce the rationale for an independent Czecho-Slovakia.

It is both clear and ironic that nationalist objectives for homelands could mesh with the ever-increasing demand for public avowals of American patriotism. Still, while activists could construct both pragmatic and emotional arguments to further their goals, ultimately support for ethnically based endeavors depended on grassroots participation. So to grasp the ethnic perspective on wartime America more fully, it is necessary to go a step further into local communities where new immigrants lived and take an even closer look at the world they were experiencing. For the reality was that, despite the national ballyhoo, it was at the local level that Americanism had to be demonstrated. It was there that Americans could keep a watchful eye and scrutinize the activities of foreign-born residents. It was there that excessive patriotic fervor, zealous Americanization, and intolerance were actually encountered. Nevertheless, a closer look reveals that the same hyphenism and patriotism evident at the national level characterized ethnic activities in local arenas.

In their communities, Slovaks, like other ethnic groups, went to great lengths to avow their patriotism. A Cambridge, Ohio, newspaper, for example, carried a lengthy English-language article by a priest from nearby Byesville. He declared that Slovaks were "prepared to do . . . [their] duty" as President Wilson "leads us to the victory against our old enemies."[67] In bold print, Slovaks in Lackawanna County, Pennsylvania, announced that, although they had contributed to the "$25,000 Fund" for Slovakia, they were loyal Americans. They also beseeched other Slovaks to make similar donations to further homeland independence.[68] This combined patriotic affirmation and political appeal on behalf of their native land was aimed at Slovaks, not at Americans. Local activists apparently wanted to reassure their compatriots that working to advance Slovak independence did not signify any disloyalty to America. Editors and organization spokespersons were thus not alone in enthusiastically heralding loyalty to their adopted country while expressing interest in homeland issues.

Local people also arranged public displays. In the summer of 1917, Slavic groups working together orchestrated an "All-Slav" demonstration, including a parade, in Pittsburgh. Organizers hoped that this "patriotic" manifestation would draw 20,000 participants.[69] Going beyond appeals to strong-arm tactics, one ad tried to boost Slovak participation by asserting that "the time has come to show clearly who is a faithful citizen of this free republic, who is the grateful guest, and who is the enemy."[70] A few days later, Slavic groups in western Pennsylvania held a week-long "All-Slav" bazaar to acquaint Americans with the Slavic peoples.[71] Youngstown, Ohio, organized a similar affair, which local English papers subsequently headlined, "Slavs Manifest True Allegiance to Adopted Country."[72] Multi-Slavic events became more common in the war years, but they did not displace ethnic particularity. During the 1917 Pittsburgh All-Slav bazaar, specific days were dedicated to single nationalities. For example, July 5, the feast of Saints Cyril and Methodius, was set aside for Slovaks.[73]

In addition to collaborative multinational displays, groups independently planned ethnic-specific activities. Scranton's Slovak Roman and Greek Catholics held their own patriotic celebration in the spring of 1918.[74] Local branches in small cities such as Racine, Wisconsin, and larger regions such as Pennsylvania's Lackawanna County sponsored fund-raising affairs to further the move for Slovak independence.[75] In the few areas where they had become a tradition, Slovak Days continued to be observed, albeit with slightly modified objectives. The 1914 Slovak Day in Mount Carmel, Pennsylvania, had been held to honor the town's "first Slovak settlers." Promoters of the 1917 Slovak Day announced that it would be similar to past events but would also be an opportunity to "show Americans especially President Wilson that we [Slovaks] are always at his service."[76] Immigrant newspapers highlighted patriotic activities and often obligingly printed participants' exuberant letters detailing the days' festivities and manifestations of loyalty. The similarity of events staged in other places revealed a ripple effect as Slovak communities apparently imitated what compatriots elsewhere were doing.[77]

While patriotic themes and affirmations characterized these ethnic affairs, what contemporaries could easily have stamped as hyphenism abounded. Even after the United States entered the war, Slovaks in local communities continued to inject Old World politics into their events. Proceeds from the 1917 Slovak Days in Whiting, Indiana, and in Akron, Ohio, as well as from the All-Slav bazaar in Pittsburgh, were designated for "political agitation" for the Slovak nation. Slovaks in Kenosha, Wisconsin, initiated Slovak Day and promised that all the funds would go toward liberating Slovakia and to help widows and children in the homeland. A Chicago branch of the Slovak League planned an extended affair to help raise $25,000 for the benefit of the Slovak nation.[78] Financial and abstract objectives inspired Slovaks in Pittsburgh energetically to promote the day set aside for Slovaks during the 1917 All-Slav bazaar. They saw it as an opportunity to assist the homeland because the event would "make news," reflect "honorably" on Slovaks, and better acquaint Americans with Slovaks as a people.[79]

Across the state border in Akron, a Slovak Lutheran was also concerned with how Americans perceived Slovaks. He hoped a Slovak Day there would demonstrate that his countrymen did "more than work with shovels." No doubt mindful of the religious differences that characterized this Slavic group and the need to show a united front on homeland issues, he declared that the day's activities would offer evidence that Akron's Slovaks lived together in harmony. Pointing to these "critical times," he called on his countrymen and countrywomen to acknowledge their "national consciousness." Scheduled speakers discussed political issues regarding the Slovak homeland but still reminded immigrants of "our obligations to our new country." Proceeds from the twenty-five-cent admission, though, were targeted for political activities for the Slovak "nation." Participants sang "Hej Slováci" and American hymns. Over the next year, numerous Slovak communities sponsored festivities to help the homeland cause.[80]

Ads and published reports suggest that promoters of local Slovak events never lost sight of the need for allegiant displays. American hymns formed an integral part of the agenda at ethnic demonstrations. Even more graphically symbolic, however, was the pervasive display of the American flag. This national emblem was a ubiquitous part of ethnic rallies, pageants, and exhibitions. For nearly six weeks before the All-Slav parade and public rally in Pittsburgh, people were told to come carrying an American flag. The Slovak Evangelical Union even encouraged its members to march behind "a huge American flag" while simultaneously carrying a small one.[81] If the 20,000 persons that organizers hoped would join in the "patriotic meeting" actually did come, this flag-waving spectacle surely must have gratified onlookers. For immigrants and their children, such fanfare reinforced the notion that displaying the national emblem could be equated with patriotic affirmations. As the Weber–Erickson–Benton Company, a Pittsburgh firm that produced flags, explained in a Slovak-language ad, its inexpensive flags meant "persons who feel like Americans could decorate their homes with the American flag."[82] The company's own commercial motives notwithstanding, its advertisement, designed to strike a responsive chord, reflected the reality of the times. As immigrants came under scrutiny, the flag was a powerful symbol individuals could bring out to display their patriotism.[83]

Immigrants understood that in wartime America actions and words were yardsticks for determining allegiance. They knew that local vigilantes, those self-proclaimed guardians of American loyalty, prowled America's communities and, therefore, foreign-born people had best watch their step. Immigrants discovered that others besides zealous neighbors might be assessing their Americanism; their employers also could be evaluating them. Thus, demonstrative patriotism was often expected in the workplace as well as at public gatherings. To understand the long-term effect that their wartime experience would have on America's foreign-born denizens, it is important to bear in mind what they were encountering when they went to work.

Some employers had gone on watch even before the United States entered the war. Although the most notorious and probably the most demeaning industrial effort at forced Americanization occurred at the Ford Motor Company's English School, companies elsewhere put pressure on foreign-born employees.[84] In early 1916, the Packard Motor Company in Detroit announced it would not promote noncitizens. Although the company would continue to employ aliens, noncitizens' "only hope for advancement and preferment lies in their speedy adoption of American citizenship and the forswearing of allegiance to other lands."[85] When it came to high-powered measures, companies backing Detroit's "English First" movement knew how to bear down hard. One establishment threatened that foreign employees who did not attend night school or an English-language class in the factory would be laid off; several others announced they would give preferences, including possible pay increases, to people who attended night classes and hence were making an effort to learn English. It is no wonder that a 150 percent increase in registration was reported for Detroit's night schools.[86] The Electric Hose and Rubber Company in Wilmington, Delaware, exerted similar pressure when it informed employees that, after they learned English, the company would increase their wages.[87]

With varying degrees of enthusiasm, industries cooperated with the mounting army of local Americanizers eager to force immigrants into civics classes and language training. Employers worked with local school systems to set up night courses and followed their employees' progress. Some companies arranged for on-site English and citizenship instructions while others adopted the strategy of "Americanization through the pay envelope." This practice entailed inserting the National Americanization Committee's series of "simple lessons in citizenship" along with the worker's pay. Produced in several languages, among other informational items, the lessons included "requirements for citizenship." Pay envelopes might also contain notices about local English and citizenship classes.[88] Immigrants, especially those who were not citizens, could reasonably view these actions with some trepidation.

After the United States became a combatant, enthusiasts continued pressing companies to support Americanization efforts. In particular, they intensified pressure to set up "factory classes."[89] The Cleveland Americanization Committee, organized shortly after America entered the international fray, pushed employers to make workers attend language and civics instructions. As a result, on-site classes for employees were set up at twenty-two industrial plants; other businesses in the region reportedly did the same.[90]

Although some businesses did capitulate to the 100-percent mentality, punishing immigrants for poor language skills or their alien status probably represented the extremes. Financial viability rested on securing a stable workforce, and especially now, with America actively engaged in the war, many industries could ill afford to adopt discriminatory hiring policies based on language or citizenship. Companies therefore often viewed Americanization from the standpoint of their financial interests and typically established educational classes as part of a safety program or as a way to stabilize their labor force or counter radicalism.[91] Still, Americanization posters hung on the walls; ads for night classes appeared on bulletin boards as well as in some pay envelopes; and bond campaigns were conducted in factories. Moreover, even if industrialists did fashion Americanization programs to coincide with their business interests, their activities contributed to the unprecedented stress on English. For foreign-born workers, the persistent emphasis on the importance of English formed part of their wartime experience.

While neither discriminatory hiring and promotion tactics nor the pay-envelope strategies were universally adopted, where they were implemented they constituted outright threats. In addition, the effects of factory-sponsored Americanization programs went beyond the individual companies as word of mouth no doubt spread news about company policies throughout ethnic enclaves. Liberty Loan drives carried out in the workplace put added pressure on the foreign born. For immigrants, the reality of wartime America was that on the job and in their daily lives they would openly have to display loyalty to the American flag and country. Furthermore, learning English was not only practical; it could be interpreted by employers and neighbors as an affirmation of Americanism. In an age that came more and more to accept Theodore Roosevelt's dictum that "there is no such thing as a hyphenate American who is a good American," immigrants everywhere were called upon to demonstrate that they were, indeed, good Americans.[92] Local circumstances, combined with the tyranny of such highly charged rhetoric, thus helped shape the wartime experience remembered by America's foreign born. Long after the Armistice ended hostilities and treaties had, for the time being, settled the fate of ancestral homelands, the memories lingered.

HISTORIANS HAVE graphically portrayed the repression that gripped the United States during perhaps the most pervasively intolerant era of American history. World War I did more than unleash pent-up antagonisms; it fused nativism and ideologically based antipathies. The injection of superpatriotism into this mixture of aversions melded hostilities into a repressive nationalism that permeated the country. As militant Americanizers targeted the country's "aliens and dissenters," the war acted as both an animus and a subterfuge for trying to repress ideological and ethnic diversity.[93]

Going beyond militant nationalism, which has left the era indelibly marked, to look at wartime America from the standpoint of the foreign born does not alter but provides an enhanced perception of the times. From the vantage point of new immigrants, the railing at hyphenism could not drown out the espoused "American" ideals activists chose to hear. Wilson's articulated sympathy for oppressed nationalities and his principle of self-determination had the unexpected effect of encouraging activists to disregard official U.S. policies and, instead, vigorously promote their homeland agendas. In the eyes of ethnic nationalists, such as Slovaks yearning for Slovakia's liberation from Hungary, Wilson became the champion of subject minorities. Thus, their goals were not at odds with American ideals. In effect, Wilson's oratory and policies allowed enthusiasts to cloak their activities on behalf of the homeland with American principles.

Interest in the Old Country was by no means the only tinder sparking activities by immigrants in America. The drive for national unity, which grew increasingly bellicose, also legitimized aggressive ethnic activities. The atmosphere of coercion and howls to demonstrate 100 percent Americanism galvanized nationality groups. Americans demanded manifestations of unqualified patriotism, but to comply with this demand, immigrants had to cultivate and openly flaunt their ethnicity. Multinational parades and actions viewed as "patriotic" helped appease the appetites of zealous Americans who craved demonstrations of loyalty by the foreign born. Ethnic groups marching in segregated divisions, wearing ancestral costumes, and waving the American flag became public avowals of collective patriotism. Thus embedded within the repression and enforced solidarity that characterized the times—and that have so captivated the attention of history—was the counteroffensive open to the foreign born under siege. It is evident that at both the national and local levels, a medley of fear, political agendas, and sincere sentiments fueled a continuous blaze of "patriotic" activities. Still, the underlying point is that, rather than scouring the country of ethnic consciousness, the wartime climate provided opportunities both to mobilize and inject life into "foreign colonies." In an ironic twist, the demands of superpatriotism, combined with the realities of wartime repression, fostered ethnic activism.

The war years also set some parameters for this activism. Embracing American principles and simultaneously using patriotic symbols legitimized ethnically oriented activities. This activism, it must also be emphasized, took place at the different levels within an ethnic community. Sometimes activists at the group's national level interacted with local communities; at other times, communities initiated their own doings. Activist rhetoric—occasionally eloquent, occasionally strident—added intellectual texture to ethnic activities, but ordinary people made up the substance. The wartime experience demonstrated that, although the lofty rhetoric of articulate national activists sifted down to the grassroots, a combination of Old World issues, assertive patriotism, and local circumstances moved the rank-and-file to action. In addition, local communities bred their own activists.

The flag-waving parades, the omnipresent wartime posters, and the demonstrations of loyalty did gratify ardent patriots. In the minds of zealots seeking to stir national unity, these displays represented a domestic victory. For people committed to Americanization, immigrant involvement in wartime patriotic activities, as well as the increased number of persons being naturalized or declaring their intention to do so, signified successes. For ethnic nationalists, achieving homeland independence was a victory. Nevertheless, once the war ended, for proponents of Americanization and ethnic activists alike there was still work to be done.

2   Unfinished Business

*The Homeland, National Identity,
and Americanization*

THE GREAT WAR left European nations bitter and exhausted; it left the United States a country suspicious and emotionally charged. Although spasms of intolerance and repression convulsed postwar America into the "Red Scare," more than ferreting out foreign or radical threats drew the country's attention. Five months after the Armistice, the government launched the Victory Liberty Loan drive to support American military personnel still in Europe and waiting to return home. This short but feverish campaign extended the wartime ardor for allegiant displays into peacetime and produced some of the era's most graphically patriotic posters. A slogan beseeched Americans to "Finish the Job." Getting the doughboys home was not the only unfinished business in postwar America. Americanizers surged forward with programs to transform aliens into English-speaking, loyal citizens while ultranationalists channeled energy into self-styled patriotic organizations. The Armistice brought an end to the fighting, but peace neither calmed the public temper nor enervated the country's nationalistic vigor.

If America found it difficult to unwind from the war, so, too, did the country's immigrants and, especially, ethnic activists. Attending to unfinished business on both sides of the Atlantic spawned a flurry of activities in ethnic populations. Their interest in homeland affairs could not easily be quashed; moreover, from the activists' perspective, the government's tolerance of wartime lobbying seemed to sanction sustained involvement in overseas causes. Exuberance over the breakup of the Habsburg Empire, together with the realization that issues involving their native lands still needed to be settled, kept nationalist activity at near-frenzy levels.

Austria-Hungary's former inhabitants quickly discovered, though, that redrawing Europe's boundaries could severely complicate questions concerning their ethnic identity. Immediately following the war, Slovak ethnicity in particular became linked to nettlesome homeland politics. With eyes gazing on Europe, Slovak activists in the United States sought to fashion a culture that would both confirm their group's distinctiveness and nurture a Slovak ethnic consciousness. Establishing a national identity grounded in history, however, was confounded by internal religious, regional, and philosophical differences that plagued this ethnic group.

At the same time that a small band of activists was trying to affirm a deeply rooted Slovak national culture, immigrants were facing relentless pressure to Americanize. Champions of ethnic group survival could not ignore this challenge, especially the penchant for equating speaking English with being Americanized. Embarking on their own Americanization programs, activists seized on loyalty to specific principles as being the more reliable measure of a true American; thus, they attempted to supplant language with a value-laden criterion. Coincidentally, this "principles" standard dovetailed with ongoing efforts to forge a Slovak national identity. Looking at the era from a Slovak perspective shows that ethnicization within the broader context of promoting "Americanism" survived the transition from war to peacetime.

THE DRIVE TO CONSTRUCT and preserve a Slovak national identity was set in motion by activists concerned about developments in their homeland. When Slovaks looked across the ocean to the newly created Czecho-Slovakia, they saw internal rivalries and external threats fracturing the country's brittle national foundation. While various ethnic animosities troubled the infant state, relations between Czechs and Slovaks were particularly vexatious. Despite closely related languages, these two Slavic groups were separate peoples whose independent histories had fashioned distinct cultures. Now that Slovaks and Czechs were joined in a single nation, their differences could outweigh similarities. Religion sharpened distinctions. Slovaks were overwhelmingly Roman Catholic. While forced under Habsburg rule to profess Catholicism, Czechs had a strong Protestant heritage that stretched back to Jan Hus, a reformer burned at the stake as a heretic in the early fifteenth century. Liberation from the Habsburgs unleashed anti-Catholic sentiment and promoted the cult of Hussitism among Czechs. In November 1918, a Czech crowd expressed its anti-Catholicism by toppling a statue of the Virgin Mary in central Prague. The next year, Czecho-Slovakia's provisional government proclaimed July 6, the day Hus was executed, a national holiday. It also initiated other policies that some interpreted as hostile to the Catholic church.

Hungary's resolve to keep its northern territories exacerbated tensions in Czecho-Slovakia. As the Hungarian government campaigned to retain its historic lands, Czechs and Slovak Protestants feared that Slovakia's large Catholic population, dominated by the clergy, might reconcile with Hungary. The belief that Slovak autonomy could lead to independence—and ultimately to the destruction of Czecho-Slovakia—intensified support for a centralized government. Looking for officials who would not fall sway to clerical influence, the provisional government installed a former Slovak Catholic to administer Slovakia, and he, in turn, selected primarily Lutherans to assist him. Making matters worse, more Czechs than Catholics were appointed as Slovakia's representatives to the Revolutionary National Assembly, the infant state's postwar governing body. Favoring these groups over Catholics angered the Slovak Catholic clergy and heightened both ethnic and religious animosities in the new nation. Mutual suspicions, then, led to a volatile fusion of religion, ethnicity, and politics in postwar Czecho-Slovakia.

The country's newly framed constitution perpetuated existing tensions. Adopted in February 1920, it established a centralized state, Czechoslovakia, with a single capital, Prague. Both directly and implicitly the constitution advanced the notion that Czechs and Slovaks were a single people. For Slovakia's Catholic nationalists, this "Czechoslovak idea," tainted in their view with Protestantism, posed a threat both to Catholicism and to the Slovak national identity. To them, their defense lay with the Pittsburgh Agreement, even though it had been drawn up in the United States without the knowledge or consent of Slovaks in the Old Country. Even before the 1920 constitution was promulgated, a small contingent of Slovaks had been demanding implementation of the agreement, which would have given Slovakia legislative and administrative autonomy within the joint Czech–Slovak state. In late 1918, the Slovak nationalist priest Andrej Hlinka revived the prewar Slovak People's Party and made the Pittsburgh Agreement the fulcrum of its platform. By 1921, Slovak autonomy was considered a "Catholic" objective. As Slovak activists in America monitored the situation in Czecho-Slovakia, antagonisms bred there rippled across the ocean to affect Slovak identity in the United States.[1]

Given the midwife role that nationals in the United States had played in birthing the Pittsburgh Agreement, they understandably took a keen interest in the fate of that accord. While achieving Slovak autonomy emerged in Czechoslovakia as a "Catholic" objective, it was also considered the Slovak American position.

Homeland politics exacerbated the already confused nature of Slovak ethnicity in America. This was a complicated matter because, on the eve of World War I, most Slovaks did not view themselves as belonging to a unique nation. The reason for this feeble ethnic consciousness lay deep in their premigration history. Slovaks had no independent ancestral homeland. Although for centuries they had lived primarily in a well-defined region of northern Hungary, they were nonetheless a Slavic minority without a sense of separate peoplehood. Despite a shared language, Slovak inhabitants of northern Hungary often identified themselves by village or county. The Hungarian government's Magyarization policies, instituted in the nineteenth century and aimed at extirpating cultural pluralism, further thwarted the development of a Slovak ethnic identity. Once in the United States, Slovaks did establish their own institutions, but persistent regionalisms, together with the effects of Magyarization and the consequences of having no independent national history, slowed the development of a national consciousness among the grassroots immigrant population.[2]

Confusion among Americans about "Slovaks" and who they were further complicated the situation. While Slovaks moved haltingly toward developing a more encompassing ethnic identity, to Americans these former residents of northern Hungary were practically invisible. When it began compiling mother-tongue data, which revealed the ethnic makeup of the migration into the country, the Bureau of Immigration did include Slovaks as a "race"; the 1910 census also listed Slovak as a mother-tongue option.[3] But for the most part, by the onset of World War I general perceptions of Slovaks remained blurred as many Americans lumped them into the amorphous category of "Slavs" and cast them into the general class of "undesirables." Still, with a vast network of secular as well as religious fraternal societies, churches, and a growing number of schools, the institutional and emotional basis for nurturing Slovak ethnicity had been planted in the United States by the eve of World War I.[4]

Ironically, the wartime move to establish an independent homeland somewhat counteracted the blossoming Slovak identity. Once immigrants who styled themselves as spokespersons for suppressed compatriots in Europe had settled on the idea of establishing a joint Czech–Slovak state, *realpolitik* shaped ethnic activities for the remainder of the war and forced Slovaks not only to lobby for but also to justify creating "Czecho-Slovakia."[5] The politics of constructing a nation-state out of the rubble of the Austro-Hungarian Empire necessitated this strategy, but it played havoc with the goal of perpetuating a separate Slovak identity in America.

The campaign for the new nation, together with the civic designation "Czechoslovak," obscured the distinct "Slovak" national identity that, theoretically, a homeland free of Hungary should have illuminated. While both Czech and Slovak organizations continued to engage in their own ethnically specific activities, the tendency was for the broader civic identity, "Czechoslovak," to supersede the ethnic particularity of the composite nationalities. Slovak organizations worked on behalf of "Czecho-Slovakia," sometimes spelled with the hyphen, many times not. National organizations as well as ordinary Slovaks did carry out campaigns to assist "Slovaks" in war-torn Europe and to further the cause of "Slovak" freedom from Hungary. Still, in patriotic exhibitions such as Loyalty Day 1918, Slovaks and Czechs typically marched together in "Czechoslovak" divisions. Relief activities were undertaken for Czechoslovaks in the Old Country; Czechoslovak branches of the Red Cross operated in local communities.[6] After the Czechoslovak National Council in Paris was allowed to recruit volunteers for its legion, the New York Czechoslovak Recruiting Office issued a spectacular poster depicting Czech and Slovak flags waving together (Illustration 2).[7]

Despite this symbolic featuring of separate Czech and Slovak flags, the national identity of the proposed joint state supplanted the ethnicity of the component populations. Thus, during the war and immediately afterward, popular literature and news reports often turned communities that had previously been Slovak *or* Czech into "Czechoslovak."[8] The new nation's inhabitants as well as former nationals in the United States were referred to as "Czechoslovaks." Activists committed to preserving a Slovak national identity realized that they needed to halt the "Czechoslovak" impulse both in Europe and in the United States. They understood that this was necessary to ensure the Slovak people's long-term existence as a distinct nationality.

Instead of unity, homeland politics created four conflicting positions on the fate of Slovakia. Two contingents favored Slovak autonomy within the new nation but differed on how quickly this should occur. One faction, led by Catholics, insisted on instant autonomy; these immediatists supported the Slovak People's Party in Slovakia.[9] They distrusted the Protestant- and Czech-dominated central government, which they feared would institute measures to "Czechify" Slovaks. Another bloc, comprising primarily Lutherans and, at least, the leadership of the

ILLUSTRATION 2.
Vojtech Preissig
poster issued by the
Czechoslovakia
Recruiting Office,
Tribune Building,
New York, ca. 1917.
Courtesy of Meehan
Military Posters.

Slovak League, favored a transition period with a temporary centralized government. Some believed immediate autonomy would unleash discrimination against Protestants; even more alarming was the fear of reconciliation with Hungary. In the view of these gradualists, the Hungarians—not the Czechs—posed the greatest threat to Slovakia's national existence. Maintaining that Slovaks were not ready for autonomy, the gradualists wanted the Magyarization legacy obliterated and Slovak national consciousness strengthened before making Slovakia autonomous. They desired provincial self-government for Slovakia but preferred moving inchmeal toward it. Another contingent, properly known as centralists, believed that a permanently centralized government was the best constitutional structure for the nation. Finally, a small group accepted "Czechoslovakism," the idea that Czechs and Slovaks were one people and that their languages were dialects of one another.[10]

It was the battle between the immediatists and the gradualists, and yet their shared opposition to the "Czechoslovak idea," that fueled efforts to shape a Slovak national identity in America. Each side believed that the survival of the Slovak people in the new state rested on asserting a strong national consciousness that would defy the fabricated "Czechoslovak" identity. As a consequence, during the immediate postwar era Old World issues continued to nurture ethnic activism, and Slovak ethnicity became intertwined with politics in the homeland.

Stirring ethnic awareness had long been the aspiration of Slovak nationalists, especially the small camp in the United States. Concerned that a pithless ethnicity would doom their institutions, leaders of both religious and secular bodies had mutual objectives. Accordingly, both types of organization promoted a national consciousness by publishing items on Slovak history and personages. Following the war and the creation of a multiethnic homeland, the move to heighten Slovak ethnicity took on immediacy and added dimensions. Horrified by reports that July 6, the anniversary of Hus's execution, had been designated a national holiday, the Federation of Slovak Catholics, an American lay and clerical organization, called for making July 5, the feast of Saints Cyril and Methodius, a day of general commemoration.[11] Prior to the Great War there had been intermittent calls for Slovaks in the United States to set aside July 5 to honor these two saints; in the postwar years, this meek cry evolved into a clamor. Catholic activists viewed the Cyril and Methodius tradition as a way to establish Slovaks as a unique people. They also endeavored to use it as a conduit to tie the Slovak national identity to religion. The argument was that the two apostles had brought not simply Christianity but "Catholic Christianity" to the Slovaks.[12] One particularly fervent spokesperson asserted that a Cyril and Methodius Day would let individuals demonstrate that they were "Catholics and Slovaks."[13] The aim was to create a cult of Cyril and Methodius akin to the popularity that Hussitism enjoyed among Czechs. Protecting Catholicism in Slovakia was a persistent refrain.[14]

The Catholics' appropriation of Cyril and Methodius widened splits among Slovaks in America. Asserting that the missionaries should be venerated for bringing Christianity to all Slavs, Protestants resented the exclusive claim Roman Catholics laid to these ancestral personages. They also maintained that the Christianity that sprang from the apostles' efforts among Slavic peoples had endowed Czechs and Slovaks with a shared history and values.[15] However, the designation "saints," together with numerical superiority, gave Catholic activists the upper hand in the campaign to capture rights to Cyril and Methodius. In addition, although Protestants believed these proselytizers had rescued Slavs from the throes of paganism, they had a more natural affinity for Hus and were eager to promote respect for this ancient figure. Consequently, as the debate progressed, the Cyril and Methodius tradition evolved into the foe of Hussitism. Moreover, while Roman Catholics spent energy aggressively claiming these apostles, Lutherans responded by celebrating their own notables and trying to build reverence for Slovak Protestants, past and present.

Despite their disagreements over the religious dimensions of "Slovakness," vying factions were dedicated to affirming a Slovak national identity. Organization newspapers and annual publications carried features on Slovak history and culture. They spotlighted literary and historical luminaries, particularly those involved in the nineteenth-century nationalist movement, which had resulted in the codification of the Slovak language. They printed Slovak literature and songs. Renewed emphasis was placed on Juraj Jánošík, an eighteenth-century bandit who, in the Robin Hood genre, purportedly fought for justice. Embellished by legend, this folk hero who stole from the rich to give to the poor symbolized the Slovak struggle of the weak against the mighty.[16] From the activist perspective, a people battling for freedom constituted the overriding theme of Slovak history. This battle, the argument went, had endowed Slovaks with an appreciation for liberty and justice and had molded the Slovak national character. Now, following their liberation from centuries of Hungarian rule, Slovaks should not be a dominated people in their own country.

The stepped-up campaign to confirm a Slovak national identity was not a coordinated effort. Rather, it was a strategy that competing activist factions independently adopted. Immediatists insisted that their distinct culture and history justified Slovak autonomy without delay; gradualists believed that Slovaks were a separate people but as yet lacked the national self-awareness vital for autonomy.[17] Nevertheless, while disagreements over the constitutional structure of the homeland as well as religious differences eclipsed the unity among these rival camps, their activities, taken in the aggregate, amounted to a general movement. For despite increased acrimony, these opposing factions had a mutual aspiration: they hoped to fashion a Slovak national identity with discernible historical roots that could effectively counter Czechoslovakism as well as destroy the legacy of Magyarization. In terms of the homeland, a desire to achieve Slovak autonomy as laid down in the

Pittsburgh Agreement drove their individual agendas. Pushing their respective programs, each side weighted its position with democratic ideals and principles of self-determination.

As divisions hardened over Czecho-Slovakia, religious activists more directly connected ethnic identity to the homeland situation.[18] The Cyril and Methodius tradition became identified with support for immediate Slovak autonomy and the Catholic political party advocating it. In June 1920, the leading Slovak Catholic immigrant newspaper editorialized that establishing a single Saints Cyril and Methodius Day in the United States would "show Slovaks in Europe the strength of religion and national convictions" that Slovaks in America had.[19] The author was essentially calling on Slovak Catholics collectively to serve, in Jonathan Winthrop's elegant phrase, "as a city upon a hill," an example and an inspiration to those in the motherland. Advocates of a Saints Cyril and Methodius Day fancied that it would evolve into the Slovak equivalent of the Irish Saint Patrick's Day, a national observance with religious overtones that would simultaneously establish a unique ethnic identity. Clearly, by 1920 Catholic proponents saw creating a nationwide day as a means both to counter Czechoslovakism in America and influence politics in the homeland.[20]

While Catholics in the United States sought to rally forces that would intrinsically link religion and ethnicity, Czecho-Slovakia adopted its constitution. The First Catholic Slovak Union expressed its dismay by enclosing *Jednota*'s front-page announcement about the constitution in thick, black borders.[21] Obviously, in the union's view, the failure to implement the Pittsburgh Agreement was cause for mourning. Neither the National Slovak Society nor the Slovak League of America, both with Catholic members, greeted the new constitution so sullenly. Instead, they accepted the centralized state as a temporary expedient until Slovakia was ready for autonomy under the terms of the Pittsburgh Agreement. "Step-by-Step Autonomy in the Czecho-Slovak Republic" read the bold headline of a description of how the president of the Slovak League assessed the situation. This notice, which appeared in *Slovenský hlásnik*, also reflected the typical Lutheran outlook.[22] These Protestants in particular had a persistent fear, which they seemingly could not shed, that the Catholic clergy would take Slovakia back into the Magyar fold. From their standpoint, Slovakia's national identity could be maintained in a joint Czech–Slovak state.[23]

Offering a contemporary perspective of how Slovaks differed on homeland issues during the years immediately following the creation of

Czechoslovakia requires mentioning how the vying factions have been historically treated. In both Slovak popular literature and historical scholarship, the sincerity of the gradualists in particular has been challenged. In the hands of nationalist writers, *all* Slovaks who supported a central government during these crucial years have been dismissed as "centralists" and simultaneously tarred as "Czechoslovaks," traitors to a Slovak national identity. But viewing issues from the contemporary vantage point and examining the ongoing discussion of homeland autonomy, which was carried on in the immigrant press into the early 1920s, reveal that many articulate Slovaks so casually labeled "centralists" did support autonomy but advocated a gradual move toward it. These were nationalists who, convinced that their overseas compatriots needed more time to cast off the legacy of Magyarization, believed the best chance for national development lay in a joint Czech and Slovak state. If centralization was a gamble, immediate autonomy could mean disaster. For the purposes of exploring ethnic activism during the postwar era, the task is not to deride either position, but instead to accept the fact that on homeland questions, each faction—immediatists and gradualists alike—was equally convinced that its assessment of the situation was correct and each acted on that conviction. As a consequence, differently based fears about Slovakia and its inhabitants' future exacerbated existing religious as well as ideological differences among Slovaks in the United States.[24]

The influence of homeland issues extended beyond the political battles within Czechoslovakia. Some activists were so fervidly committed that they viewed contemporary American politics through a lens shaded with interest in Old World matters. The 1920 presidential election succinctly illustrated this. Commenting on the presidential campaign, *Jednota* was neither timid about telling readers how they should vote nor was this official organ of the First Catholic Slovak Union shy about its reasoning. In describing Warren Harding's "principles" as "narrow-minded chauvinism" and "plutocracy," one reporter did seem interested in social policy. The commentator's depiction of the Democratic candidate James Cox, however, more clearly revealed the extent of his concerns. Cox exemplified the principles of Woodrow Wilson, he declared. Making an indirect reference to foreign policy, and more specifically to the fight over the League of Nations, the columnist portrayed the election as a battle between the ideals of humanity and national selfishness. In a strongly written editorial, the paper subsequently clarified its position by endorsing Cox because the Democratic

Party supported the League of Nations, "the most important question of this era." A vote for Cox was a vote for Wilsonian principles and, equally important, for the league. In this instance, the First Catholic Slovak Union conceptualized issues from the vantage point not of what was good for the United States but of what its spokespersons believed would benefit the homeland. League principles, meaning self-determination, the editorial concluded, would secure the freedom of "our nation under the Tatras [mountain range]." Although *Jednota's* readership was overwhelmingly foreign born, during the campaign the newspaper assigned immigration issues a back seat to procuring a mandate for the League of Nations. After the election, it did predict that a Harding victory "would mean bad times for immigrants."[25] Still, for this Catholic paper's editors and the activists who contributed to its pages, matters that touched the homeland had taken precedence during the presidential campaign.

The secular *Národné noviny,* the official publication of the National Slovak Society, took a more circumspect approach. Instead of endorsing a particular candidate, it contrasted party stands on various issues. While it enunciated the differences between the two major political parties on the League of Nations and clearly supported creating it, *Národné noviny* laid more emphasis on stances concerning America's immigration policy. After the election, the paper's front-page story brooded over what the Republican victory would mean for the country's foreign born.[26]

Highly placed partisans used the immigrant press to trumpet their positions and take swipes at the opposing views of other prominent spokespersons, but they also wanted to draw rank-and-file Slovaks to their cause. Self-preservation on both sides of the Atlantic rested on instilling a sense of peoplehood into the ordinary masses. Activists knew that. Surely to their delight, the drive initiated by Catholic activists soon after Czecho-Slovakia's birth to establish a national holiday did spark some popular reaction at the community level. In 1919, Slovaks in several regions sponsored a "Saints Cyril and Methodius Day." The events often had combined purposes. Slovaks in Torrington, Connecticut, for instance, coupled a celebration of the saints with a parade honoring countrymen who had fought in the war. The day ended with a banquet arranged by the local Slovak Catholic parish. Although observances held elsewhere were less elaborate, the religious and political objectives were equally conspicuous. The Slovak League organized Cyril and Methodius Day in Pittsburgh, where festivities consisted of songs and political speeches about the homeland. Slovaks in Whiting, Indiana, devised a modest program comprising songs, speeches, and the Catholic mass to carry out their annual commemoration of the saints' feast. Celebrating Slovakia's freedom from Hungary, however, was the day's theme.[27] During the next two years, sporadic observances of the saints continued.

Slovak activists also sought to attract grassroots support by resorting to the wartime strategy of organizing local public rallies. Community activities, however, were not controlled by the leadership of national organizations. The influence local activists could exert was evident in different events arranged by regional divisions of the Slovak League in the early 1920s. In some areas, league branches sponsored "Czecho-Slovak" Days. Western Pennsylvania held its first Czecho-Slovak Day in 1920, and all Slavic groups that had fought for the creation of the Czecho-Slovak republic were invited. Publicity promoted the day as one that would demonstrate unity among these nationalities. Although announcements used the hyphenated spelling, "Czecho-Slovak," even after the 1920 constitution had deleted the hyphen, the event was nevertheless designed as a show of support for the new nation. In addition to drawing Slovaks from throughout the region, outspoken national activists, including the president of the Slovak League, participated in the day's activities.[28] At the same time, league affiliates in the state's eastern section held a Slovak Day. Reportedly, among the speakers was Jan Masaryk, son of Czechoslovakia's president who was being much maligned by immediatists for having signed and then later rejecting the Pittsburgh Agreement. Meanwhile, league affiliates in Cleveland also organized Slovak Day, an event initiated during the war. The theme, commemorating Slovakia's fight for freedom, was the same as the previous year's. The 1920 affair differed slightly because the proceeds were designated for a fund to establish a memorial in Cleveland to Milan Štefánik, the Slovak member of the Czechoslovak National Council who had recruited personnel in the United States for the Czechoslovak Legion and had died in a plane crash in May 1919.[29] Clearly, in 1920 the homeland figured prominently in public activities. In this respect, the agenda that had captured the attention of national activists did enjoy some grassroots interest. The events indicate that, at the community level, Slovak political activities reflected the platform or interests of whichever local faction was the most energetic in pushing its agenda.

For nearly half a decade following the Armistice, Old World issues helped propel efforts to shape a Slovak national identity and gave impetus to local activities as well. Even during this phase when homeland affairs dominated, however, Slovak enthusiasts had to remain sensitive to conditions in America. In essence, despite their aggressive plans, the aspiring sculptors of a Slovak identity could not fashion with unfettered creativity; they had to reckon with conditions on both sides of the Atlantic Ocean. However much immigrants remained interested in their native lands, they could not escape the realities of the society in which they now lived, especially the ongoing pressure to Americanize. Immediately after the war, Americanizers, too, had an agenda of unfinished business. Although tarnished by the wartime excesses of its offspring— 100 percent Americanism—the Americanization movement retained vigor. Dealing with this fact added yet another dimension to efforts to forge a Slovak national identity.

The vitality of the Americanization impulse was apparent in the spring of 1919 when more than 400 men and women convened in Washington, D.C. Representatives of civic organizations, people from immigrant-welfare agencies, educators, social-service workers, home missionaries, visiting nurses, Red Cross volunteers, and interested observers trekked to the capitol for the conference "Methods of Americanization."[30] From the welcoming address by the Bureau of Education's Director of Americanization, Fred C. Butler, on Sunday, May 12, to adjournment on Wednesday, May 15, participants mulled over Americanization. Differences were clearly evident, but, as parties bandied ideas about and either nodded in agreement or shook their heads in dissent, the proceedings revealed some fundamental unity.[31] People generally accepted the premise that being Americanized entailed learning English. They also agreed that Americanization included gaining a knowledge of American history and government, embracing "American" principles, and, of course, becoming a citizen. Participants further concurred that Americanization needed national standards. While recoiling from extremes labeled "chauvinism," the general mood was still an aggressive one, advocating, for example, compulsory adult education.

The penchant for equating English with being Americanized rankled some liberal critics, but devoted Americanizers raised a cautionary hand as well.[32] Addressing the gathering, Secretary of the Interior Franklin Lane counseled against treating English as the gauge of Americanization. It was abhorrence of radicalism, not forbearance for immigrants, that moved this long-time supporter of English-language instruction to admonish his audience. For Lane, radicalism, not foreign-born people, posed the real threat to the nation. The secretary belonged to that band of contemporaries who believed every American needed to be Americanized, needed to be imbued with American principles and an unflinching loyalty to the country's political and economic system. He called for instilling a "supreme allegiance to the flag of the United States" into all Americans, native and foreign born.[33]

Following the conference, the disciples of Americanization spread out into local communities to continue their proselytizing. The Department of the Interior's Board of Education kept up its support for community-based activities, especially an emphasis on factory schools in companies employing large numbers of immigrants. In its year-end report, the bureau claimed that in 1919 more than 800 Americanization committees were hard at work in industrial plants. This federal agency also continued publishing handbooks and guides to assist Americanization efforts.[34] At the same time, the apostles of anti-radicalism were laying emphasis on ripping out the roots of un-American ideas and embedding unwavering loyalty to "American" principles and "the flag."

Collectively, then, the broad spectrum of Americanizers—ranging from the liberal-minded to the nativist fanatics—reflected the general tendency to equate English competency, citizenship, and adherence to fixed political and economic principles with being "American." Although disavowing the excesses of wartime extremists, proponents of tolerant Americanization, including those who attended the 1919 conference, actually revealed an essential mutuality with the 100-percenters. While superpatriots were fond of intimidation, reformers espoused more constrained but nonetheless high-pressure tactics as they sought mandated language training and citizenship education. The continuing stress on Americanism and English-language proficiency was part of the popular climate shaping the real-life existence of ordinary immigrants in the early 1920s. It was in this atmosphere that Slovak activists at both the national and local levels were trying to shape an ethnic identity that would suit homeland and, not incidentally, new-land needs.

One activist who directly confronted the Americanizers was Albert Mamatey, a naturalized citizen and president of the Slovak League of America. Mamatey was among the few representatives of the country's ethnic groups who took part in the 1919 Americanization Conference. When he addressed the gathering, he espoused what at first glance was a seemingly contradictory position. Mamatey flatly stated that he neither opposed Americanization nor wished to "dampen" the enthusiasm of people participating in the effort; instead, he applauded "praiseworthy efforts" to uplift the foreign born. Indeed, lamenting "race hatred" as well as the contempt and indifference toward "foreigners," he welcomed a more active, sympathetic interest in them. Laudations aside, however, Mamatey offered a blunt yet measured attack on the supposed relationship between Americanization and English literacy. Seizing on the theme that Americanism was based on adherence to ideas, he warned that equating language with patriotism constituted a flawed assumption. His underlying rationale coincided with Interior Secretary Lane's admonitions, especially as Mamatey recited names of "radicals," both native-born and English-speaking naturalized citizens, who had opposed the war. He pointedly reminded his audience that immigrants and their children had served in the military and contributed to the war effort in other ways. While conceding that learning English was practical, he cautioned against an overzealousness requiring language instruction for all non-English-speaking people. Asserting that complete Americanization would be impossible to achieve in the first generation, he told the audience that "the transformation ... into Americans will be accomplished in the second generation" and "nothing will stop" this process.[35]

Mamatey's assertion about a generational process was meant as an assault on using English as a criterion of what constituted being American. He was not voicing some inner hope or even resignation that the second generation would shed its ethnic identity. He was merely explaining that he had no problem with the fact that the children of immigrants would speak English. Learning English was not only unavoidable; it was practical. Moreover, his comments were by no means an admission that foreign-born people could not be Americanized. Instead, he was joining company with anti-radicals who believed that "an American [is a person] who has American ideals" and that the real "foreign" persons were those who clung to or were "activated by un-American or anti-American ideas." Immigrants who had fled repression in their homelands, he declared, appreciated the liberty America afforded them. In addition, based on criteria rooted in *principles*, he wanted the second generation to become "American." Significantly, Mamatey did not voice the same contempt for the citizenship criterion that he did for the language standard. On the contrary, as "proof of our willingness to push Americanization," he detailed ethnic organizations' citizenship requirements for membership and their "efforts to fit them [their members] for the duties of life and citizenship with our English-speaking people."[36]

Although Mamatey did not represent all foreign-born people—or even all Slovaks—his address at the 1919 conference outlined the philosophical underpinnings of what would become their response to Americanization. In addition, his speech embodied the strategy that ethnic activists would employ to make Americanization and ethnicization complementary processes. His comments were equally prescient about how his ethnic group would confront the generational issues it would soon face. The tactic was in part to promote ethnicity by stressing ideological components of the American identity.

Within the context of the early 1920s, the objective was to challenge the premise that learning English was integral to being Americanized. From the standpoint of Slovak national activists of virtually all religious, political, and ideological views, language was the linchpin of Slovak ethnicity. Preserving the ancestral tongue was key to warding off Czechoslovakism. Thus, not surprisingly, spokespersons took particularly close aim at the English-language aspects of "Americanization." In the opinion of these nationalists, countering Czechoslovakism on both sides of the Atlantic depended on strengthening loyalty to the Slovak language among the generations. Although disagreements over Slovakia's autonomy had sharply divided Catholic and Protestant activists, a Lutheran minister expressed a point of agreement when he stated that there was no "Czechoslovak" language and that the use of the term "Czechoslovak" would mean "the end of Slovak identity."[37]

In defending against the assault on immigrant languages, the writers for *Národné noviny* were apparently not intimidated by the country's intolerant temper. They went on the offensive. Instead of masking views in Slovak-language pieces, the paper brazenly used English in editorials about Americanization. In one particularly bold commentary, an essayist lambasted proposed legislation that would make studying English obligatory for every non-English-speaking person between age twenty-one and forty-five. He denounced the idea as "inhumane" and "stupid," especially for laborers who toiled ten to fourteen hours every day or for women who would have to leave children and household duties to attend school. There was, the writer conceded, no quibbling with the premise that "every resident of this country should have a command of the English language." The editorialist even admitted that the lack of competency in English had been a "great impediment" to immigrants and that everybody should be encouraged to study English "as a matter of expediency."[38] However, the commentator assailed claims that language competency or studying English were measures of individual or group patriotism. Americanism, he insisted, could be demonstrated in other ways. Slovak critics thus did not question the practicality of knowing English or challenge its standing as America's premier language. Instead, they called for encouraging the study of multiple tongues. Promoting bilingualism was not a response solely to Americanization. It was also a reaction against Slovaks possibly being lost in an indistinct Czechoslovak identity both in their homeland and in the United States.

While, with eyes fixed on Czechoslovakia, articulate activists tried to shape a national identity, rank-and-file Slovaks coped with everyday life in postwar America. Homeland issues did arouse interest, and local communities even organized public rallies, but ordinary Slovaks did not necessarily share the fiery passion evident in the vitriolic exchanges among partisans. Perhaps even more important—from the perspective of national activists—it was possible that many Slovaks were not worried about fostering the mother tongue. The robustness that characterized efforts by individuals who themselves clearly possessed honed language skills subtly exposed a difference between them and the general Slovak populace.

From the outset of their campaign to establish a distinct national identity, activists encountered problems grounded in the Slovak historical past. Their experience under the Magyars had shaped the cultural values, especially attitudes toward education, of Slovaks living in the United States. Hungary's policy of forced assimilation had by 1905 reduced the number of elementary schools providing any Slovak-language instruction to 241, an enormous decline from 1,822 institutions in 1869. Only 7 percent of the Slovak children enrolled in primary schools in 1905 were being instructed in their native tongue. The continuous decline over the quarter-century after 1879 in the number of youths who attended Slovak schools meant that most Slovaks developed only minimal competence in their own language.[39]

Slovak immigrants obviously carried the effects of a steadily worsening literacy rate with them. The growth of foreign-language newspapers indicates that some Slovaks learned to read their mother tongue in the United States, but how many did so cannot be ascertained. Nationalist priests, believing there was a close link between language and the preservation of religion, had pushed for Slovak parochial schools. Congregations, however, did not always share their pastors' ardor and thus had to be pressed to support what were often clergy-initiated endeavors. Moreover, in some parish schools Slovak-language instruction was not part of the curriculum.[40] This ambivalence toward education in general, and toward Slovak-language training in particular, resulted from a convergence of values, experience, and new-world realities. Coming from primarily agricultural backgrounds and generally with little formal education, Slovaks characteristically sought security. Stable employment and home ownership ranked high among individual and familial goals; formal education typically did not.[41] If reading and writing Slovak had been unnecessary—indeed, a potential hindrance in their homeland—these skills seemed even more inconsequential to the practical goals of working-class people in the United States.

The simultaneous, sometimes conflicting, dynamics that were influencing attitudes about language and national identity were evident in articles that appeared in the 1924 *Kalendár ženy*, the yearly almanac of a female mutual aid organization. A four-page article titled "The Woman and the Nation" surely delighted those who believed that sustaining Slovak was vital to nurturing a Slovak identity. Concentrating on cultural retention and language maintenance, the author reminded women of their responsibilities to their people. She appealed for Slovak elementary schools and for women to take steps to keep children, the prospective "bulwark of [Slovak] national life," from being estranged from their people.[42] As the "soul of the family," mothers in particular were obliged to cultivate both moral principles and a national consciousness in their children.

Only a few pages away, *Kalendár* readers encountered a Slovak-language article, "Why Slovak Women Ought to Learn English," flatly stating that English was necessary for women to understand "the new world they live in." The author methodically cited practical reasons associated with women's maternal responsibilities and household chores. Shopping, banking, and conversing with teachers and doctors all required using English, she wrote. Traveling to visit family living in other locales as well as sending money via the postal service would be much easier. In addition, knowing English could let those working outside the home earn more money "in factories." Understanding English would help them avoid accidents because they would better understand rules and their fellow employees. Finally, with competency in English, women could take out citizenship papers and understand laws and American government.[43] In sum, for broad pragmatic reasons, women needed to master English.

The author was not advancing elitist, philosophical arguments or even promoting a political agenda. In their attacks on zealous Americanization, Slovak critics had usually conceded the necessity of knowing English. The *Kalendár ženy* author, however, went further by offering a matter-of-fact perspective and shedding light on what was significant to ordinary immigrants. Coping with routine tasks in the home, community, and workplace was a reality of daily life; raising American-born children was another. She, and those who accepted her line of thought, were more likely to be receptive to the notion that, if it meant learning English, they were not adverse to being "Americanized." There was nothing in her argument, though, that hinted that Americanization entailed rejecting the mother tongue or, perhaps even worse, rejecting one's ancestral heritage. On the contrary, the author seemed comfortable with the idea that people could remain loyal to their ethnic identity while following the practical approach of embracing the language of their adopted land. But her arguments also underscored the difficult task that articulate champions of promoting the Slovak language faced when it came to eliciting support from practical, ordinary Slovaks.

Taken together, the *Kalendár* commentaries reflected present realities and underlying anxieties about the future of ethnic life in America. It was possible that parents who were either illiterate or who possessed minimal reading and writing skills in Slovak would not feel passionately about making children acquire these abilities. They were certainly inconsequential to achieving material security in America. The ongoing animosity toward foreign ways, together with lingering memories of the wartime experience, surely slanted attitudes about language. Values rooted in the Slovak historical experience further affected individual perspectives. There were, then, early signs that some Slovaks might not be convinced that ethnic identity and mother tongue were inextricably linked. As a result, the postwar crusade to create a Slovak national identity augured the possibility that preserving the mother tongue would be more than a matter of "intergenerational conflict" in which immigrants would try to force American-born children to learn something the youths would prefer to forget.

Although Slovaks differed in their passion for promoting the mother tongue, during the early 1920s the alleged correlation between English proficiency and "Americanness" became the foundation for activists simultaneously to attack and embrace "Americanization." As they went on the offensive against overzealousness, national activists seized on the wartime concept of Americanism and formulated arguments to support language maintenance.[44] Within these standards, true Americans were adherents to tolerant, democratic ideals and would never deny basic freedoms by compelling persons to forswear ancestral languages and attachments in the way Old World tyrants had tried to do. As one

Slovak commentator succinctly put it: "Americanism and intolerance cannot grow on the same tree."[45] Organizations championed their own Americanization programs. The National Slovak Society, determined to demonstrate that "holding on to our mother tongue does not weaken our citizenship nor love of this republic," encouraged immigrants to become citizens.[46] Other Slovak societies did the same. At its 1921 convention, the Slovak Evangelical Union included "Americanization" on its published agenda. Reports presented at this annual meeting proudly informed members that the Slovak Evangelical Union had continued its Americanization program "in the true American spirit." Summarizing the preceding year's activities, the minutes, which were also reproduced in the official organ, noted that the mutual aid society's newspaper had published articles on how to become a citizen and about America's institutions, constitution, and economic system.[47]

Some ethnic activists joined hands with those Americans who pointed to bigotry, industrial exploitation, and the country's socioeconomic inequalities as being what were truly "un-American." They also found company with critics who flayed Americanization as a subterfuge to counter labor unrest and produce a quiescent labor force. Charges that Americanization was a stratagem to control the working class were voiced in 1920 following the nationwide steel strike.[48] Angered by the injustices inflicted on immigrants, an English-language editorial warned that the Slovak League would instruct Slovaks about their "constitutional rights" and would "Americanize them on a basis of absolute equality." The writer defiantly stated, "If there is any Americanization to be done, we will do it ourselves."[49] This bold claim was grounded in the premise that citizenship and adherence to principles, not their language, made individuals "American."

By defining Americanization in terms of ideals and citizenship, Slovak activists were simultaneously attacking both the movement's moderate and extreme elements. Proclaiming intolerance "un-American" and tarring the emphasis on English as bigoted, naive, or perhaps both, they tried to turn the tables on Americanizers, and especially the superpatriots. Within this line of thought, challengers to "chauvinists" and "professional Americanizers" became the truly Americanized, the true Americans. Constructing their points to oppose what Mamatey had assailed as overzealousness, ethnic activists were trying to stave off the excesses of Americanization while at the same time advancing efforts to shape a distinct Slovak identity. As activists built their argument for principles and citizenship—not language—as the heart of Americanization, they stressed the compatibility of the Slovak character with American principles, especially a love of liberty and democracy. Hammering on a theme common to immigrant dialogue, they alleged that, as fugitives from oppressive regimes, their appreciation of freedom surpassed that of Americans whose democratic experience caused them to take their liberties for granted. Nevertheless, because the two peoples had each struggled for their independence, a comparable historical experience, the argument went, had similarly shaped the Slovak and American psyches.[50] There were also transatlantic overtones to this assertion about liberty-endowed characters: both immediatists and gradualists saw it as a rationale for Slovak autonomy and a justification for their ongoing political involvement in homeland affairs.

Ethnic activists understood that, if they were to fend off the extremes of Americanization and perpetuate a Slovak identity, they had to do more than fire obloquy at zealots; they had to stir ethnic pride among ordinary Slovaks. From their standpoint, they needed to nurture the idea that Slovak uniqueness rested on an estimable ancient culture *and* a dedication to Americanism. Drawing in the masses, though, required broadening the boundaries of Slovak culture beyond intellectual, literary, and artistic achievements to embrace the common arts. In 1919, an essayist for *Slovenský hlásnik* represented this approach when, denouncing efforts to make immigrants forsake their native tongues, he boasted that Slovaks had a deeply rooted culture and, as evidence, singled out exquisite Slovak needlework.[51] Stressing folk arts, this author was articulating a view that had gained a faint voice in popular thought. Some Americans had already accepted the notion that immigrants had made significant cultural contributions to America. From this perspective, rather than depriving immigrants of the cultural "gifts" they bore, Americanization had to be a reciprocal process based on mutual respect.[52]

The "immigrant gifts" concept held that preserving ancient, premigration traditions, together with an appreciation of their positive impact on American culture, would promote assimilation. This philosophy, which had actually originated in the social settlements of the Progressive Era, stimulated a small wave of postwar multiethnic exhibitions featuring folk arts, crafts, music, dances, and costumes. In 1921, planners in several cities secured the cooperation of ethnic communities to put on displays of handicrafts and customs. Twenty-two countries and at least half again that number of foreign-language groups were represented in Buffalo's Exhibition of the Arts and Crafts of the Homelands. In the fall of that year, thirty-three groups participated in New York

City's "America's Making Festival," two weeks of pageantry and exhibitions. Events elsewhere reflected the ethnic composition of their respective areas.[53]

Because participants were typically identified by country instead of ethnic group, the multinational festivals exacerbated the ongoing problem of asserting a distinct Slovak identity. Country of birth meant that the wartime practice of including Slovaks under the "Czechoslovak" appellation continued. Categorized by country, even separate Czech and Slovak displays, art, crafts, music, and costumes became Czechoslovak. Event catalogues, reports, and subsequent publications might note the Slovak and Czech components but again typically described the contribution as Czechoslovak. This usage further muddled general perceptions of Slovak identity and advanced a concept that since the war had bothered Catholic and Protestant activists alike. "South Slavs," whose homelands had also been incorporated into a single state, experienced the same treatment.[54] Still, for Slovaks the expositions' stress on cultural pride neatly corresponded with the activists' agenda to fashion a unique national identity. Festivals generally aimed to elicit appreciation for the nationalities' individual traditions, and by highlighting culture, multiethnic exhibitions allowed people to emphasize the give and take between adopted and ancestral lands.

In significant ways, the postwar affairs were similar to the wartime allegiant displays. By seeking to punctuate the diverse contributions to American culture, the events galvanized the individual groups in local communities and encouraged them to flaunt their ethnicity. Indeed, the success of multinational exhibitions depended on groups asserting ethnic particularities. Also, boasting, which regularly appeared in the immigrant press, shows that these multiethnic affairs fostered friendly rivalries among local nationalities. *Slovenský hlásnik* captured the competitive spirit when it reported that twenty-eight nationalities had participated in New York's "America's Making Festival" but that Slovaks and Czechs had "distinguished themselves the best." They could make this claim, the article implied, because their "costumes, songs, needlework, and music" had merited the special attention and admiration of American spectators. The event, the reporter gushed, had provided a rare opportunity for these two groups "to distinguish themselves" and elevate their "work, culture, and enlightenment in the eyes of Americans and other nationalities."[55] On another occasion, the paper crowed that folk-art exhibitions provided Slovaks with opportunities to demonstrate that they had brought more than "hands, legs, a stomach and pockets for the

American dollar."[56] Spokespersons for other ethnic groups probably offered the same assessments of their displays. These were early hints of the "other nationalities" theme that would influence ethnic activism at the community level for decades to come.

Even as they participated in multinational undertakings, ethnic groups arranged their own nationality affairs. As we have seen, following the creation of Czecho-Slovakia, agendas for the homeland inspired local Slovak activists to arrange various "days," especially in 1920. But, despite ardent efforts, the immediate postwar attempts by Catholics to establish a countrywide Cyril and Methodius Day essentially to help advance a political agenda for the homeland failed. This failure did not mean that Slovaks totally ignored appeals to honor the apostles; instead, in the early 1920s some communities responded by fashioning "days" that, while incorporating Old World or Cyril and Methodius themes, were increasingly shaped by American circumstances.

Between 1920 and 1923, the Slovak League's Cleveland affiliates continued to sponsor Slovak Day and to designate the proceeds for a memorial to the Old World hero Milan Štefánik. In 1923, however, a "Slovak Catholic Day" for the Cleveland diocese was held on July 4. Despite the anniversary of America's independence, ads touted the event as honoring Saints Cyril and Methodius, whose feast was the next day. Organizers no doubt were seeking to capitalize on an American holiday when many workers might have the day off. An estimated 1,000 persons turned out for the occasion, which promoters described as an opportunity to exact respect from other denominations for the way Slovak Catholics joined together to demonstrate a love of their faith and Slovak nation.[57]

For Slovaks elsewhere, Independence Day's falling on the eve of the observance of Cyril and Methodius also proved a fortuitous coincidence. That same year, Slovaks in eastern Pennsylvania, too, sponsored Slovak Day. Fifteen thousand persons from throughout the area reportedly gathered on the Fourth of July to join in festivities advertised as both celebrating America's national holiday and commemorating Cyril and Methodius. A Catholic mass launched the day's activities. The tendency to present nationality events as joint ethnic and patriotic affairs persisted. The next year, planners in eastern Pennsylvania explained that it was practical to hold Slovak Day, which celebrated Cyril and Methodius, on July 4 because it was a nonworking day for many and thus provided an opportunity to combine a national holiday with a commemoration of these august figures.[58]

Some local promoters chose not to exploit the proximity to America's holiday but instead highlighted only the religious and ethnic significance of Cyril and Methodius by honoring them on a separately dedicated day. Instituting their first Slovak Day in 1924, local organizers in Westfield, Massachusetts, hinted at what had moved them to action and what they hoped would excite fellow Slovaks in their vicinity. They believed the events held on Sunday, July 6, would show "others" the respect Slovaks had for their patrons, Cyril and Methodius.[59] The same year Pittsburgh's Czecho-Slovak Day, traditionally sponsored by the Slovak League, yielded to a Slovak Day dedicated to Cyril and Methodius. People who attended the festivities at Kennywood Park received badges with the apostles' pictures. Bishop Boyle, prelate of the Pittsburgh diocese, addressed the participants, who reportedly had come from throughout western Pennsylvania for this first Slovak Day. He praised them for honoring their saints.[60]

By 1924, Slovak Catholic activists were retreating from their push for a "Cyril and Methodius Day" but clearly had not abandoned their objective of trying to link ethnicity and religion. In addition, more and more, local days were supporting a Slovak Catholic agenda. For example, organizers of the 1923 Slovak Day in Wilkes-Barre, Pennsylvania, gave equal portions of the $2,000 proceeds to the Sisters of Saints Cyril and Methodius; Scranton's Catholic bishop for orphans; a fund for Slovak American students; and a bishop in Slovakia for "Slovak youth." Pittsburgh's 1924 revenues went to Slovak nuns in the city and to two religious orders planning to build convents in the diocese.[61] Although Slovak Days spotlighted ethnicity, in the early 1920s they were increasingly taking on strong religious overtones—specifically, they revealed a decidedly Catholic pitch. Moreover, they reflected the growing influence of local people and community-level concerns on Slovak activism.

As Slovaks organized nationality days, they could not ignore the contemporary craving for patriotic expressions. Slovak events, even when not held on July 4, obligingly acquiesced in this yearning. Postwar "days," including the early Cyril and Methodius commemorations, incorporated "American hymns" into their programs. Slovak Red Cross volunteers carried a service flag in Torrington, Connecticut's 1919 Cyril and Methodius Day parade; singing "My Country 'Tis of Thee" was on the program. In 1921, Slovaks in Pittsburgh's South Side observed the feast of Cyril and Methodius by blessing Slovak and American flags. At a Slovak Day in Wilkes-Barre, people heard a senator praise Slovaks for their loyalty and sacrifices during the Great War.[62] Americanism and underscoring their contributions to the war effort became themes that activists, eager to fend off nativist critics as well as to impress second-generation Slovaks, would vaunt throughout the interwar era.[63]

FOLLOWING THE ARMISTICE, most Americans wanted to turn away from European affairs; immigrants typically did not share that aversion. From a realistic standpoint, homeland affairs were not as relevant to new immigrants as situations they were confronting in the United States. Yet "American issues" such as the Red Scare, which targeted aliens, and the nationwide steel strike, which forced thousands of Slovaks onto picket lines, received secondary coverage in the immigrant press. Although the major Slovak organizations supported the 1919 steel strike, it was homeland news that dominated the headlines, front pages, and editorials.[64]

Rather than uniting Slovaks, though, interest in the mother country tore them apart. Catholics fueled a bitter controversy by linking religion to national identity and aggressively tying both to Old World politics. Differences notwithstanding, gradualists and immediatists agreed that achieving Slovak autonomy depended on exploding the "Czechoslovak" idea. In the United States, however, activists faced the twofold task of discrediting the ambiguous Czechoslovak identity and countering Americanization zealots. These individual yet companion objectives rested in part on asserting Slovak uniqueness, exposing the hoary roots of a well-developed culture, and thus invigorating a languid national consciousness. Nationalists believed that success depended on sustaining the mother tongue on both sides of the Atlantic.

Published statements indicate that Slovak activists in the United States acknowledged the benefits of knowing English but rejected the abandoning of ancestral tongues. Preferring bilingualism and facing resolute opposition, the more aggressive sought to define Americanization in a way that emphasized citizenship and principles over language. Stressing the tolerant dimensions of Americanism, they lashed out at those who equated language with loyalty. Within this liberal paradigm, the promoters of extreme and forced Americanization became the "un-American."

The emphasis on American principles grounded in a devotion to democracy dovetailed with political agendas for the homeland. Taken as a whole, the prolific commentary, vitriolic exchanges, and identity-boosting prose created during the transatlantic period formed a body of literature as well as rhetoric that provided the intellectual underpinnings for promoting Slovak ethnicity in America. Only a small contingent of committed advocates became vigorously involved in homeland and identity debates; nevertheless, during the first half-decade after the Armistice, they constructed an intellectual foundation for the ethnic activism that would flow through the interwar years and reach high tide when the country once again went to war.

Homeland politics and aggressive Americanization stimulated efforts to fashion a Slovak national identity, but tolerant strains of American popular thought also nourished the impetus. The "immigrant gifts" concept, which gained some respectability, provided a justification for promoting cultural pride among immigrants in general. Moreover, albeit in a modified form, multiethnic folk art exhibitions extended the wartime habit of demonstrating a common purpose by accentuating ethnic particularities. Notwithstanding the xenophobia that characterized contemporary American society, the popular milieu was sufficiently broad to countenance manifestations of ethnicity. The "immigrant gifts" idea, however, enjoyed a following because it focused on cultural impact and left American principles untouched by foreign influences.

Even as ethnic activists, both national and local, pushed their agendas, they could not ignore issues that American society was thrusting on them. Although people remained concerned about their mother country, in the early 1920s they were being forced to shift away from homeland matters to focus more closely on the realities of American society. For years, new immigrants had been struggling with the impact of the Great War and its legacy. As the mid-1920s approached, they were engaged in another battle: the battle of the "undesirables."

3   Memories, Principles, and Reality
The Postwar Era to 1924

During the years immediately following the Armistice, the United States came face to face with festering tensions—those bred by war and those more deeply seated in America of the early twentieth century. Countrywide labor strikes; exploding bombs, together with plots fortuitously uncovered; and nationally orchestrated searches for alleged radicals kept the nation's nerves on edge well after the guns fell silent in Europe. As social and political ferment unsettled their postwar world, Americans remained apprehensive about entanglements with Europe and ever wary of foreigners in their midst. After nationwide explosions and strikes forecast for May 1, 1920, failed to materialize, the national "Red Scare" did quickly subside. A peaceful May Day enervated the hysteria that had gripped an anxious nation for more than a year; nevertheless, an underlying animosity toward the foreign born persisted.[1]

Fears about immigrants inundating America intensified this hostility. In late September 1920, a reported "near riot" at Ellis Island caused the commissioner of immigration to halt temporarily the landing of passengers so the unprecedented "congestion" at the receiving depot could be relieved. "So many immigrants" had arrived that inspectors could not expeditiously process them; consequently, people outside, weary of waiting for relatives or friends, stormed the gate.[2] Several weeks later, Americans went to the polls to elect Warren Gamaliel Harding, whose party had called for a "return to normalcy." The appeal of this beguiling slogan lay in its ambiguity. This catchphrase left definitions of normalcy to individual interpretation; in it, Americans of various and diametrically opposed ideological persuasions could find solace. Rather than curing America's problems, the call for normalcy further cultivated underlying divisions and nourished the yearning for conformity sowed during wartime.[3]

Xenophobia, which pervaded the nation, made it inevitable that assessing immigration would constitute part of the impulse to restore a romanticized traditional stability. For nativist devotees of racially based eugenics, the objective went beyond merely limiting entry into the United States to establishing permanent control of the nation's ethnic composition. Demands to curtail immigration thus evolved into nationality plans grounded in a bigotry that would stigmatize nearly 18 percent of the contemporary population. The stigma perforce would be passed on to subsequent generations.

Throughout the immediate postwar era, while Slovak activists had been concentrating on Europe and defining ethnicity within the paradigm of homeland issues, they had not been oblivious to conditions affecting their compatriots in the United States. The same was true for other nationalities, especially those with roots in the former Austro-Hungarian Empire. Spokespersons did occasionally speak out on behalf of the much maligned new immigrants. It was the drive for immigration restriction, though, that caught the notice of articulate new immigrants and caused them finally to focus more sharply on this side of the Atlantic. As anti-foreign sentiment deteriorated into calls for a racially based immigration policy, activists would turn their attention to that issue and, more specifically, to its inherent long-term impact.

During the half-decade following the Armistice, as national activists dealt with homeland issues, immigrants throughout American society were coping with everyday realities and, especially, the runnels of wartime intolerance and ultranationalism streaming into their postwar world. Following passage of the 1924 national origins law, Slovak activism, which had been dominated by national activists first focusing on international issues and then on American immigration policy, would ebb into an undertow moved by community activities. A view of American life from the local arena during the time leading up to the 1924 national origins legislation reveals intertwining factors at work shaping the ethnic activism that would subsequently characterize the 1930s.

THE NEW YORK TIMES'S front-page report about a "near riot" at Ellis Island in September 1920 no doubt created a disturbing image in the minds of people already panicky about a postwar surge of immigrants into the United States. Although the Times story could catch the eye of only a small portion of the country's newspaper readership, the event itself incarnated fears lurking in the popular mind. Even some traditional sympathizers with the foreign born were wondering whether, perhaps, the time had come for a numerical reduction or temporary suspension of immigration.[4] Long-time foes, of course, were already convinced that something must be done. Since the war's end, the nation's lawmakers had been grappling with ways to forestall the anticipated rush of Europeans to America's shores. The growing number of new-comers intensified this legislative momentum. In the twelve months before Congress began its third session in December 1920, nearly 464,000 persons entered the country, and the influx seemed likely to continue. Legislators reacted by stepping up debates on limiting, and perhaps even suspending, immigration. Wilson's pocket veto of a quota plan did not deflate restrictionists' efforts. Regulation remained high on the congressional agenda until, in May 1921, Congress succeeded in passing an immigration quota bill, which the recently inaugurated Harding obligingly signed. A drive to prolong regulation realized quick success when, one year later, Congress extended the Immigration Act of 1921 to June 1924. Although the new policy aimed temporarily to reduce immigration into the country, in both legislative deliberations and in public opinion it was clear that limiting migration from eastern and southern Europe was the major objective.[5] Immigrants and their children who followed the debate realized that. They understandably took umbrage at the underlying premise that, in contrast to the groups that preceded them, the so-called new immigrants were "inferior" and "undesirable."

Slovak activists initially interpreted the growing clamor for restriction as an assertion by descendants of earlier immigrants that they were *the* true Americans and thus had a more legitimate claim to the country. From the standpoint of the foreign born, another implication of the rising xenophobia seemed to be a claim that, historically, it was native-born people—not immigrants—who had made significant contributions to America's development as a nation. Reacting to these inferences, critics began rummaging through U.S. history for examples to challenge such pretensions to anteriority. In 1920, a Slovak Lutheran newspaper tellingly used the upcoming celebration of the Fourth of July as an occasion to remark, in an English-language editorial, that eight signers of the Declaration of Independence were foreign born.[6] *Národné noviny*'s editor combined the anniversary of two historical events to malign detractors of the contemporary immigration. After congratulating America for "[one] hundred and forty-four years of Independence" and adherence to democratic principles, the commentator, in a thinly veiled reference to the tercentenary of the Pilgrims' landing at Plymouth, turned derisive as he mocked the idea that descendants of people who had come 300 years earlier should "feel that they are better than those who arrived three hundred weeks ago." This expositor of the American experience was clearly speaking about more than the direct-line posterity of the Pilgrims. Like critics of restriction before him, he was hammering on the old theme that all Americans, including prominent citizens, traced their origins to immigrant ancestors. "The earlier arrival may consider himself more fortunate," he observed, "but not superior."[7]

The activists' rhetorical cannonade ranged from thoughtfully crafted essays to pointed witticisms. In 1920, *Národné noviny* regularly carried English-language quips displaying a contemptuous attitude toward present-day issues and especially matters related to immigrants. Subtly addressing the previous-arrival notion, one pithy gibe wryly taunted, "Don't tell an Indian to go back where he came from if he is dissatisfied with conditions."[8] Exuding even more sarcasm, another scoffed, "Of course, we understand that the 'Hunkey' and the 'Dago' are foreigners. But what are the McWhatyoumaycallens and the O'Whoesits?"[9] The paper's quipster, like so many others, knew that nativist sentiments were not directed equally toward all nationality groups. More and more they sensed that, in the popular thought of the early 1920s, the previous immigration from northern and western Europe had in effect bequeathed a most-favored status not only on successive generations but on the contemporary foreign-born population from those countries. Given this, they wanted to quash any action that might perpetually leave "new immigrants" on the lower ranks of America's nationality scale.

The battle, therefore, was as much against popular attitudes that touched the lives of ordinary immigrants residing in America's cities and towns as it was against legislative initiatives. The "Nordic theory," a supposition alleging the superiority of "races" from northern Europe, was infiltrating not only Congress. The media had helped spread this nativist canon into the homes of the general public. In 1920–1921, for example, readers of the anti-foreign *Saturday Evening Post* encountered Kenneth L. Roberts's ominous predictions about a deluge of undesirables to America's shores. This maligner of the new immigrants spiced "emergency" warnings with his own vivid eyewitness accounts of embarkation points in Europe, where thousands were supposedly poised to leave. He was putting the country on alert. Infested with contagious diseases, a filthy, ignorant humanity, Roberts declared, was eagerly waiting to swarm into the United States and sink into America's slums.[10] These were not oppressed human beings seeking asylum; no, they were economic refugees who would turn into "parasites on the community." In his scenario, the new immigrants, unlike Nordic peoples of the past, became "unsightly indigestible lumps" floating around in the melting pot. Measures were necessary so "that refuse might be refused and deposited in the customary receptacle for such things."[11] For a mere

$2.50 per year, the *Post*'s subscribers automatically received Roberts's denigrating fulminations as well as other anti-immigrant materials the magazine chose to print. Americans who preferred to let content determine their purchases could obtain a newsstand copy of the weekly for five cents. For those who wanted to indulge in lengthier and more theoretical but no less disdainful commentary on the new immigration, a bounty of publications grounded in pseudoscientific racism appeared in the early 1920s.[12]

The initial response by Slovaks to calls for changes in the country's immigration policy reflected the fact that they knew American popular opinion was demanding some type of restriction. In late December 1920, one quipster sardonically captured the country's general nativist temperament when he sneered that perhaps restricting immigration was "almost a blessing" because it would "remove the bone of contention" that was aggravating "meddle-someness and intolerance in American public life."[13] After Congress imposed the 1921 law limiting immigration, some Slovaks actually voiced a reconciled support for temporary restrictions. Whether bending over backward to seem reasonable, cognizant of popular sentiment, or expressing sincere convictions, a few observers openly acquiesced in the idea that a nation should regulate entry into its territory. For example, in 1922 *Jednota* merely pointed out to readers that the traditional source of the membership of the First Catholic Slovak Union had "dried up," and, now, their organization's future rested with "our youth."[14]

Any early acquiescence in the seemingly inevitable, however, gave way to bitterness. When Congress extended the expiration date of the 1921 immigration law to June 1924, the decision roused scant interest among Slovak activists. This nonchalance in part reflected a preoccupation with homeland issues, but also the legislation did not flagrantly target new immigrants, and so it apparently did not excite alarm. Subsequent rumors about proposed revisions were not so cavalierly ignored. Reports that the House Committee on Immigration was weighing proposals to alter the formula that the 1921 legislation had established for calculating annual quotas triggered swift reaction.

Congressional moves to change immigration laws reflected a popular mood willing to brand nationalities as undesirable and countenance a national policy skewed against them. Slovaks and other new immigrant groups therefore faced a two-front battle. They had to fight discriminatory legislation specifically targeting them, and they had to counter the potentially long-term invidious effects that codifying racist theory into law would have on popular thought—specifically, on perceptions of them and their descendants. New immigrant spokespersons could not ignore the underlying premise that the so-called Alpine and Mediterranean peoples whose origins lay in eastern and southern Europe, respectively, were biologically and culturally inferior. Nor could they close their collective eyes to the ancillary assumptions that the new immigrants were less assimilable, would adulterate the American population, and would debase American civilization. By ranking nationalities according to desirability and linking their fitness to supposed inherited characteristics, the proposed immigration policy laid the foundation for permanently stigmatizing particular ethnic groups. This blotch would not fade with the demise of the foreign-born population but would taint its descendants as well. As the push to place numerical restrictions on immigration evolved into a drive for an allotment plan hinged on the theory of Nordic superiority, new immigrant activists fashioned their rejoinders accordingly.

Slovaks did not resort to public manifestations like those employed during the lobbying efforts for the homeland. But with a vigor reminiscent of their wartime endeavors, activists plunged into the rhetorical fray over immigration policy. They denounced suggestions that the law be amended so that the 1890 instead of the 1910 census would be used to assign quotas and the annual allotments would be lowered from 3 to 2 percent. Organizations sent memoranda to congressional representatives, and when invited, spokespersons testified at congressional hearings.[15] The most dynamic campaign against revising America's immigration policy was carried out in fraternal newspapers. By the fall of 1923, the Slovak press was printing articles lambasting the proposed revisions in yearly allocations.[16]

As momentum for quota legislation gained force, Slovak commentators became more impassioned and increasingly more indignant. In early 1924, the major newspapers featured two particularly scathing sets of essays sponsored by the Slovak League. One series, a six-part sequence titled "Restricted Immigration," exuded indignation.[17] Representative of the rhetoric that reverberated through the immigrant press, the articles provided a particularly illuminating ethnic perspective of the iniquitous effects racially based immigration laws would ultimately have. The author declared that the current bid to revise America's immigration policy stemmed from a "mental attitude" with deep historical roots. This was evident in the fact that, seesawing with the times, the popular predisposition traditionally had been to cast foreign groups in an unfavorable light, only to have subsequent generations do an about-face. He reminded readers that this national propensity formerly had thrust English-speaking Irish immigrants into the ranks of the "undesirable."[18] Of course, the point was that many contemporary critics of immigration were themselves descendants of previous "undesirables."

This writer, along with other advocates, was also aware of allegations that recent arrivals had not contributed to the country's development. Despite strained efforts to single out foreign-born individuals who had participated in historical events, they knew that, within the context of the country's founding and democratic development, the charge was true. Defenders, like the Slovak League spokesman, asserted, however, that the new immigrants had contributed mightily to America's remarkable industrial growth. As manual labors they had been crucial to expanding the nation's factories, working its mines, and manufacturing its finished goods. He went on to recite Slovak military service and domestic activities to support America's wartime effort.[19]

The Slovak League's commentator minced no words in assaulting the proposals under consideration as "discriminatory." Combining emotionalism with cold facts, he shrewdly presented evidence demonstrating that the intended revisions would decrease allocations for Belgium and France. Lest anyone miss the point, he elaborated by using apt references to the war. Close analysis revealed that Germany, the former detested enemy, would receive a higher immigration allotment than two countries that had been "allies of the United States."[20] He denounced the plan as a subterfuge to let more Germans into the country. This league agent asserted that the Nordic theory, which alleged the superiority of particular races, constituted part of an insidious scheme to discriminate against eastern and southern Europeans while favoring Germans.[21]

From the Slovak—and, indeed, the new immigrant—perspective, this seemingly preferential treatment of Germans was particularly hard to swallow. The league's spokesman reproached congressmen for such partiality "only five years after the war." "Not one of these legislators," he asserted, would have considered according Germans such a preferred position at a "time when the casualty list of this country read like a pay-roll of our large industrial plants." Carrying the allusion to wartime contributions by eastern and southern European immigrants further, he again deftly combined military service and domestic support for the war effort by reminding readers that just five years earlier "posters for the promotion of war loans bore the legend, which since then has become legendary: 'Americans All.'"[22] Whether intending cynicism or righteous indignation, the point was evident: when new immigrants had sacrificed for victory against the vicious "Hun," they had been embraced as "Americans." Now that the war was over, these former patriotic "Americans" were to be spurned as inferior, as undesirables.

As Slovaks weighed the immediate and long-term effects of the proposed revisions of immigration law, umbrage generated bitter, impassioned entreaty. Modify existing policy or, if necessary, suspend immigration entirely, but do not, the Slovak League's representative implored, frame legislation "based on a principle of prejudice." Congress must fashion a law "that will not leave any feeling of bitterness, resentment and objection to being classified as undesirables." Speaking on behalf of Slovaks, he emphasized that they took exception to "any law which would set up an arbitrary mark of distinction between us and our non-Slovak neighbors—a mark which would entitle them to throw into our face that we are less desirable because we came here later." The basic point was: "a law which tends to create a division in our citizenship cannot be a good law."[23] The proposed legislation thus was not only callous in design; it was callous in intent. Critics knew that. From the standpoint of new immigrant America, the law, if enacted, would sow the seeds of contempt and would be an indelible badge of degradation.

Slovak activists realized that a further reduction in immigration was inevitable. The task was to persuade Congress to impose an equitable quota plan instead of one that would stigmatize individual ethnic groups. From the Slovak vantage point, negatively branding new immigrants would have ramifications beyond eternalizing bigoted attitudes among old-stock Americans. It could affect the Slovak self-image as well.[24] The move toward a nationality-based immigration policy and the ascendancy of the Nordic theory took place almost concurrently with the ongoing campaign to forge a Slovak national identity and bolster ethnic consciousness. The ideological assumptions fueling restriction in the early 1920s undermined this effort. Ethnic activists could expect a lukewarm response, at best, to attempts to create pride in an ancestry that popular opinion deemed inferior, especially when American law formalized that inferiority. Certainly, nativist tirades predicting the "mongrelization" of America represented the antithesis of the "immigrant gifts" concept that ethnic activists had latched on to to promote their cause. In countering an idea that ranked nationalities and implicitly pit "new" and "old" immigrants against one another, activists resorted to the same rationale employed in the battle against zealous

Americanization. The strategy was to portray restrictionists and "rabid extremists" as un-American while holding up their critics as defenders of Americanism. In the struggle over immigration policy, adherence to ideals—not ancestry—was, these writers collectively maintained, the sign of a true American.

Activists presented their arguments in both Slovak- and English-language articles. The Slovak columns clearly aimed to keep immigrants informed about legislation directly touching their lives.[25] Their authors no doubt hoped to influence naturalized citizens who ideally would work to defeat politicians who had voted for the offensive legislation. The English-language articles were different; they targeted other readers. To be sure, these pieces constituted part of the lobbying effort directed at American politicians. However, readers of English-language items consisted of the American-born second generation and probably immigrants who had come at a young age and were proficient in English.[26] Reminders that some of the most vociferous restrictionists were themselves descendants of former "undesirables" were intended to chide native-born restrictionists. Such remarks, however, also formed part of a preemptive strike to thwart the negative impact that the "undesirable" tag might have on younger Slovaks. Activists needed to stem what they feared would be a rush by second-generation Slovaks to disassociate themselves from a denigrated nationality and its institutions. They were telling them not to shun their ancestral heritage because, despite the contemporary disdain, they, like nationality groups before them, could ultimately gain respectability. Taken on the whole, the thrust of their commentary strongly suggests that the English-language articles were intended to sway a second-generation readership.

The effort to block discriminatory legislation failed. The immigration bill, which Congress finally passed in the spring of 1924, drew reactions ranging from resentment to resolve. The Catholic *Jednota* declared the law "a defeat for Slavs and Latin peoples" and "the victory of an idea" that Americans have to be Anglo-Saxon or Nordic. In essence, the newly devised plan, with its aim ultimately to maintain an ethnic status quo, created a permanent affront to persons of eastern and southern European heritage. A few weeks later, the paper also reiterated the same point it had made after Congress first instituted quotas in 1921. Because it strangled a vital source of new membership, the law could potentially doom ethnic organizations. The future "is now in our own hands," the columnist resolutely proclaimed.[27] That future, of course, rested in large measure with Slovak youths. A Slovak from the industrial town of Maltby, Pennsylvania, added a local voice to the discussion about immigration policy. In a published letter, he decried the potentially destructive effect of the new law. He was particularly distraught about its impact on the mother tongue. Lamenting that the Slovak language "will die out," he called on Slovaks to get classes established in high schools and colleges.[28] This man represented those rank-and-file Slovaks who were concerned about language retention as well as cultural maintenance, and who undoubtedly would be willing to engage in efforts to fight the negative impact of the national origins legislation.

Some particularly indignant critics tried to call Slovaks to action. Denouncing the "so-called 100 per cent Americans," a writer for *Slovenský hlásnik*, who signed his letter "a citizen," urged Slovaks to become citizens. They could then coalesce into a political force and influence legislation. He also opined that, if massive numbers became citizens, then Americans would consider their electoral strength and "stop calling us 'hunkies.'" "Become citizens," he entreated.[29] Given the wartime experience with Americanizers, this admonition made sense. After all, persuading new immigrants to naturalize had been a primary objective fueling both tolerant and fanatical Americanization. Also looking to create political pressure, the Slovak League tried to convince Slovak organizations to unite in a concerted effort to lobby for changes in the 1924 bill and to discredit the nefarious idea that Nordic peoples were the only desirable immigrants. Others stepped up assaults on 100 percent Americanism and pounded on the well-established theme that "chauvinism" and intolerance were un-American.[30]

In fighting the discriminatory legislation, Slovak activists framed the issues within the parameters of ethnic diversity because they saw the legislation as an invidious comparison of nationalities. At the same time, since America's naturalization laws recognized all former European nationals, regardless of country of birth, as white and eligible for citizenship—a fact seemingly reinforced by the current zealous efforts to get the "new immigrants" to naturalize—there was no reason for Slovaks to conceive of the debate within confines other than those of "nationality." The "undesirable" label did not make them ineligible for citizenship, and in that sense it did not set them racially apart from other white Americans, including the old-stock native born. On the contrary, naturalization elevated them to a status equal to these Americans. They did not, therefore, perceive issues in terms of their "whiteness." As articulate Slovaks saw it, the contemporary debate about immigration was rooted in alleged inherited cultural differences among nationalities and among people from different countries.

The trenchant attacks on the Immigration Act of 1924 and the Nordic theory, together with ruminations about political redress, constituted an intellectual response to America's newly formalized immigration policy and the prejudices underpinning it. Carried out primarily in the newspapers, the endeavor involved a comparatively small number of well-informed and probably better-educated activists who, albeit for different reasons, had a shared agenda: creating and perpetuating a Slovak ethnic consciousness. Officials of secular and religious fraternal societies feared for their own future viability, while the politically oriented looked to the broader ramifications of a devitalized ethnicity. From all these perspectives, though, the national origins idea and its formalization into American law stigmatized Slovaks and their descendants. In a heterogeneous society comprising "many peoples," the new policy rated them "inferior" and possibly forever relegated them to the class of "undesirables."

Thus, by 1924, the era of unrestricted immigration had come to an end, and it had faded in a way that besmirched the image of people who traced their heritage to eastern and southern Europe. Despite some feeble calls to lobby for legislative changes, after the spring of 1924 immigrants accepted the reality of restriction; they were, however, less docile about the attached stigma. The battle against the national origins legislation demonstrated that activists could not afford to focus so closely on the Old Country. The campaign against the legislation signaled a refocusing of priorities from homeland issues to matters developing out of conditions in the United States and to the growing challenge to group survival in a multicultural country.

Despite their concern with Old World politics, national activists, whose words filled the immigrant press, had not been out of touch with life at the community level. Instead, they had given some voice to that experience. "If you haven't yet found your place in your community, just pick on the foreigners," one *Národné noviny* commentator sneered in the spring of 1920.[31] Proclaiming that "we are living in an age of confused slogans" and "are still living in the atmosphere of the war," another writer was portraying what ordinary immigrants were coping with daily.[32] Whether incisive discourse or bluster, such rhetoric flowed from reality. Immigrants lived in a hostile world. The writer knew it, and they knew it. Self-appointed protectors of Americanism and supposed traditional values heightened the hostility that characterized the early

1920s. As national activists fought against revisions in immigration policy or engaged in efforts to fashion a Slovak national identity, average foreign-born persons dealt with these local realities. To gain a rank-and-file perspective on what would influence their views and help shape interwar Slovak activism, it is necessary to turn to the local arena where immigrants had to negotiate the currents of wartime xenophobia and hyped patriotism that flowed strong into the 1920s.

For ordinary immigrants, the Red Scare and 100 percent Americanism helped keep alive memories of the aggressive wartime drive for national conformity, a drive animated by nativism. During the war, immigrants had been required to exhibit their loyalty by marching in parades and purchasing war bonds. The fondness for patriotic manifestations trickled into peacetime. Wentworth Stewart, a critic of equating naturalization with being Americanized, revealed this popular appetite as he described witnessing "an exhibition of spontaneous Americanism." It had happened when hundreds of boys of different nationalities abruptly stopped playing and stood at attention when a band began playing a national hymn. Stewart could hardly contain his exuberance over this event on Boston Common. He reveled in this impromptu action, which he defined as a "manifestation of natural Americanism." For him, the spectacle conjured up memories of a similar satisfying wartime incident when Slavs in a midwestern town had marched in a drenching sleet storm "in honor of their country of adoption." Stewart asserted that "when aliens *by their own initiative* give evidence of Americanization," their sincerity "cannot be questioned."[33] The spontaneity, together with the fact that the actions were generated from within the foreign-stock population, was key to Stewart's exhilaration. Such happenings would similarly gratify other zealous patriots, especially in the belligerent supernationalism that carried over into what the historian John Higham called "the tribal twenties."[34]

The English-only tidal wave that had swept over the country became another wartime current that streamed into postwar America and into the 1920s. Exemplifying the country's nativist temper and unrelenting hostility toward foreign tongues, states passed stringent language laws.[35] Jobs could still be linked to language competency or foreign-born status. Stories in the immigrant press revealed that some employers were continuing the practice of discriminating against both aliens and naturalized citizens. In 1920, the National Slovak Society let its members know that equating immigrants with radicals had prompted a Newark, New Jersey, firm to advertise for "only Americans" and to declare that it would employ only individuals who "can talk the English language." A Baltimore company announced that it planned gradually to "discharge all foreigners, even if naturalized" and to replace them with "genuine Americans."[36] Workers who did not lose their jobs might still expect pressure to attend Americanization classes. Factory schools sponsored by employers gained popularity as Americanizers emphasized their potential for reaching larger numbers of immigrants. While certain employers openly targeted non-English-speaking immigrants, some states continued to enact laws sanctioning discrimination against, for example, foreign-born professionals.[37]

How many people were directly affected by discriminatory state legislation or employer pressure in the workplace is secondary to the reality these actions reflected and to the climate they helped foster in immigrant communities. Reminiscent of what had happened in wartime America, stories in the foreign-language press and word-of-mouth reports among the immigrant populations served as warnings even for those who escaped a personal experience.[38] The relentless stress on English and the sanctioned mistreatment of non-English-speaking people were components of immigrant life in contemporary America. While national activists had been beating the propaganda drum to ward off the English-language criterion and to hail instead the "principles" determinant of Americanness, main-street new immigrants had been dealing with real pressures in their communities—especially the demand to become literate in English.

The wartime drive for national unity had revealed a society in which vigilante actions could be countenanced, and this perverse indulgence also carried into peacetime. Scholarly accounts have vividly exposed the frenzied intolerance that swept over America. Despite its spectacular nature, the Red Scare, which gripped the nation in 1919–1920, was also local. It brought government agents and their civilian accomplices into people's homes and gathering places. Even after the Red Scare subsided, belligerence lingered as superpatriots stalked communities. And in the early summer of 1920, the penchant for stalking got a gigantic boost. While Americans were gearing up for summertime events, and political parties were preparing for their national conventions, two men and a woman in Georgia were quietly conducting negotiations destined to touch the lives of many Americans, particularly the foreign born. On June 7, William J. Simmons, the Imperial Wizard of the Ku Klux Klan, finalized an agreement with two charlatans, Edward Young Clarke and Elizabeth "Bessie" Tyler, that paved the way for the Klan to slither north of the Mason–Dixon line. Astute and unscrupulous, Clarke and Tyler successfully exploited the temper of the times. The tenacious quest to impose conformity on American society meant that, under the guise of Americanism, the Klan and other vigilante groups could recruit foot soldiers from the country's broad populace.[39]

During the first half of the 1920s, the Ku Klux Klan was indeed one of bigotry's most successful recruiters. Its nationwide activities notwithstanding, individual Klan actions were parochial. When Klansmen burned crosses, punished errant members of a community, paraded in hoods through the streets, instigated boycotts, or displayed window signs identifying the proprietor as a Klansman, the activity was local. When klaverns went after violators of Prohibition, became the self-appointed upholders of traditional morality, or declared themselves enforcers of law and order, the action was local. Thus, although couched within the Klan's national objectives and garbed in the rhetoric of 100 percent Americanism, individual Klan agendas were often shaped by locally bred conditions.[40]

Slovak activists derided restrictionists and "100 percent Americans," but, with few rare exceptions, the Slovak press proved hesitant to fire shots at the Klan. In 1921, as the Invisible Empire was gaining notoriety, the Lutheran *Slovenský hlásnik* did characterize the Klan as un-American and undemocratic.[41] *Svedok,* the organ of the conservative Slovak Synod, however, actually expressed sympathy with the Klan's anti-Semitism and anti-Catholicism but pointedly rebuked its anti-foreign bias and the 100 percent Americanism that fed it.[42] Generally, though, the press criticized the Klan in coded phrases denouncing "chauvinism" and the general intolerance in the nation. Falling into the category of bigoted 100-percenters, the Klan was just another in the panoply of fanatical anti-immigrant forces in American society. But for ordinary immigrants living in ethnic neighborhoods, witnessing Klan activities could be a reality of their existence. The evidence suggests, however, that while foreign-born individuals might have feared the Klan, they also seized on American principles to defy it.

Although the full story remains untold, snippets indicate that communities did not necessarily cower before vigilantes, especially the Klan.[43] The Invisible Empire's growth was accompanied by massive initiations, "konklaves," and huge public demonstrations. When these occurred, opponents showed up to jeer. Consequently, regions where immigrants and their children dwelled saw both Klan and anti-Klan activities. For example, in Steubenville, an Ohio industrial town inhabited by large numbers of new immigrants, local Klansmen's self-assigned mission to enforce Prohibition and cleanse municipal government of alleged corruption sparked a violent confrontation in the summer of 1923. An estimated 2,000 to 3,000 people were ultimately involved in an August nighttime melee that left four men shot and an undetermined number beaten. Ten days later, a riot broke out when a small crowd prevented Klan members from parading through nearby Carnegie, Pennsylvania, after a massive initiation reportedly attended by Klansmen from Steubenville and other towns in Pennsylvania, Ohio, West Virginia, and Kentucky. Elsewhere in 1923, angry confrontations led to violence. In Perth Amboy, New Jersey, police used tear gas to disperse a crowd after thousands descended on a Klan meeting and beat or pelted fleeing members with stones.[44] These crowd attacks on marchers reflected—and, indeed, contributed to—what was seemingly a growing disposition to curb the Klan's inflammatory public activities. Attempting to foil events that could trigger disorder, several states literally tried to unhood Klan paraders by passing legislation making it illegal to wear masks in public. Localities also sought injunctions to prevent Klan marches. Despite legal efforts to check its public activities, the Klan continued to creep north and west. Flaming crosses let local residents know when it had arrived.[45]

Although assaults on the Klan occurred in communities inhabited by large numbers of new immigrants, the involvement of foreign-born persons and their children in these incidents remains largely unexplored. In Steubenville, though, the four persons arrested for shooting Klansmen had Italian names, and vague descriptions suggest that a significant portion of the attackers lived in one of the town's foreign quarters. In Carnegie, a felled crowd member was Slavic. Whether new immigrants or their second-generation children actively engaged in anti-Klan activities remains secondary to the reality these incidents represented. For even if they were not directly involved, the violent confrontations and blazing crosses unavoidably touched the consciousness of immigrants and their children. The riots and cross burnings served as reminders of the Klan's presence. Moreover, local Klansmen liked to let communities know they were on guard. In the words of one historian: "the Klan watched everybody."[46]

While white robes, hoods, and burning crosses were Klan insignia, the Invisible Empire also appropriated the American flag as its banner. The flag appeared in Klan literature, on its paraphernalia, and in its public demonstrations. The Klan's obsession with waving the flag and espousing Americanism reflected a contemporary national passion for patriotic exhibitions. The Klan's commandeering of America's symbol, however, provoked hostile reactions that revealed how closely ordinary people, especially in ethnically diverse communities, identified the flag with "American" principles. Local Klan chapters parading behind the national emblem created flash points in already volatile situations. Crowds challenging Klansmen seemed particularly galled by their display of the flag. For instance, bantering over the flag touched off the violence in both the Steubenville and Carnegie anti-Klan incidents in 1923. Accosting paraders, people specifically objected to the Klansmen's use of the American flag and demanded that they remove it from their motorcades.[47] Whether these protesters had read anti-Klan materials or immigrant-press columns on what constituted true Americanism is incidental. These street-level critics clearly considered the Klan and the values it represented un-American. In their opinion, promoters of intolerance had no right to march under the symbol of the country's sacred principles. These local confrontations thus represented broader disagreements over the significance of the American flag. With vying factions trying to usurp the nation's standard as symbolizing their particular breed of Americanism, the fight was not over displaying the flag but, rather, over what principles it stood for.

From a palette of media reports and advocatory rhetoric, then, a portrait of life in ethnic America emerges. The wartime experience with demands to manifest loyalty, the ongoing threats of job discrimination, the unrelenting pressure to learn English, and the necessity publicly to show off their Americanism were neither easily ignored nor easily forgotten.[48] Since the war, the foreign born had lived with the clamor for explicit expressions of Americanism and loyalty. They also resided in a society that countenanced vigilantism and overt discrimination against non-English-speaking people and noncitizens. The Ku Klux Klan and superpatriotic organizations, as well as leery neighbors, constituted a felt presence in polyglot cities, industrial towns, and rural America. Along with seeking financial security, raising families, and even enjoying leisure-time activities, this was reality for average immigrants in the early 1920s. Federal legislation implicitly branding new immigrants as inferior and undesirable added to the already hostile atmosphere. The unfriendly ambiance might not have controlled their lives, but it had to be reckoned with nonetheless.

Thanks to the repressive atmosphere the Klan symbolized, manifesting Americanism became a necessary aspect of nationality-based activities for the foreign born. By incorporating the Stars and Stripes into purely Slovak affairs, local organizers tried to give ethnic events an "American" look. Honoring the American flag was not new; it was a Slovak tradition that stretched back to the late nineteenth century. Ever since Slovak immigrants had established their national fraternal organizations, local lodges had commonly held flag blessings. Wartime patriotism and its progeny, 100 percent Americanism, essentially ensured that Slovaks would not easily abandon but, more likely, broaden their public flag-waving.[49] For example, celebrating their lodge's silver anniversary in 1920, members of a Yonkers, New York, branch of the First Catholic Slovak Union carried what one reporter called "the holy and American flag" as they marched into the church.[50] In the early 1920s, the enthusiasm for demonstrating respect for the country's national standard filtered into other ethnic activities. Both the Slovak and Czecho-Slovak nationality days—public rallies with clear-cut political aims—incorporated the American flag and patriotic songs into their events. The Saints Cyril and Methodius Days, with their combined religious and political objectives, did the same.

While Slovaks increasingly were imbuing their public activities with patriotic tinges, especially flag-waving, in the early 1920s local organizers were finding a place for the national emblem in children's activities as well. This was evident when Slovak publications began including pictures of youths holding the American flag. For example, readers of the April 1920 issue of *Kruh mládeže*, a monthly segment for young members of the National Slovak Society, were treated to photographs of two young boys, each proudly holding a flag. Even more impressive was a telling photograph submitted two months later by the society's Young Folk's Circle in Kenosha, Wisconsin. Taken at the circle's picnic, the photograph showed at least twenty-three of the approximately forty-five smiling youths holding miniature American flags (Illustration 3).[51] In addition to food and leisure-time paraphernalia, preparations for this day of American-style recreation on a farm had included taking tiny flags for the obligatory group photograph.

These "loyalty pictures," which were reproduced in nationally distributed Slovak publications, shed light on what was influencing locally sponsored ethnic activities.[52] Supplying the young people with flags was likely a ploy to convince them that ethnic activities were also "American." Trying to manipulate situations to impress upon participants that they could be both "American" and "Slovak" had undoubtedly motivated the local planners who had packed flags along with

ILLUSTRATION 3. Loyalty photograph of the National Slovak Society's Young Folk's Circle of Kenosha, Wisconsin, taken at a picnic held in 1920. From *Kruh mládeže*, 15 June 1920, 14. Courtesy of the Immigration History Research Center, University of Minnesota.

other fare for leisure-time outings. Publishing such loyalty pictures suggests even more far-reaching but no less subtle objectives. Commentators could assume that immigrants and their children made up the readership, as they did for articles on Americanism in the Slovak press. For, even in the suspicious, watchdog atmosphere of the early 1920s, few nativists probably took the time to peruse the vast array of foreign-language publications.[53] Both the pictures and the activities they documented were aimed inward at second-generation Slovaks. The Kenosha group picture practically screamed out to readers that Slovak children could be proud Slovaks *and* loyal Americans. Pictorial propaganda was not limited to capturing youthful subjects. Group photographs of adult lodges often showed members holding small American flags or included a prominently displayed standard-sized one.[54]

Items about the American flag regularly appeared in materials printed by religious and secular organizations. A 1922 children's publication included a two-page article explaining the national emblem's colors and symbolism.[55] The immigrant media also took steps to educate readers about the correct handling and displaying of flags. Given the popular climate of opinion in the early 1920s, these instructions fittingly took on a cautionary as well as a didactic tone. For instance, a front-page article in *Slovenský hlásnik* advised, "It is in the interest of all foreigners in America to be acquainted with rules regarding the hanging of a foreign flag in the United States." The non-American standard could not be larger or fly higher than the American flag.[56] Admonitions about properly venerating the flag were not the idle musings of overly jittery activists. They reflected a calculated assessment of the modern-day temper and especially of life in local communities. Proposed legislation to deport "undesirable" aliens also had made mention of the need "to protect . . . [the] national emblem."[57]

FOR NEW IMMIGRANTS, the 1924 quota legislation was a turning point. It marked the end of the spirited, albeit unsuccessful, battle to thwart pernicious immigration legislation and ushered in an era of dealing with the immediate and potential long-term effects of the defeat. Indeed, as the surge toward restriction gained momentum, activists progressively changed their emphasis to issues that directly affected their populations in America.

While 1924 was a crucial moment in a historical sense, the era leading up to it had set the stage for the interwar era. Themes that would run through ethnic community life and influence both ongoing Americanization and activism during the interwar era had been laid out. Since the onset of the Great War, being patriotic *and* ethnic had actually been the norm. Popular enthusiasm for patriotic manifestations—combined with a decade of intolerance, an equally long drive for conformity, and unrelenting demands to manifest "Americanism"—had a cumulative effect on ethnic communities. For example, whether they were caving under pressure, expressing heart-felt sentiment, or perhaps both, national and local ethnic societies routinely incorporated the American flag into public activities.

The fight against the "undesirable" label had compelled new immigrants to develop a strategy of touting their contributions to the nation. They highlighted their military activities during wartime primarily by stressing that immigrants and their children had served the flag in the World War. Looking to their positive impact on society, they trumpeted the theme that the foreign born had been vital to the industrialization of the United States. During the interwar years, military service during the Great War, domestic support for the war effort, and contributions to America's industrialization would become the oft-chanted reminders of what one commentator described as the "offering[s] of the foreign

born to America's shrine."[58] The reaction to being designated "undesirable" thus encouraged what would become commonplace over the
coming decades: scavenging American history for examples of foreign-
born or ethnic-specific involvement in significant events.[59]

If the 1924 legislation stabilized the ethnic composition of the United
States, it similarly fixed a generational trend within ethnic populations.
For Slovaks, the new calculations meant that, beginning in the middle
of 1924, the annual quota for Czechoslovakia plummeted from 14,557
to 2,031, and in 1929 the allocation was set at 2,874.[60] With allotments
based on country, not ethnic group, Czechoslovakia's puny allocation
was shared by Slovaks, Czechs, Carpatho-Rusins, and a few other
nationalities. As a result of annual quotas, just under 55,000 Slovaks
immigrated to the United States during the 1920s.[61] Ethnic populations
were by no means static, because as the number of foreign-born declined,
the size of the second generation increased. The ramifications of this
swelling generation gap would become more important over time.

In the aftermath of immigration restriction, ethnic organizations as
well as the viability of ethnic cultures became endangered. Cultivating
ethnicity over the long term necessitated instilling pride in ancestry in
the second generation. "Our future rests with the youths" went the cry.
The Slovak newspaper *Jednota* was expressing resolve when, reacting to
the national origins legislation, it proclaimed that "if, over four generations" the Irish could maintain "an affection for their own people," then
Slovaks could do the same.[62] Immigrants knew that America was in fact
a multiethnic society. The aim was to preserve their ethnic group as part
of this heterogeneity.

For nativists, the Immigration Act of 1924 had the desired results. It
drastically reduced migration from eastern and southern Europe, and,
with the national origins formula finally implemented in 1929, the ethnic composition of the United States for the time being seemed stabilized. Gloating over their success, restrictionists sought unsuccessfully
to broaden their victory by trying to impose quotas on the Western
Hemisphere as well, but after 1924, immigration faded as an issue from
the national agenda. The country turned its attention to other interests.
New consumer products helped improve the standard of living while
pockets of the country suffered economic decline; movies, sports, and
amusement parks added variety to American leisure-time activities;
individual exploits and spectacular trials captured the headlines. New
immigrants participated in the events and changes sweeping over
American society in the 1920s.[63]

At the same time, life in ethnic communities moved on much as before. National and local organizations celebrated anniversaries; churches arranged fund-raising socials; and congregations maintained religious traditions. Ordinary immigrants, however, also had to live with the lasting effects of the nativism that had surfaced during wartime and flowed full force into the 1920s. In particular, they had to cope with a national psyche that cast them as "inferior" and thus "undesirable" additions to the nation. They also had to contend with generational changes and "Americanization" pressures that threatened group survival in America's ethnically diverse cities and towns. Dealing with these realities in the post-1924 era would see national activism, in which an articulate elite set the agenda, established the parameters of discussion, and fashioned the debate, give way to local vigor.

The following chapters offer an investigation primarily of local activism during the nearly decade and a half between the national origins act and the resurfacing of homeland issues in the late 1930s. The early battles stressing the ideological component of American identity did have a prolonged effect on ethnicization during the interwar period. Nevertheless, until the late 1930s, ethnic activism was an undertow in which the din of national rhetoric remained constant but local actions mattered much more. As we shall see, in the decades following passage of the 1924 national origins law, the ethnic impulse was very much alive among first- and second-generation new immigrants.

II. TURNING INWARD: 1924 THROUGH WORLD WAR II

4 Manifesting Pride, Power, and Patriotism

Nationality Days in Local Communities

FOLLOWING THE PASSAGE of the national origins law, Slovak publications teemed with indignant references to immigration restriction. During the next ten years, allusions to the law's adverse impact were common; clearly, this was not something aggrieved persons easily shoved aside. Resentment over being ignobly classified "inferior," together with a keen awareness of the long-term effects of the severely curtailed immigration, characterized the commentary. Combining gloom with resolve, articulate Slovak activists developed strategies for perpetuating group identity in a country unfriendly to "foreignness."[1] Despite popular antipathy toward the foreign born, one strategy Slovak enthusiasts followed was to arrange events flaunting ethnicity and drawing attention to their collective presence. Believing that a single nationwide "day" would both affirm and stimulate ethnic consciousness, activists carried out a campaign to institute Slovak Day. Appeals to organize annual manifestations of ethnicity generated a positive response at the local level. Consequently, the late 1920s witnessed an ever-increasing rise in the number of Slovak Days. By 1931, this drive, launched at the national level, had been taken over by local activists.

Until the late 1930s, when resurfacing homeland issues again embellished public activities, Slovak Days became parochial affairs influenced primarily by local circumstances. Rivalries among Slovaks spawned conflicting days, but the proliferation of the events demonstrated a striking copycat effect as communities followed the examples of fellow Slovaks in other areas. Community activists viewed these once-a-year happenings as a way to bolster ethnic consciousness and inspire self-respect among Slovaks of both the first and second generations. Local planners also fashioned days to impress outsiders, meaning "other nationalities." In addition, these events provided opportunities for Slovaks to demonstrate the compatibility of their Americanism and ethnicity. As displays of pride, power, and patriotism, local Slovak Days nurtured a Slovak activism spawned during the war and cultivated through the nativist 1920s.

THE CONCEPT OF A SLOVAK DAY had shallow historical roots. Before World War I, a few Catholic clergymen had made appeals for Slovak immigrants to establish a national day dedicated to Saints Cyril and Methodius. As previously noted, they wanted to imbue a religious fete with clear-cut ethnic overtones. In essence, the goal was to use a nationwide commemoration to link Slovak ethnicity to Roman Catholicism. These clerical entreaties went largely unheeded, but conditions spawned by the war finally spurred some communities to arrange Slovak Days.[2] In shows of patriotism and hyphenism, the wartime demonstrations reflected dual desires to forward homeland independence and comply with the popular demand for manifestations of loyalty to America. Toward these ends, the few Slovak Days born during the Great War openly espoused political and patriotic objectives.

The war did not beget a national Slovak Day, but the friction over Czecho-Slovakia did lead some Slovaks to devise various "days" to publicize their political stances. For half a decade after the Armistice a threefold concern with Old World issues, countering Czechoslovakism, and manifesting American patriotism influenced the character of the few nationality days that Slovaks organized. During this interim, however, neither religious nor secular activists forcefully advanced the idea of establishing *Slovak* Day, a single nationwide event specifically designed to accentuate Slovak ethnicity. Catholics in particular had continued to focus on creating a Cyril and Methodius holiday. Fears that immigration restriction heralded the end of Slovak ethnic identity in the United States finally prompted a shift away from an emphasis on Cyril and Methodius to one that more emphatically stressed nationality. Calls to hold Slovak Days escalated from faint whispers to nearly an all-out clamor.

In the aftermath of the 1924 immigration law, Slovak enthusiasts, motivated by disparate and occasionally conflicting objectives, collectively laid down the ideological rationale for establishing a Slovak Day. For advocates of a nationwide observance, the Irish Saint Patrick's Day became the quintessential model. In a campaign that had gained force by 1927, champions of an annual Slovak holiday trumpeted the Irish example. From their perspective, this annual Celtic observance was evidence of the durability of an Irish American consciousness. Slovak commentators mentioned that those affirming their ethnic pride on Saint Patrick's Day were fifth- and sixth-generation descendants. They told their compatriots that Americans interpreted the Saint Patrick's Day celebrations not as a rejection but, rather, as a reaffirmation of the group's Americanism. Revealing admiration mixed with jealousy, advocates pointed to Saint Patrick's Day observances as proof of the respectability and political power Americans of Irish descent had achieved.[3] Publicists for a Slovak Day were convinced that a national observance could have the same consequences for Slovaks. For them, the Irish experience offered reason to hope that Slovaks could indeed survive wide-ranging pressures to assimilate.

Supporters went beyond calls to mimic the Irish. Reiterating themes common to the booster literature, a 1927 editorial synthesized the rationale generally advanced for instituting a Slovak Day. It would, the writer opined, "strengthen Slovak solidarity and national consciousness." Citing local observances such as the 1926 event in Pittsburgh attended by 18,000 persons, he asserted that creating a Slovak Day would transcend social differences by bringing together all classes of Slovaks, ordinary workers as well as professionals and intellectuals. Benefits could reach beyond ethnic communities because huge annual gatherings would highlight their numbers and "show the world" Slovaks merited respect, he declared.[4]

Although national activists had their own agenda, their rhetoric did not merely reflect the ideological fixation of an elite minority detached from its grassroots society. Pleas for Slovak Days clearly fell on sympathetic ears in local communities. How many people were converted to the notion cannot be determined. To have an impact, the call to organize local days needed to strike a responsive chord with only a small, energetic segment, especially if it included pastors who could mobilize networks of local parishes. Still, the subsequent evolution of Slovak Days offers evidence that activist rhetoric either reflected existing views or was able to arouse sentiments already lurking among rank-and-file Slovaks. Within just a few years, the campaign for Slovak Day was clearly enjoying marked success. In 1925, only a handful of local days were held, but by the summer of 1931 so many were being planned that some Slovak newspapers had regular Slovak Day columns. Fraternal publications and, later, local radio programs included items about them. The Slovak media thus formed an information network reaching communities countrywide and nurturing enthusiastic cores of activists devoted to these episodic manifestations.[5]

All the publicity revealed that, contrary to the hopes of early advocates, local activists had taken over Slovak Days. Trying to turn back the tide, a proponent of a nationwide observance again attempted to use the Irish example to inspire, and maybe even to shame, Slovaks into accepting his position: March 17 is "the one day when the Irish prove to the rest of us that they are proud of their ancestors and of the Emerald Isle from which they came." He lamented that the "purely local aspect of our 'Slovak Day' defeats its own end." Pleas like his fell on deaf ears, though, as local activists continued to treat Slovak Days as parochial affairs.[6]

Activists, both local and national, lamented the development of seemingly haphazard and competing Slovak Days. Visionaries had always preferred one event, like the one the Irish held, to the hodgepodge of randomly scheduled celebrations that developed. Despite aggressive Catholic efforts, the attempt to turn Slovak Days into a Cyril and Methodius feast also failed. Although the majority of Slovak Days did take on religious overtones, some local areas managed to keep their annual events secular by stressing ethnicity instead of religion. A sterile cultural tradition was one factor thwarting the effort to blend religion and ethnicity to create a single national observance. Unlike the feast of Saint Patrick, which had been a holy day in Ireland, the feast of Cyril and Methodius had not been universally observed in the Slovak region of northern Hungary. For ordinary immigrants, revering the ancient apostles was therefore a novel concept. Lacking the thread of a premigration custom, advocates were unable to weave veneration of Cyril and Methodius into the fabric of Slovak popular culture in the United States.[7]

Circumstances in America also undermined the feasibility of establishing July 5 as a national Slovak Day. In theory, this day in a warm-weather month suited the outdoor activities that typically characterized Slovak Days. But the observance of American Independence Day created complications. As local nationality days evolved into recreational events, it was unrealistic to hold two amusement-oriented affairs back-to-back. Hence, instead of competing with Fourth of July celebrations, organizers in many communities opted to integrate Slovak Days into them. In other places, planners let parochial factors, which might change from year to year, affect when they scheduled their annual event. During the 1930s, some locales combined Slovak and Labor Day observances.[8] Promoters of a single Slovak Day were unable to triumph over weak cultural traditions and complications created by American society.

Although attempts to institute a nationwide observance failed, there was widespread positive reaction at the community level to the *idea* of a Slovak Day. Persons there did take up the cause. Because activists were community residents hoping to attract fellow inhabitants to their cause, they fashioned public notices specifically to appeal to the local masses. The promotional literature for Slovak Days therefore gives voice to what was motivating committed activists, and equally important, to what their experiences told them could prick the sentiments of fellow Slovaks. An investigation of such materials thus provides a grassroots perspective of these events and sheds particularly illuminating light on the dynamics nurturing routine displays of ethnicity. It is important to keep in mind that, regardless of whether it encompassed regional or small-town affairs, irrespective of whether it was for a first-time day or for long-established events, and without respect to geographic area, the publicity for Slovak Days displayed an astonishingly marked similarity.

Once the idea took hold, the ardor for Slovak Days spread. By 1933, Slovaks in cities as well as small and midsize towns such as Coaldale, Pennsylvania; Raritan, New Jersey; and Kenosha, Wisconsin, were arranging annual celebrations. Local events also evolved into region-wide affairs attracting people from a broad geographic area. The Pitts-burgh function, for instance, became Slovak Day of Western Pennsylva-nia, and Slovak Day for Luzerne and Lackawanna counties drew from the state's numerous northeastern towns. Slovak Days in Michigan, New Jersey, and New York encompassed wider areas. During the 1930s, the momentum to institute Slovak Days remained steady. In 1935, the first Ohio Valley Slovak Day for those living in towns along the river was held. That same year, people in Cicero and Berwin, Illinois, joined together to arrange their premier celebration; one year later, Slovaks in Bridgeport, Connecticut, organized a day.[9] The claim by one jubilant observer that Slovak Day celebrations "have suddenly bloomed in pop-ularity" and had sprung up in areas where large numbers of Slovaks lived was indeed correct.[10] By the early 1930s, sales of admission tickets revealed that, depending on the weather, large regional events could attract 10,000 to 40,000 persons, and small, locally sponsored days could draw as few as 300 or between 2,000 and 3,000 participants.[11] Reports that crowds were growing each year induced an exuberant observer to chor-tle, "One wonders where our alarmists and scoffers get the idea that the Slovaks' pride in their nationality is quickly dying out in this country."[12] The ongoing popularity of Slovak Days did suggest a persistent rather than a waning ethnicity in local communities. Even if arranging the events relied on a small cluster of people, the turnout was the result of arousing ethnic feelings among an area's Slovak populace.

The proliferation of Slovak Days reflected steadily growing enthusiasm for the idea as well as the discord that these affairs could generate. Practically from the outset, denominationalism undermined the unity that a national day was ideally supposed to promote. Even in the mid-1920s, as enthusiasts were shifting away from the religiously oriented Cyril and Methodius Day to events emphasizing ethnicity, Catholic inroads into what would eventually become Slovak Days were already evident. As early as 1925, publicists for Slovak Days were inadvertently admitting that denominational differences were sowing dissension. The first days scheduled for Youngstown, Ohio, and Bethlehem, Pennsylvania, were advertised as "purely national." Local arrangement committees elsewhere called for all Slovaks, "without regard to religion," to participate in upcoming events.[13] Over the next decade this entreaty— "without regard to religion"—became an incessant theme in announcements of Slovak Days. Promoters were not merely engaging in overblown rhetoric; they were forging arguments specifically to deal with what they knew were realities of Slovak community life and the sources of local friction. In addition to typical faith-based differences, disagreements over autonomy for the homeland, which had generated divisions primarily along religious lines, had trickled down to the local level and endured into the 1930s.

Ironically, even as they pleaded for inclusiveness, planners could exemplify a Catholic bias. Organizers of the 1926 event in western Pennsylvania admitted that, because four bishops from Slovakia would be attending, the day might give the appearance of being a Catholic affair. They were quick to declare that this was not the case; a visit by prelates from the Old Country, they asserted, should please all Slovaks.[14] Disclaimers notwithstanding, the presence of these bishops, together with Pittsburgh's Bishop Boyle, gave the occasion a distinctly Catholic look. In addition, the souvenir badges carried a picture of seven bishops— six Slovaks and Boyle. Despite claims of nondenominationalism, pre-event publicity linked the affair to celebrating Saints Cyril and Methodius. One zealous planning-committee member went so far as to refer to the "enemies of Catholicism."[15] It appears that fellow residents viewed the day in the same manner. In his post-festivity euphoria, a happy participant took the time to write a letter expressing his pleasure and praising the day as one that had successfully celebrated "our apostles," Cyril and Methodius. Seventy-five thousand to 80,000 persons reportedly came to Kennywood Park for Slovak Day in 1926.[16]

The bishops' American visit acted as a catalyst furthering the transformation of Slovak Days into Catholic-dominated events. Their presence inspired people in South Orange, New Jersey, to hold their first Slovak Day on July 5, 1926. Several American bishops joined in celebrations in their respective dioceses as well. Although he did not schedule his traveling to coincide with local Slovak Days, Andrej Hlinka, head of the Slovak People's Party and leading advocate for Slovak autonomy, was among the bishops visiting the United States in the summer of 1926. The excitement aroused by his trip revealed the ongoing relevance of Old World politics for some people, especially for the Slovak Catholic clergy who enjoyed significant influence at the local level. As the importance of homeland politics was subsiding for ordinary Slovaks and certainly for their children, Hlinka's presence still helped invigorate the nascent enthusiasm for Slovak Days in the mid-1920s.[17] Their subsequent expansion, though, was the product of circumstances and activism in local communities.

Nationally minded Slovaks in some areas continued to arrange secular days, but more and more their successes represented the exception rather than the rule. During the four years after Hlinka's visit, the Catholics' appropriation of Slovak Days continued, especially as organizers turned these days into fund-raising events. In addition to admission fees, the sale of food and souvenirs yielded profits. By the late 1920s, revenues from some days were going toward Slovak Catholic orders, institutions, or local churches and schools. Seeing what was happening elsewhere caused people with religiously based interests to begin contesting the secular days in their areas. As a result, Slovak Days in places such as Cleveland, which had traditionally been nonreligious, came under attack. For a dozen years after the Slovak League had inaugurated the city's first Slovak Day, the event was promoted in Catholic, Lutheran, and secular newspapers as a purely national event; the profits had gone into a fund for a statue of the Slovak wartime leader Milan Štefánik. In 1929, however, Catholic parishes scheduled a Slovak Day for July 7, more than a month before the Slovak League's annual affair would be held. Organizers of the July 7 event left no doubt about its Catholic orientation. Souvenir badges would feature a picture of Saints Cyril and Methodius; organizers hoped Cleveland's bishop would return from Rome in time to say the opening mass; and finally, revenues would go toward a Slovak Catholic school. Sponsors of the league's August affair reacted by pleading with Slovaks to support the traditional day, which had been held yearly since 1917. Slovak Day ought to be "without regard to religion," asserted one clearly distressed Slovak League member.[18]

Elsewhere, disagreement over how to distribute revenues aggravated religious divisions and sparked competing events. This happened in Detroit where, since its first Slovak Day in 1927, the proceeds had gone toward establishing a special section in the city's art museum that would feature Slovak artifacts and folk crafts. During the next two years, Detroit's organizers continued to emphasize cultural objectives and dedicate revenues to the hoped-for exhibition. In 1929, however, the city's Slovaks scheduled days for two successive weekends. Ads made it clear these were competitive undertakings. One arrangements committee announced that its proceeds were intended for the Slovak exhibit at the art museum; its rival advertised that revenues would go toward a Slovak Catholic school. The programs further revealed the fundamental differences between the two days. Religious services had not traditionally been part of the city's Slovak Days; but by including a Catholic mass, speeches about Cyril and Methodius, and souvenir badges with the apostles' pictures, founders of the newly instituted event left no doubt about its religious orientation.[19]

By the following year, the rift between the two Detroit factions was complete. Some individuals who had abandoned the traditional celebration were willing to explain why. Helping to arrange what was now being called Slovak Catholic Day for the State of Michigan, disaffected former supporters expressed their displeasure with the secular nature of the past Slovak Days. They were miffed when organizers rejected their suggestion that some of the profits from the previous year's event be earmarked for a Catholic school. Instead, all the proceeds went toward the proposed cultural exhibit in the city's art museum. In an astounding, if not disingenuous plea, they called on Slovaks not to let religion divide them. Yet they informed readers that the day's celebrations would start with a Catholic mass. They coolly remarked that Lutherans need not be bothered by this because they could "come to the picnic."[20] Naiveté turned into an affront as the boosters of the new, rival day proceeded to tell Catholics they made up 90 percent of the Slovak population and should be aware of their strength. Adding injury to the insult Protestants must already have been feeling, organizers announced that revenues would go into a fund for a proposed Slovak Catholic school. Promoters of the Fourth Detroit Slovak Day, scheduled for two weeks later, appealed to people of all religious persuasions to attend their affair. Local clergymen evidently felt differently about interreligious activities. Not only did Roman Catholic priests reportedly decline invitations to participate in National Slovak Day 1933, at least one apparently warned parishioners that he would not grant absolution to laypersons who went.[21] Detroit Slovaks kept holding competing functions throughout the decade. As the Depression deepened, the nationally oriented event redirected its funds to help Slovaks adversely affected by hard economic times. The Catholic-sponsored affair continued to donate its earnings toward a school.[22]

In Chicago, where religious differences also spawned disagreements over proceeds, the same rivalry developed. Beginning with their first celebration in 1929, organizers of Slovak Day in Chicago contributed the proceeds to the Slovak American Charitable Association, which provided assistance to needy Slovaks. By 1931, however, Catholics complained that their interests were not receiving an ample share of the profits, even though they had worked hard to make the annual events successful. Their denomination represented more than 75 percent of the city's Slovak population, they observed. This alleged slight, in the face of the Catholic numerical superiority, intensified their pique. As a result, they wanted to "demonstrate our strength and our loyalty to our people and church."[23] Upholding the precedent set by the two previous annual days, the receipts were given to charity; they went, however, to the Slovak Catholic Charitable Association.[24] Decrying religious divisions wrought by the Catholic day, sponsors of the nondenominational event renamed theirs "Slovak National Day." Stressing the purely ethnic character of the celebration, they consistently pleaded with Slovaks to set aside religious differences for one day out of the year to celebrate the nationality that united them.[25]

Protestants could hardly have been pleased when proceeds went to Slovak Catholic institutions. Consequently, many shunned the Catholic-dominated days. Nevertheless, how profits were allotted was not the principal cause of rival local days. Instead, disagreements over revenue reflected the animosities generated by a stalwart clergy and laity bent on instituting a Catholic day and clothing it in their particular sectarian purposes. From the Catholic vantage point, a nationality day with religious overtones could reinforce the link between Catholicism and "Slovakness." These events also provided a means for shoring up Catholic institutions.

In 1936, Slovak Lutherans began adopting the Catholic strategy. That year, Lutherans in Pittsburgh inaugurated Slovak Lutheran Day of

Western Pennsylvania and launched a campaign to get their religious brethren elsewhere to follow suit. Catholic dominance, together with the success other nationalities were having with their annual events, prompted the move. However, led by the Slovak Evangelical Union, proponents of a Lutheran day also candidly admitted that they wanted to bolster lagging fraternal membership. Specifically, they hoped to attract youths.[26] The union's headquarters were located in Pittsburgh, which probably explains why the effort was initiated there. With national officers residing in the area, the city's Slovak Protestant community harbored a small circle of people naturally inclined to promote their organization by cultivating a Slovak Lutheran consciousness. Advancing fraternal interests notwithstanding, the day was also envisioned as a counter to the perception that "Slovaks" were "Catholic."

The hope that other regions would imitate their efforts met with some success. Admitting that they were following the Pennsylvania example, the next year Lutherans in Cleveland, Newark, and eastern Pennsylvania sponsored Slovak Lutheran days. Cleveland and Pittsburgh engaged in a friendly competition as advertisers for each city urged Slovaks in their region not to let themselves be put to shame by their brethren in the rival city. In 1938, regional days were held in six areas where large numbers of Slovak Lutherans had settled.[27] By that time, a desire to counter Catholic dominance and bolster their fraternal membership with youthful members, together with the reemergence of Old World issues, was nurturing these days. Still, the spread of Lutheran days exemplified the same type of copycat phenomenon that characterized Slovak Catholic and national days. With an eye cast on what Slovaks elsewhere were doing, community activists arranged their own particular ethnic manifestations.

While internal differences helped fuel the growth of Slovak Days, local circumstances encouraged their expansion as well. Indeed, forces within Slovak communities blended with realities of the "outside" world to generate the energy for nationality days. For example, large regional events spawned offshoot celebrations, especially in the early 1930s, when tight finances made travel difficult.[28] Elsewhere, local conditions animated Slovak Days. This happened, for instance, when Slovak enthusiasts wanted to make their ethnic group part of regional history or other public commemorations. The city's centennial provided the impetus for Slovaks in Bridgeport to call for a Slovak Day in 1936. They asserted that it would highlight their presence and remind people how Slovaks had helped build this Connecticut town and had contributed to its history.[29] In Philadelphia, Slovaks organized their first day to coincide with the city's observance of the 150th anniversary of the U.S. Constitution, a national event closely linked to local history. For them, ethnicity and Americanism were not incompatible. They wanted to draw attention to themselves and prove that "not only are we good Slovaks but also good Americans." A year later, publicists were still boasting about the extensive coverage local newspapers had given their well-attended Slovak Day.[30] In their view, while displaying their Americanism, they had asserted a *Slovak* presence in the city.

The continuing proliferation of Slovak Days in the 1930s revealed a pervasive copycat phenomenon. The publicity generated by newspapers, which regularly printed ads, programs for local celebrations, and letters from jubilant participants, inspired Slovaks in other areas to organize celebrations. Planners of the first Slovak Day in Sharon and Farrell, Pennsylvania, described their joint venture as "following the example of brothers and sisters in other cities." They, too, wanted to demonstrate to others that "we are faithful sons and daughters of our new country and are proud of our Slovak origins."[31] During the late 1920s and into the mid-1930s, remarkably similar pronouncements threaded through publicity for Slovak Days. Seeing what people elsewhere were doing emboldened Slovaks to establish rival events. Slovak Catholics in Chicago, who broke ranks with sponsors of the traditional secular day, were, as they put it, "following the example of other large Slovak colonies" when they decided to hold their first Slovak "Catholic" Day.[32] When they established their own days, Lutherans were imitating Catholics and nationalists as well as trying to influence other Slovak Lutheran communities.

However much they might disagree about religious or national agendas, promoters of Slovak Days viewed them as manifestations of ethnicity. This was evident in the notices urging people to attend. Time and again, ads described the days as a means of demonstrating "national consciousness." Publicists repeatedly presented the events as opportunities to show "other nationalities" residing in the area that Slovaks "are alive." The phrase *"iné národnosťi"*—other nationalities—flowed constant in the steady stream of publicity for Slovak Days. A large attendance, organizers promised, would gain the notice and by extension the respect of the non-Slovak population. Cleveland's activists, for example, reminded area residents that a huge turnout for their 1933 event would cause municipal newspapers to report on it.[33] At the same time, planners of Slovak Day in Pennsylvania's Westmoreland County were employing a blatantly competitive tone to prod their fellow Slovaks. "If other nationalities are able to have huge turnouts for their celebrations, then why cannot Slovaks do the same?" they asked. "Let's not lag behind ... other nationalities," they pleaded.[34] Enthusiasts routinely called on Slovaks not to be put to shame by other nationalities who held successful events. With constancy bordering on harping, publicists appealed to Slovaks to demonstrate that they were not "ashamed" of their nationality. The terms "shame" and "ashamed" permeated the publicity. Living in a diverse society, one impassioned advocate declared, means that Slovaks "must have the respect of all nationalities here in America."[35] Obviously, such entreaties grew out of a sense of competition as well as some awareness of an ethnic pecking order.

The incessant references to "other nationalities" in ads for Slovak Days throughout the 1920s and 1930s did not cite specific groups. Instead, they used general descriptions: "other nationalities," "Americans," or the "American public." The ambiguity and prevalence of "iné národnosti" indicate that, rather than a universal competition between specific groups—for example, between Czechs and Slovaks—the heterogeneity of individual regions forged the specific rivalries that developed in local communities. What constituted "other nationalities" varied and was a product of migration patterns and the power structure of the respective geographic areas. The phrase, though, reveals that America's nationalities viewed their world through the lens of ethnic diversity. From this perspective, annual communal displays such as Slovak Days could evince respect from other ethnic groups as well as the American public.

The motives for staging Slovak Days could be blatantly political. Again, implicitly reacting to the ethnically diverse society they inhabited, planners of these annual communal events believed that well-attended gatherings would demonstrate "strength and unity."[36] They also could "show the public how many of us there are and how well we work together."[37] Over the years, such reasoning constantly ran through the publicity. Support Slovak Day, one local committee openly admonished, because "it will mean a great deal for us in the political field."[38] Speakers used the occasion to call on Slovaks "to wake up ... politically and get what belongs to us."[39] Reflecting on the recent successful Slovak Day in his town, one commentator asserted that, despite a few disinterested persons, "on the whole," Slovaks, including the second generation, were "enthusiastic about any measure which will make Connecticut aware of its Slovak citizens who pay taxes, support excellent church edifices, and vote regularly."[40] By and large, public commentary reveals that these days were seen as vehicles for manifesting ethnic fervor, engendering respect, and vaunting potential political strength. They aimed to cultivate Slovak consciousness and build ethnic cohesion.

For their part, politicians and public figures quickly grasped the potential benefits of nationality days. By participating in them, local luminaries added credence to assertions that these celebrations were as much "American" as Slovak. Appearances by mayors, council members, commissioners, judges, district attorneys, and local law-enforcement officers became commonplace. Slovak Days also drew an array of state representatives and senators who took advantage of these opportunities to mingle conspicuously with voters in their districts. Organizers of one event reported that it was impossible to accommodate the eighteen non-Slovak city, county, and state officials who attended and wanted to speak.[41] Some governors also accepted invitations to address local constituents. As early as 1928, Detroit Slovaks boasted that Michigan's governor had bestowed "honor" on them by speaking at their annual day.[42] During the 1930s, the governors of at least five states participated in one or more Slovak Days in their states. Representatives to the U.S. Congress sometimes gave speeches at these annual fetes in their home districts. Occasionally, even a U.S. senator reportedly graced the day with an appearance.[43] In election years, candidates for public office seemingly scrambled to these nationality days. To assure "candidates for office [and] those seeking nominations in future primaries" that they had found the right place on the right day, organizers of Michigan's 1930 Slovak national day placed a "big sign" in English at the park entrance.[44] Attentive politicians unable to show up for Slovak Days sent representatives or greetings, which were dutifully read during the days' speech segments and often summarized in the Slovak press. Cleveland Slovaks certainly must have aroused the envy of Slovaks elsewhere when they published President Roosevelt's salutations for their day in 1933.[45]

Civil servants were not alone in apprehending the potential benefits of the day. In at least some areas, union activists could be equally savvy. John L. Lewis, president of the United Mine Workers, spoke at the third annual day in Wilkes-Barre, Pennsylvania, in 1925. During the 1930s officials of miners' locals spoke at other Slovak Days in Pennsylvania's coal region.[46]

Attendance by politicians or their acclamatory messages thus became intricate parts of Slovak Day programs. Civil dignitaries could expect to address Slovak Day crowds because planners reserved special places on the program for speeches. Over the years, regardless of how religiously or how nationally oriented they were and regardless of where they were celebrated, the form and content of these days were strikingly similar. The Catholic-dominated events typically began with the "*nabožená časť*"—the religious part—comprising a mass and sermon. This was followed by the "*národná časť*"—the national part—featuring Slovak speakers, political figures, civil servants, and aspiring officeholders. The secular Slovak Days usually commenced with the "*národná časť*."

Although Slovak newspapers typically described only snippets, the themes that reporters from wide-ranging geographical areas chose to accentuate are illuminating. Based on what eyewitnesses related, politicians had strikingly similar messages. They flattered Slovaks by lauding their sense of civic duty. Over and over they described Slovaks as "good citizens" and praised them for fulfilling their "citizenship" obligations. Party leaders and elected officials who believed Slovaks had been their backers openly thanked them for their past support. Law-enforcement officials called them "law-abiding citizens." Reiterating an oft-chanted theme of the interwar era, some speakers cited the military and domestic sacrifices Slovaks had made in support of the war effort.[47]

Participation by public figures had the practical effect of sanctioning Slovak Days and making these local events part of the political milieu. Instead of shunning them as un-American, prominent civil servants embraced these collective manifestations of ethnicity and tried to reap political benefits from them. At the same time, their involvement suited the multifold desires of Slovak promoters because they could credibly assert that these yearly outbursts of ethnicity brought attention to and served the interests of Slovaks. Appearances by governors and members of Congress in particular received special publicity in the Slovak media. Newspaper editors and local enthusiasts eagerly used such appearances to promote Slovak Days, but the benefits went beyond bolstering attendance. Promoters aggressively seized on these gestures as opportunities to try to impress both Americans and other nationalities, as well as to motivate Slovaks throughout the country to follow their example.[48] The fact that political notables took part reinforced the notion that Slovaks were viewed as important in local, state, and national politics. This attention not only enhanced the possibility that residents would participate in future Slovak Days in their respective areas; it also nurtured the copycat phenomenon, as Slovaks in various locales vied for the same attention from their civil luminaries. The self-satisfaction that crept into publicity and after-the-fact commentary also subtly reflected an underlying competition with other nationalities and heightened a sense of Slovak "otherness" in an ethnically diverse society.

For their part, Slovak activists were not shy about exploiting the political potential of their local nationality days. In addition to accommodating a wide range of speakers, participants at Fayette County's 1933 Slovak Day paid respects to Franklin Delano Roosevelt by approving a resolution assuring the new president of their allegiance to the U.S. Constitution and of their willingness to perform their civic duties.[49] The resolution, expressing the twin themes of loyalty and good citizenship, carried the claim of having been approved by the 40,000 persons attending the day. Slovaks in Lackawanna County saw an opportunity for subtle political lobbying when they passed a resolution praising Pennsylvania's governor for his "progressive, humane, liberal and social program." Their declaration assured the state's chief executive that he could rely on the cooperation of the "75,000 loyal citizens . . . of Slovak birth or ancestry" participating in Slovak Day 1935.[50]

Accommodating politicians and passing resolutions constituted one aspect of the subtle Americanism that came to characterize Slovak Days. There were other, more demonstrative expressions. Since the war, activists at the national level had been countering "chauvinism" and "overzealous Americanization" by promoting the notion that Americanism meant adherence to principles and becoming citizens. For their part, local activists bent over backward to ensure that they projected a patriotic image. Slovak Days were chances to do this. As noted, practical considerations caused some local planners to blend Fourth of July and Slovak Day celebrations. Certainly, fusing ethnic and patriotic displays on Independence Day was nothing new. The practice reached back at least as far as the Great War, when nationally coordinated patriotic exhibitions had been scheduled for July 4. On Loyalty Day 1918, immigrants had labored to portray images linking their people's past to a historical struggle to achieve democracy. With the emergence of nationality days, this tradition was carried on in the postwar era.

During the 1920s and 1930s, local communities jointly celebrating the Fourth of July and Slovak Day found it easy to blend expressions of Americanism and ethnicity. Catholics were particularly delighted with a date placing Slovak Days so close to the feast of Cyril and Methodius because it allowed participants collectively to exhibit their Americanism and promote a religiously based ethnic identity. Using the combined celebrations to their advantage, Catholics attempted to equate

Cyril and Methodius with the revolutionary themes attached to the Fourth of July. Again and again, Slovaks heard that their participation had the dual effects of celebrating American independence and their own ancient forefathers. In eastern Pennsylvania, where Slovak Day had regularly been held on July 4, organizers of the 1928 event told their compatriots that "as American citizens we are celebrating the most important American holiday, . . . but as Slovaks we are celebrating the most important Slovak feast . . . , [which commemorates] the christianization of our ancestors' culture."[51]

In 1932, captivated by the national observance of George Washington's 200th birthday, Slovaks practically everywhere incorporated commemorations of America's leading founding father into their annual days, especially those held on Independence Day. Enthusiasts claimed that Cyril and Methodius had possessed the same virtues and principles as Washington. The "father of our adopted country" was repeatedly hailed as a person worthy of honoring on Slovak Day. For Slovaks in Chicago, commemorating Washington was touted as a "chance to prove our patriotism." Organizers in Perth Amboy included a "George Washington Parade" on their Slovak Day program. It should be emphasized that there is no evidence in the local publicity for 1932 Slovak Days that Slovaks were bestowing adulation on this founding father because they were "yearning . . . for 'Nordic' ancestors." On the contrary, to instill an abiding pride in *Slovak* ancestry, the publicists strove mightily to stress that Slovaks as well as their ancestors symbolized the same principles as this "hero" of American history and the father of this democratic nation. The emphasis was on principles and Washington as an American hero. It is important to underscore that Slovaks universally and consistently presented Washington in terms of the father of the country—not as an ethnic type or in terms of "race" or ethnicity.[52]

Although the July 4 fetes were particularly conducive to patriotic themes, Slovak Days were not universally scheduled for that date. Except for the few held on Labor Day, these nationality events often took place at times with no connection to American history or culture. Still, promoters never lost sight of the fact they had to present an image that blended Slovaks' Americanism and their ethnic identity. Regardless of when Slovak Days were held, the publicity, speeches, and after-the-fact reports pounded on themes praising Slovaks, their good citizenship, and their adherence to American principles (Illustration 4). Rhetoric for affairs large and small continually reminded Slovaks that they could be both good American citizens and ethnics proud of their nationality.

Prvý Slovenský Deň v Chicagu 1918. Oznam slovenského Válečného šporenia.

ILLUSTRATION 4. The ongoing effort to demonstrate Slovaks' patriotism by stressing their support for the home-front effort during the Great War is evident in this Chicago Slovak Day poster of 1918, reprinted in *Slovenský Deň* [Slovak Day at the] *Coliseum Chicago, Illinois 1930: Souvenir Program of Slovak Festival Commemorating 50th Anniversary of Gen. Milan R. Stefanik* (Chicago: Mally Press, 1930), 35.

Exhibiting Americanism, then, was an integral theme woven into the religiously as well as the nationally oriented affairs. This interweaving was evident in the rhetoric associated with Slovak Days, but it was equally conspicuous in the days' activities. With stunning similarity, published programs announced that the national segment of the programs would commence with the "The Star-Spangled Banner," "America," "My Country 'Tis of Thee," or simply an "American hymn." With equal consistency, programs advertised speech segments as ending with "Hej Slováci." Whether the songs were performed by choral groups or the audience, the inclusion of American patriotic melodies and the Slovak national ballad symbolized the American and ethnic character of the events.

The penchant for equating flag veneration with adherence to American principles also filtered conspicuously into Slovak Day activities. With Americans—both the friendly and the suspicious—looking on, a mix of prudence and genuine feeling, no doubt, induced a profusion of American flags. In symbolism equal to including two national hymns on the program, the American and Slovak flags waved ostentatiously at many local days. More than 20,000 persons reportedly "marched proudly" under the American and Slovak flags at a 1927 New York–New Jersey Slovak Day. In Milwaukee, where a gala parade became a regular part of Slovak Days, participants in 1932 were asked to put Slovak and American flags on their cars. Slovak veterans of the Great War carried both national emblems in the cavalcade launching Bridgeport's 1936 annual event.[53]

Even without parades, the flags were conspicuous. One observer was moved to report that the American and Slovak standards waved proudly by the altar at Detroit's 1929 event. Chicago girls and boys had to learn the American and Slovak anthems so they could take part in dual-flag-raising ceremonies.[54] Evidently trying to combine every possible expression of patriotism, at Detroit's 1933 national day, children pledged allegiance to the American flag and sang "My Country 'Tis of Thee," and an orchestra played the "The Star-Spangled Banner" and "Hej Slováci." In a similar joint display of patriotism and ethnicity five years later, a Binghamton, New York, Slovak Boy Scout troop, carrying both national flags, regaled onlookers with "America the Beautiful," "The Star-Spangled Banner," and "Hej Slováci."[55] In what was no doubt an impressive show of patriotic excess, Bridgeport's local lodge members marching in one parade wore white shirts and blue hats and carried small American flags.[56] But by displaying the flag at a Slovak event, participants were continuing a practice that had been going on for the previous two decades.[57]

These joint demonstrations of Americanism and ethnicity were attempts to accommodate the realities facing new immigrant America. Slovaks, like other ethnic groups, were undoubtedly aware of the popular disposition for flag-waving. In local communities, so-called patriotic organizations regularly exhibited the national emblem. The flag flew at war memorials and was intrinsic to commemorative events. The Ku Klux Klan made sensational use of it in its 1926 march down the streets of Washington, D.C. Although at times skewed to conform to bigoted ideologies, throughout the interwar era, displaying the flag was an expression of patriotism, adherence to "American" principles, and good citizenship. The publicity for local Slovak Days clearly indicated that, regardless of where they occurred, organizers tried to make these events a positive statement of Slovak Americanism. They wanted to impress others as well as Slovaks with the idea that ethnicity and being American were compatible. Displaying the American and Slovak flags was a symbolic statement of this compatibility.

As SLOVAK DAYS EXPANDED in the 1930s, it became evident that national proponents did not merely represent a fringe element out of touch with the ordinary population. These annual events nourished cadres of local activists aware of what was happening elsewhere and willing to work to mobilize Slovaks in their areas to ethnic causes. Indeed, the nearly identical programs, together with the similar rhetoric used by enthusiasts living in different areas, show that local populations set examples imitated by others. This awareness and mimicking reveals that, collectively, Slovak communities constituted a self-conscious subculture within the larger American society. A copycat phenomenon made ethnic displays, tinged with patriotic expressions, part of this Slovak subculture. Moreover, rather than being an exception, Slovaks were representative of what other new immigrant groups were doing.[58] For Slovaks, periodic demonstrations of ethnic solidarity constituted an ongoing adaptation to a multiethnic society. Throughout the interwar era, national enthusiasts did not hesitate to promote the idea that a nationality day was a manifestation of consciousness. Local organizers, however, were the ones who dwelled on impressing "others"—meaning Americans and other nationalities. In a country where people were being judged by their ancestral origins, they wanted to emphasize a Slovak presence in their heterogeneous communities.

It was also local people who pressed patriotic themes. Displaying the flag and incorporating various "American hymns" reflected a hard-headed assessment of local life since the war. It was in communities, after all, where, to varying degrees, foreign-born persons had experienced threats to their jobs or witnessed expressions of overt bigotry. The impact of this real-life existence influenced nationality day rhetoric and programs. Exhibiting the flag at Slovak Days demonstrated the ongoing influence of the wartime propensity to use public exhibitions to demonstrate collective loyalty. By the 1930s, however, what had been in part a response to coercive nationalism had evolved into a customary feature of ethnically sponsored events.

Clothed in combined political and ethnic purposes, nationality days were cultural scions of America's wartime demonstrations, which had first sanctioned collective ethnic actions as patriotic. While no longer straining under the kind of pressure brought to bear during the Great War, the ethnic activities of the 1930s nevertheless meshed several objectives. Slovak Day advocates perceived the events as a weapon in the struggle to break out of the ranks of the "undesirable." As they promoted the idea that mass actions reflected well on group respectability, activists worked assiduously to link Slovak Days to Americanism and good citizenship. Clearly unable to prove the claim, commentators nevertheless constantly described participants as "citizens," a term that resonated in speeches and print reports about the days' events. From the standpoint of Slovak activists, society's ongoing affinity for patriotic expressions, combined with the cumulative experiences of wartime America and the nativist 1920s, necessitated pounding these themes. Why individual people attended nationality days is an inscrutable question, but their presence helped project images that enthusiasts, especially local advocates, wanted to present to Americans and other nationalities.

Promoters of Slovak Days hoped to impress more than non-Slovak onlookers. They also aimed to influence their own people. Besides demonstrating cohesion to the outside world, Slovak Days were perceived as ways to advance ethnic consciousness within Slovak communities, especially among young immigrants and the second generation. The twin goals of conveying group patriotism and impressing youths had spawned the type of expressions depicted in the "loyalty pictures" that graced the pages of Slovak fraternal publications immediately after the war. Over time, both foreign- and English-language promotional literature for nationality days presented the events as American *and* Slovak, opportunities to be good Americans and express pride in ancestry.

Slovak enthusiasts could hammer on patriotic themes, wave the flag, and proudly point to American luminaries who honored the day with their presence, but they still had to design days that would entice people—especially the "Americanized" youths—to attend. With this purpose in mind, organizers planned recreational activities, which ultimately formed the crucial segment of annual nationality days. As the Slovak Day programs moved from speeches to entertainment, local promoters mingled popular culture with ethnic activities and traditions. Slovak activists realized they had to do this if they hoped to attract their "youthful element."

5 Maintaining an Ethnic Image
Fashioning Nationality Days for Local Youths

"COME, AND BRING THE ENTIRE FAMILY, you will not regret it," the ad for Mahoning Valley's 1934 Slovak Day trumpeted. The description of the day, scheduled for July 25 at Idora Amusement Park, did indeed suggest that the "excellent program" included something for everyone. The enthusiastic as well as the indulgent could expect speeches by priests, senators, judges, lawyers, and mayors. For those seeking a good time, the entertainment segment contained an array of possibilities. Parish choirs would perform. There would be "old country entertainment," including a folk-dance exhibition and a foreign-language "100% sound film." Spectators could watch gymnastic performances, a baseball game, and other athletic competitions. There were wide-ranging activities for those who preferred participating to watching. Young children and adolescents would discover that planners had paid particular attention to them. A combination of ethnic and "American" activities would finish off the day. Following the crowning of the "Queen of Slovak Day," those with the stamina could trip the light fantastic into the night. An "American orchestra" would play American tunes, but there would also be traditional Slovak dancing.[1]

Throughout the summer of 1934, the thousands who trekked to local Slovak Days could anticipate similar programs carefully attuned to entice the first and second generations, old and young. To excite all ages, especially those commonly referred to as "youths" or "the youth," during the 1930s, architects of local Slovak Days revamped insipid, speech-dominated programs and turned these events into fun-oriented occasions. Consistently promising a "rich program," Slovak Day organizers maintained the days' ethnic image but, to lure the generations, blended "Slovak" and "American" activities. Relying on favorite pastimes and contests, they involved youths in ways designed to foster an ethnic identity without rejecting their Americanness. By combining ethnic and American activities to suit the occasions' cultural and practical objectives, annual events further nurtured ethnic activism. These yearly manifestations of ethnicity also serve as windows to view how ordinary people were adjusting to generational and cultural differences in their communities.

LOCAL ACTIVISTS MIGHT well be pushing political, religious, or ethnic agendas; however, personal reasons caused individuals to attend Slovak Days. Organizers realized that. Accordingly, regardless of their motives, promoters had to design days that would appeal to the different generations—young and old. Publicists for local days targeted the foreign born by tapping into emotions and following a strategy of reasoned, but sentimental, persuasion. For instance, advertisers reminded people residing in communities "scattered" around the region that Slovak Days in Windber, Pennsylvania, meant they could get together at least once each year.[2] In general, publicity for Slovak Days stressed how they provided unique opportunities "to renew old acquaintances and make new ones." They constituted family reunions for relatives living in different towns.[3] They were occasions for "old timers to reminisce."[4] Surely, some immigrants felt pangs in their hearts as they read about one Slovak Lutheran Day bringing together persons separated for years. Several participants allegedly had not seen one another since they had departed their homeland thirty-five years earlier.[5] These sober, yet subtly emotional, descriptions both voiced and reflected maudlin tendencies lurking among the communities' aging—even if not old—foreign-born populations. They certainly imparted the personal, intangible benefits that might flow from attending a local Slovak Day.

Some enthusiasts chose to emphasize reality. The "immigrants are dying off," one especially straightforward ad warned; it was necessary, therefore, to establish a solid "foundation among our youth."[6] Implicitly, getting the younger generation to take part in Slovak Days would be an important step toward achieving that goal. Underscoring the need to win over young people in the community, these promoters were articulating a pivotal concern that resonated through the rhetoric for annual days. Both local organizers and proponents of a single national observance agreed that youths must become involved. Political or sentimentally geared publicity might sway a foreign-born cohort, particularly older people, but it was less likely to influence the second generation or perhaps even younger immigrants.

From a practical standpoint, local planners realized that getting children to Slovak Days meant they had to make them family affairs.

Effecting a lasting interest depended in part on convincing parents to establish Slovak Day as a tradition when their children were young and impressionable. The planners also recognized that parents, especially the working class, wanted to spend free time doing more than singing patriotic hymns and listening to religiously or politically oriented speeches. Demonstrating their grasp of reality, organizers of the Luzerne and Lackawanna counties' 1930 day incorporated a variety of contests that accentuated its family thrust. Prizes were awarded for "the most beautiful baby" as well as for the largest and second-largest families. The prospect of winning a baby beauty contest or receiving recognition for their family size probably had little, if any, appreciable impact on whether parents decided to attend; nevertheless, these particular competitions revealed the underlying goal of transforming Slovak Days into family-oriented events. This was evident in other amusements designed to pique the interest of young and old alike. The program included a pie-eating contest, various age-based races, and, finally, two baseball games.[7] The 1927 New Jersey–New York committee expressed what became the combined objective and strategy for local promoters. The day, the ad proclaimed, will "give our young people the chance to appear in their most popular sports, which so many of our youth like.... Let it be that there will not be one young boy or girl who does not participate."[8] Parents could expect Slovak Days, wherever held, to amuse their young children. The program has "ANYTHING OUR YOUTHS' HEARTS DESIRE," a 1928 English-language ad proclaimed.[9]

Similar claims echoed through the publicity for these yearly happenings in other communities. Committees arranged egg-rolling, coin-hunting, pie-eating, and pop-drinking contests. There were tugs-of-war and ball-throwing competitions. Foot races, however, were by far the most common individual competitive events. These running meets generally involved adolescents and teenagers. Separate matches for young boys and girls were also typically age based, dividing, for example, children eight to fourteen years old into distinct groups. Occasionally athletic activities reached out to adults. In some cases, there were races limited to men over twenty years old or to married men. In the late 1920s, a few planners ventured to schedule "fat men," "fat ladies," or "old men's" races.[10] Prizes for the victors ranged from the sheer satisfaction of winning to cash awards.[11]

By the late 1920s, the speech-dominated programs of a few years earlier were clearing giving way to leisure-time entertainment. Throughout the 1930s, regardless of whether Slovak Day was a small-town or region-wide affair, parents and the children who accompanied them could expect afternoons with abundant opportunities to have fun. For Slovak Day planners, filling children's time with recreational games became a regular objective.

Sundry contests remained central features, but team sports emerged as the most widely advertised athletic activity for Slovak Days. Planners of a 1927 Gary, Indiana, event organized an interethnic football game between a Slovak sokol and a "Spanish American Team."[12] Other communities, however, did not incorporate that sport into their programs. Committees occasionally included mushball, but while this softball-like game enjoyed more popularity than football, it did not become a universal or even highly promoted activity for Slovak Days. The reason was simple: it was baseball that excited enthusiasm among the younger generation. Although they were ethnic events, Slovak Days took place within the broader context of a contemporary society enthralled by baseball and enamored of its celebrities. A few organizers grasped this fact in the early 1920s and included a baseball game in their otherwise speech-laden political days.[13] During the mid-decade, however, when local enthusiasts began launching their own Slovak Days, the idea did not initially catch on. By the end of the 1920s, this was changing.

Hoping to stimulate excitement for their 1929 day, planners in western Pennsylvania finally seized on the present-day fascination. Straining to imitate the current journalistic style, the English-language publicity trumpeted in eye-catching type the "BALL GAME YOU WAITED FOR SO LONG." Sprinkling the column with verbal sparring between the two managers, the ad sensationalized the upcoming confrontation pitting a sokol group against the Slovak orphanage team that had "carried off high honors in the Harrisburg [Pennsylvania] region." The committee once again had prevailed on Honus Wagner, a former Pittsburgh Pirate great and future Hall of Famer, to umpire. This year, Johnny Baker, who was described in the ads as a Pirate, would assist Wagner. Adding grandeur to victory, the winning team could lay claim to a "beautiful silver loving cup."[14] Planners continued to use imagination to promote this annual game. In 1932, they persuaded two professional players to umpire the Slovak Day game: Steve Swetonic, a right-handed pitcher for the Pirates, and William Urbanski, shortstop for the Boston Braves, would be calling the pitches and working the bases.[15] The publicity did not tout their ethnic heritage, but two Slavic players implicitly served as role models and examples of individuals who had gained entry into "American" sports while apparently not disassociating themselves from their "new immigrant" roots. Their success was individual, but the pride they could evoke was collective.

Western Pennsylvania's committees may have been unique in attracting sports personalities to participate, but they were not out of the ordinary in making baseball integral to Slovak Days. By the early 1930s, both the secular and religiously oriented events were featuring this sport. Integrating the games into programs followed the same copycat tendency evident in promotional ads and speech segments of Slovak Days. When Ohio Valley Slovaks included baseball in their inaugural nationality day in 1935, they were merely imitating what had become commonplace. By regularly scheduling games in subsequent years, the eastern Ohio affairs further reflected the normal pattern for Slovak Days in the United States.[16] Others, too, learned by example. The "youth wants sports," publicists for Cleveland's First Slovak Lutheran Day declared in 1937. Probably trying to convey an image of quasi-professionalism that would spur more youth involvement in ethnic teams, publicists for the next year's event heralded the fact that "all baseball players, managers, and coaches will be dressed in their flashy new uniforms."[17] Stylish outfits, friendly bantering between managers, and hyperbole about teams' reputations provided fodder for Slovak Day publicity mills.

To find competing squads, planners initially relied on Slovak sokols and parishes. By the mid-1930s, they were also turning to local teams affiliated with national fraternal organizations. With each aiming to keep people actively involved in ethnic undertakings, Slovak Days and fraternal organizations developed a natural mutuality. In 1932, for example, the First Catholic Slovak Union paid travel expenses to allow forty-one youths from Pittsburgh and four nearby towns to participate in Slovak Day baseball games. Teams merely described as "from the Slovak Baseball League" played at one eastern Ohio annual day.[18]

While persons of all ages watched baseball games, playing was typically limited to adolescents and young adults. Western Pennsylvania, for example, restricted eligibility to individuals under age twenty-one.[19] For youths captivated by America's popular summer pastime, these ethically dedicated days offered a vicarious experience. Some organizers even turned Slovak Day competitions into tournaments by holding several elimination contests before the championship game.[20] Teams that might otherwise compete with one another on a semi-organized basis could meet for tournament play. These matches were not tantamount to winning a junior-league title; nevertheless, young Slovak athletes enjoyed the thrill of playing in ballyhooed local games where the victors walked away with some kind of a championship. Winner recognition varied. Victors might be afforded honors ranging from champions of that year's Slovak Day to broader, typically regionally and ethnically defined titles. Since triumphant teams were expected to return and defend their titles, championships had a built-in mechanism for spawning future games and, not incidentally, attendance at the next year's Slovak Day. Playing baseball on Slovak Days thus presented the chance for "Slovak" teams to engage in an "all-American" experience, but one intrinsically linked to an ethnically defined event.

Some planners wanted to include leisure-time activities more in line with traditional Slovak culture. In particular, they preferred highlighting Olympic-style contests or gymnastic exhibitions by sokol teams. From their perspective, displaying healthy bodies, and by extension admirable values, served the twofold purpose of involving youths in Slovak events and encouraging exhibitions that reflected well on their ethnic group.[21] At least one sober-minded advocate revealed that sokol zealots were not necessarily out of touch with the times. He was happy, he explained, that Slovak Days sponsored baseball games; he just wanted more sokol-style events.[22] National organizations joined the effort to make team drills and gymnastic exhibitions intrinsic to Slovak Days. In 1931, for instance, the First Catholic Slovak Union amended the bylaws for its sokol division and, among its other objectives, added "to hold gymnastic and athletic exercises on 'Slovak Day.' "[23] Efforts to highlight culturally rooted activities enjoyed mixed results. While some days regularly included gymnastic exercises together with baseball games, the latter triumphed in terms of popularity and publicity. Planners realized that a significant segment of youths would rather play or watch the immensely popular American sport. To attract young people to Slovak events, activists had to acquiesce in their preference for American games to ethnically rooted activities.

Advocates apparently did not make the argument that, because sokol exhibitions could include both males and females, they had the potential to draw both girls and boys into Slovak Day activities. If they adopted this tack, they did not press it in their published commentary. There certainly is a basis, though, for observing that the highly touted baseball games were gender restricted. Youngstown's program reportedly sponsored a girls' baseball game in 1936, but this was an exception, not the norm.[24] So while baseball gave young males the opportunity to participate in a popular "American" pastime during Slovak Day, there was no comparable activity for young females. Local promoters instead attempted to capitalize on contemporary American culture to coax girls and young women to get involved in these yearly occurrences. Specifically, they recast "beauty contests" in ethnic molds.

Beauty pageants started to become part of Slovak Days in the late 1920s. Announcing that the program would include a "beauty contest," planners of Luzerne and Lackawanna counties' 1927 day were the first publicly to advertise this kind of event. They failed, however, to publish any further description or qualifying criteria. By 1930, in addition to the most beautiful baby, judges at this eastern Pennsylvania day were selecting winners in two categories, tersely described as "single" and "married" woman.[25] In 1931, Pennsylvania's Fayette County committee left no doubt about its upcoming competition. Demonstrating that they were attuned to contemporary popular culture, the planners sponsored a "bathing beauty contest."[26] This published program also lacked particulars, but the publicity suggested that organizers were mimicking the Miss America Pageant. Fayette County's imitative effort was most likely an isolated attempt. The clergy as well as more reserved adults probably recoiled at the idea. While no other Slovak Day publicized a bathing-beauty contest, clever promoters quickly grasped the potential appeal of this mainstream activity.

The ambiguity characterizing the earliest beauty contests soon gave way to better-defined objectives. Winners, for example, could expect a named honor. Presumably for the entire year, the victor of western Pennsylvania's 1931 day would be "Miss Slovakia." Chicago Slovaks bestowed the same honor on their winner in 1933. Other communities chose more modest titles. One young woman, for example, would be designated "Miss Slovakia of Detroit"; another would be "Miss Slovakia of Canonsburg, Pennsylvania." Many did what Milwaukee did in 1933 and merely crowned the young woman "Queen of Slovak Day." People attending Ohio Valley's 1937 Slovak Day also saw the crowning of several "princesses." Without providing descriptive details, a large number of committees simply listed "queen crowning" as a separate item on the announced agenda. Regardless of title designations, the programs implied that winners and spectators could expect some kind of special ceremony during the Slovak Day festivities; candidates also might have their pictures published in souvenir books (Illustration 5).[27] Developing into standard features of Slovak Days, beauty contests underwent a progressive yet relatively quick transformation as they were modified to suit Slovak Days' multifaceted purposes.

ILLUSTRATION 5. Photograph of candidates for the title of "Miss Slovakia" that appeared in *Pamätník Piateho Slovenského Národného Dňa* (Souvenir Program of the Fifth Slovak National Day) (Chicago: Mally Press, 1933), 3.

Soon after the contests were introduced, some planning committees began replacing physically based standards of American beauty pageants with ethnically rooted criteria. To enter western Pennsylvania's 1931 contest, for example, young women were required to wear "Slovak, old-country regional clothes." The crown would go to the contestant with the prettiest costume.[28] Because finalists were the winners of competitions sponsored by individual parishes, this particular contest reached beyond that year's Slovak Day and the people who actually attended it. Promoters most likely hoped to broaden interest in Slovak Day while simultaneously keeping the final pool to a manageable number. Judging costumes instead of "beauty," in the abstract, removed potential subjectivity and rancor. But in an ethnic population traditionally characterized by Old World regional rivalries, selections based on ancient costumes could be equally subjective and possibly more contentious than evaluating comeliness. Judges' decisions probably rankled some regional chauvinists, but friction among Slovaks smarting from slights to their particular origins did not fuel the ongoing transformation of these contests. Instead, local organizers seized on the queen contests as opportunities to blend ethnic agendas with another Slovak

Day objective: to raise money. For instance, the young lady who sold the most ballots, at five cents apiece, was crowned Detroit's 1934 "Miss Slovakia." One year later, an Ohio Valley youth earned the title by selling the most raffle tickets for a car.[29] Rather than peddling votes outright or vending chances for a raffle, marketing admission tickets became the standard practice. The rules were simple: the girl or young woman who sold the most tickets won.

While some organizing committees relied on the personal initiative of individual contestants, most planners devised competitions that drew in local institutions. Joining in a shared cause to promote their Slovak Day, parishes, fraternal lodges (both male and female), and various Slovak groups put forth candidates. As a result, the quest for queen titles evolved into what were often advertised as "popularity contests." By turning the contests into friendly rivalries among individuals and local groups, promoters hoped to spark more widespread enthusiasm for Slovak Days. The contests, which generated several weeks of pre-event ads—including appeals from aspirants and their sponsors—helped pique interest. And, of course, they enhanced the fund-raising aspects of Slovak Days. The competitions also inadvertently nurtured a tradition of local Slovak institutions vying among themselves for bragging rights about which had done more to advance an ethnic cause.

When they set up contests, the architects had more in mind than raising money or stirring interest by pitting local Slovak groups against one another. Publicists were not shy about admitting that young people were the targets of these popularity schemes. They wanted to give them a reason, even in the form of a potential reward, for taking part in Slovak Day. The lodge backing a Miss Slovakia candidate in Detroit frankly admitted that it considered the competition a way "to interest our youth."[30] Sponsors in Chicago had even grander intentions. They explained that they wanted "to involve youths" in Slovak Days; but, because the proceeds went to the Slovak American Charitable Association to assist needy Slovaks, the popularity contests also aimed to make "those children who want to contribute . . . feel like they are contributing" to their people.[31] Echoing the same point as fellow enthusiasts in Chicago, Detroit's committee exclaimed that, not only was it "an honor to be Miss Slovakia," the contest, which that year had garnered $219.25 for "the poor fund," provided "young people" with an opportunity "to work for the good of our people."[32] Promoters in each city believed that they in particular had attracted an energetic segment of young women. In 1938, one Chicago enthusiast boasted that during the previous half-decade, "the contribution of the Slovak youth has chiefly been represented by the work of the girls who took part in the annual contest." Indeed, "these contests always provide the largest part of the financial proceeds of the day."[33] While the revenues from the Slovak "national" days in Chicago and Detroit went to charity, profits generated from events elsewhere typically were given to Slovak local and national religious institutions. Based on published accounts, contests in which the money went for religious endeavors were as successful as the ones with a philanthropic aim.

Popularity competitions, then, served multiple purposes. They accommodated the days' fund-raising agendas, but more important, they stimulated the support of young people for a *Slovak* event. Since committees rarely gave elaborate prizes, the incentive for becoming involved was not material. A 1933 winner in New York did receive an engraved compact, and the Ohio Valley's 1936 queen won a diamond ring. These examples, though, underscore the more general rule that winners could expect a title and recognition but little else.[34] In reality, the contests' primary reward was personal gratification. The potential for self-satisfaction resonated in the pre-event publicity. The actual "crownings" were prominent items on Slovak Day programs, and the winner bore the title for a year with the distinct possibility of attaining it again. These intangible prizes obviously came from participating in annual manifestations of Slovak ethnicity. By patterning their beauty and the offshoot popularity contests after American pageants, Slovak Day promoters were unabashedly exploiting popular features of American culture but refashioning them with an ethnic twist. The fact that young women worked to win titles in their region points to the fact that there were young people who were not running away from their ancestral origins.

Established notions concerning gender roles influenced but did not fully control women's involvement in Slovak Days. It is not surprising that women might be charged with handling the food-related aspects of these annual affairs. In 1934, Milwaukee advertised that "refreshments and snacks would be prepared by our women and young girls."[35] The only women acknowledged as involved in a Bridgeport, Connecticut, event were the four serving on the refreshments and food committee.[36] Women, however, were not restricted to kitchen-style duties. Although published ads for Slovak Days did not usually disclose the names of entire committees or other persons connected with the preparations, the evidence suggests that women's involvement defies generalization. Their participation as well as responsibilities varied by locale and over time. Women did serve on organizing committees. Since women's lodges had vested interests in events promoting Slovak ethnicity, they sent representatives to planning meetings and boosted the affairs to their members, within their parishes, and among local communities.[37] Women's lodges sponsored contestants for the queen competitions. Women were in charge of soliciting businesses and lodges for ads in the souvenir program for Chicago's 1934 Slovak Day. In the late 1930s, a second-generation woman replaced the long-time male secretary of western Pennsylvania's Slovak Day committee.[38] Local Slovak Days, then, nurtured ethnic activism among first- and second-generation females. Their participation blended activities that, taken as a whole, helped project the days' "Slovak" image. These annual affairs also fostered a tradition of Slovak women canvassing among cohabitants of their community specifically to advance ethnic causes.

Advocates understood that to succeed as ethnic manifestations, Slovak Days had to project a visibly discernible "Slovak" image. The move to transform speech-heavy affairs into displays of ethnicity therefore necessitated incorporating cultural symbols aside from the Slovak flag. The queen contests and subsequent "crownings" did highlight the distinctive ethnic thrust of Slovak Days, especially in places where contestants wore Slovak folk costumes.[39] Some planners, however, wanted to make ancestral folk apparel an intrinsic part of the entire Slovak Day, not something limited to the queen and her court. Believing that their traditional folk dress, "národný kroj," set Slovaks apart from other nationalities, they decided that having participants attend in ancestral costumes would have the practical effect of enhancing the day's "Slovak" image. This approach was not entirely new. During the Great War, Slovaks, like other nationalities, had donned folk attire when they joined in patriotic pageantry. This tradition, however, did not carry over into the early 1920s. Publicity for one particularly lackluster 1929 program of speeches, music, and American hymns did advertise that some men and women would be wearing Slovak costumes, but there was no call for all people to come garbed in Old World clothes. Event organizers, though, soon decided that everyone should, indeed, dress in the *kroj* of his or her homeland region. Two years later, ads announced that cash prizes would be awarded to the four women in the "prettiest costumes."[40]

Communities elsewhere followed a similar pattern. In 1932, promoters of western Pennsylvania's day pleaded for all Slovaks to come in traditional folk dress. Aiming to pressure, the committee resorted to the familiar ploy of comparing Slovaks unfavorably to other ethnic groups. They griped that Slovaks were unique among the country's nationalities in their reluctance to wear national costumes. The next year, the committee redirected its focus. Instead of a general call, it appealed to "young girls and young women" to put on traditional Slovak apparel for the occasion. This time it tried to combine persuasion and a competitive spirit. Asserting that Slovak *kroje* were more beautiful than those of any other nationality, the publicists no doubt hoped to convince females that they would be seen in something elegant instead of merely outmoded clothes that could embarrass young people sensitive to modern American fashion.[41] By drawing comparisons with other nationalities, these enthusiasts wanted to bolster pride in traditional Slovak culture.

During the decade, local promoters tenaciously strove to make wearing folk costumes part of Slovak Days. They advanced wide-ranging arguments to induce people of all ages, male and female, to come in *kroje*. Their appeals again suggest that they were trying to assert a respectable Slovak presence in America's diverse communities. Ohio Valley organizers, for example, wanted to showcase exquisite costumes "so that Americans can see who Slovaks are." This plea alone apparently did not work well, so the next year, the committee decided that families wearing Slovak *kroje* would be admitted free to the dance in the evening.[42] Milwaukee's Slovak schools cooperated in 1935 by getting children to dress in ancestral costumes for the event.[43] Slovak Day organizers also proved to be realists. They knew that many of their compatriots probably had not brought festive folk apparel when they immigrated. One committee therefore asked women to make "old-country costumes," and judges would determine the prettiest.[44] The emphasis on folk attire intensified in the middle to late 1930s. This stress reflected a continuation of the "immigrant gifts" concept that national activists had so vigorously embraced in the early 1920s. It also was part of a now increasing effort to instill pride in ancestry. The evidence indicates that local organizers were generally unsuccessful in convincing large numbers of people to wear *kroje* to Slovak Days. As a result, enthusiasts in some places narrowed their goals to getting children—and even more pointedly, girls—to attend the annual event in national costumes. Their focus, like the various popularity competitions, thus ultimately centered on girls and women.[45] This was part of the trend toward Slovak women playing a more visible role in local manifestations of ethnicity.

Although Slovak Days were viewed as ethnic events, except for encouraging the wearing of costumes, committees did not typically plan programs featuring Slovak culture or history. Catholics tried to foster devotion to Saints Cyril and Methodius, but this was done through speeches, or sometimes by putting their pictures on badges sold during the day. In the 1920s and 1930s, Slovak cuisine was not made an attraction. Because it was still part of the family diet, traditional food did not have the allure it would enjoy several decades later, when authentic cuisine would create nostalgia among American-born generations and turn ethnic events into food festivals. A few organizers did accentuate Slovak handiwork. For one Pennsylvania day, the Vincentian Sisters prepared a display of needle crafts.[46] Promoters elsewhere occasionally delighted in featuring fancywork. One particularly zealous committee arranged an exhibition of Slovak paintings and embroidery as well as an "old country wedding" with the entire party clothed in ancestral dress.[47] A traditional wedding ritual was also staged at an Ohio Valley day.[48] Planners no doubt hoped that the fanfare and vivid costumes would instill respect for ancient traditions and perhaps even inspire youths to maintain some of them. Highlighting Old World ceremonies reinforced the perception of ancestral traditions, including folk attire, as being quaint but appropriate for "Slovak" occasions.

As they evolved into the 1930s, local nationality days were clearly envisioned as being both Slovak and American affairs. To further excite widespread interest—but, it seems, with a special eye on young adults—organizers enhanced programs with dancing. "Attention Slovak Young People," the English-language ad for Masontown, Pennsylvania's 1928 day exclaimed, "there will be dancing."[49] One firsthand observer happily recounted that youths at Cleveland's 1928 Slovak Day danced while the elders "chatted and joked." Promoters definitely got the message that people enjoyed dancing, and by 1930 they had added dancing as a regular part of the program.[50] Planners in other areas started to do the same. Some announcements merely noted there would be dancing, but in the majority of instances, they heralded the fact there would be music to suit different tastes.[51] There would be a "Gypsy band" for people who want "to dance to the old-country čardáš" and a popular local band "for our Slovak young people," one ad guaranteed. In a subsequent letter to two Slovak newspapers, a participant rejoiced that the committee, for a second year, had been sensitive to what people wanted. "The old danced to Slovak music while our young people entertained themselves again with American dances," he happily related.[52] Securing two bands, with each catering to the preferences of its respective audience, became common practice. Of course, some youths joined in the folk dancing. Still, time and again, Slovak Day ads revealed an acute sensitivity to the generational distinctions within Slovak communities. Launching their first Slovak Day, Philadelphia's organizers followed the already typical pattern when they hired two orchestras, one for "the young" and one for "the old."[53]

Throughout the 1930s, organizers unquestionably used dancing as another ploy to entice young people to attend. The committee for one day increased the incentive by holding a dance contest. Proclaiming the 1932 competition "a hit," it scheduled one for the next year. While immigrants reminisced and danced the čardáš to music played by a Gypsy band on one pavilion, youths on another floor vied for a championship to tunes played by a local orchestra. One firm rule, however, governed eligibility: to qualify for the 1933 contest, "couples . . . are to be of Slovak descent as no other couples will be officially recognized."[54] Planners were willing to accommodate different tastes in music, but, at an event aimed to advance Slovak ethnicity, they were not willing to promote interethnic socializing in a potential courtship situation. The contestants might be dancing to modern music, but the winners would have to have the proper ancestral background.

The language advertising the dance options revealed changing perceptions of immigrant culture and an increasing awareness of what constituted generational differences. Taken as a whole, the publicity and the Slovak Days themselves nurtured these fundamental distinctions. While some ads and firsthand accounts referred to "Slovak" and "American," they also, with equal regularity, described the dancing as "traditional" versus "modern" or "old" versus "new." With rare exceptions, committees pointedly advertised there would be "modern" or "American" music for "the youths." This was more than merely the jargon of publicity; the terms were applied far too precisely for that. They were uniformly linked to dancing. Generational differences, which the locally produced literature openly acknowledged, were not simply between being Slovak or being American; rather, they were between "traditional, old" and "modern, young." The publicity shows that Slovaks saw that their ethnic community was evolving into one characterized by clearcut generational differences that went beyond the kind of sparring that had historically tormented parent–children relationships. These were distinctions spawned not by progressive changes in their ancestral culture but by the intrusion of a foreign culture. Turning Slovak into "traditional" and American into "modern" could remove some of the taint associated with ancestral traditions or expressions of Slovakness.

The engineers of local Slovak Days, then, realized that cultural differences separated the generations in their communities. In drawing up plans for Slovak Days, they generally accommodated the younger generation's preference for the "American." Promoters did not insist that only traditional music be allowed at what were clearly designed to be displays of ethnicity. Rather than fight reality, community activists tried to use American music to attract youths. It was a calculated attempt to employ American popular culture in an effort to ethnicize the younger generation. And it was an approach that corresponded well with the patriotic symbols and good-citizen references that also filtered through these nationality days.

As we have already seen, the entertainment segments of Slovak Days revealed a stark tendency by communities to copy what their compatriots elsewhere were doing, but there were differences. Geographic location in particular provided different opportunities. Slovaks in Youngstown and Pittsburgh, for example, held their events at Idora and Kennywood amusement parks, respectively, where participants could enjoy various types of rides. Apparently, in some years the committees negotiated special rates for these amusements. At least twice, Ohio Valley's committee chartered a boat to ferry people to West Virginia's Rock Springs Park.[55] Most nationality days, though, were held in local public parks or at farms with grounds suited to picnics as well as sundry games and contests.

Site accommodations were not the only minor variations among local Slovak Days. Committees relied on available local resources. In a few instances, they secured a movie to show during the day.[56] Planners for one community arranged a vaudeville production, and in another the committee engaged a magician who, promoters promised, would perform tricks people had never before seen.[57] Parades constituted the most conspicuous regionally based difference. Despite some variations stemming from local resources or traditions, throughout the 1930s the entertainment segments of Slovak Days in the United States were remarkably similar.

Almost universally, Slovak Day organizers developed strategies specifically to attract youths. What degree of success they enjoyed, however, cannot be gauged. Firsthand commentaries on youth attendance were in the main impressionistic. For example, lamenting what it saw as a declining interest in its region, one 1935 committee called on "Slovak Americans to cooperate with . . . [their] elders" to ensure the future of their annual Slovak Day. Three years later, an observer in another city praised the extensive involvement of youths, especially young girls, during the previous five years.[58] Delighted reporters often alluded to young people having enjoyed themselves playing games and dancing at Slovak Days. The evidence thus indicates that youth participation probably varied by locale. Some communities most likely boasted a large turnout, and others a small one; moreover, attendance differed over time. Nevertheless, the fact that year after year committees were able to include baseball games and sponsor well-supported popularity contests suggests that efforts to entice a younger crowd enjoyed a measure of success. Slovak Days seemingly did help cultivate a contingent of young people willing to become involved in "Slovak" activities. Those attending nationality days were exposed to all that went into these manifestations of ethnicity: the flags, American hymns, politicians lauding Slovaks, and the highlighting of some cultural traditions.

The focus on young people points to the conclusion that Slovak Days transcended class interests. Some historians have maintained that middle-class individuals took over the commemorative activities of their respective ethnic groups and shaped them to conform to the image they wanted to project. Looking at both the publicity and the programs for Slovak Days reveals, however, that these were not commemorative events dedicated to celebrating a historical occurrence or venerating a heroic figure. They were leisure-time affairs meant to bolster ethnicity and assert a Slovak presence in local communities.[59] Certainly, Slovak professionals and business owners welcomed activities that would project a positive image of their ethnic group and perhaps shore up their client base. It seems that they were especially active in Chicago's 1933 secular and religious days. Contemporary accounts, however, implied that Detroit's effort that year was handled by a cross-section of the Slovak community.[60] Of course, clergymen served on many committees, but there is in fact little information about the socioeconomic status of people who worked so hard to arrange and promote these events. In 1936, one second-generation man actually suggested that the Slovak middle class was not as involved in Slovak Days as it should be. Enumerating the myriad "benefits" of Slovak Days, he alluded to the favorable publicity "young American-born Slovak" business owners and professionals could get from their active participation. He opined that the days had "a noble purpose" because they showed "the world" that young Slovaks could boast the same achievements as "their neighbors."[61] Despite its ostensibly class-oriented thrust, this man's concerns actually belonged to the seemingly perennial comparison-with-other-nationalities genre that permeated Slovak public dialogue.

Exploring the content of the publicity and the programs for Slovak Days thus throws a different light on community-generated displays of ethnicity and the motives behind them. Given the overwhelmingly working-class makeup of the Slovak population and the widespread celebration of Slovak Days, it would defy reality to suggest that middle-class people, who made up only a small—and, in some small industrial towns, minuscule—segment of this ethnic group, regularly took charge of these community events and shaped them to suit their own agendas. The activist promoting a single nationwide day more accurately depicted the situation when, in 1927, he asserted that nationality days drew together "not only the intelligentsia but also the masses."[62] With different agendas in mind, but always hoping for a public display of ethnicity, Slovak Day enthusiasts universally drafted programs to entice the native and foreign born—young and old.

SLOVAK DAYS occurred only once a year, but, like Saint Patrick's Day, these observances provided evidence of ethnic durability. As one 1933 ad ebulliently put it, the event was "a powerful Slovak manifestation."[63] The publicity makes it clear that people promoting Slovak Days were anxious to counter contemporary negative attitudes toward Slovaks, eager to preserve Slovak institutions, and set on advancing ethnic pride. They hoped to ensure group survival. For nationality days to help achieve these aims, organizers knew they had to attract both the young and the old. So to boost attendance, planners made sure the day's entertainment blended "the Slovak" and "the American." Folk dancing and wearing traditional costumes helped give days a distinctly "Slovak" flavor. The queen crownings also embellished the events' "Slovak" image. The competitions, however, represented an attempt to refashion a popular American activity to suit Slovak Days. To attract—and, in effect, ethnicize—youths, planners grafted a Slovak veneer onto an element of American popular culture. They also used baseball games, which were thoroughly "American," to achieve those ends. Organizers did not tinker with this "American" image; they exploited it.

By offering both "traditional" music for the "old" and "modern" tunes for the "young," local activists were again demonstrating a willingness to employ mainstream American culture to foster enthusiasm for intergenerational ethnic undertakings. More than any other activity, the dance portions of the programs shed light on how Slovaks viewed generational differences. They realized that fundamental distinctions between the "young" and "old" were linked in part to cultural tastes. Over time, it appears, ordinary Slovaks—and other nationalities as well—ascribed a quaintness to folk culture that made it apropos to ethnic fetes. Folk costumes, dances, and music became nostalgic vestiges of the older generation's ancient culture, and, in the proper setting, they became acceptable means for acknowledging one's ancestry.[64]

The historical record yields stingy information about the ordinary people who participated in Slovak Days and other ethnic undertakings. Still, the evidence points to the conclusion that, during the 1920s and 1930s, arranging nationality days helped nurture local activism. It needs emphasizing that these single-day events typically entailed months of preparation and publicity. In addition, the various popularity contests, which often went on for lengthy periods prior to the events, reached out into communities. By fostering friendly rivalries, these yearly occasions challenged individuals as well as lodges to get involved in an ethnic cause. They also encouraged women to work on behalf of ethnic interests. In short, they motivated people—and in many areas, probably a core of activists—to devote energy to rouse cohabitants of their communities to action. The popularity contests, which were carried on through the 1930s, indicate that this nucleus embraced at least a portion of local youths. Overall, the successful holding of Slovak and other nationality days year after year, together with their fixed yet pliant programs, suggests that these annual events bridged the generations.

Certainly within the broader lives of the first and second generations, Slovak Day was a single annual incident. Throughout the calendar year there were also parish and other social functions not specifically designed to manifest ethnicity. For the many who did not participate, and in the towns where there were few or no nationality days, these affairs were largely irrelevant. Still, annual days show that nationalities wanted to maintain a felt presence in ethnically diverse communities. As the Slovak emphasis on youths revealed, ensuring that that presence would endure over time rested on keeping the second generation in the ethnic fold.

6 Language and Leisure

Getting the Younger Generation's Perspective

SOUNDING A VENERABLE nativist theme, Billy Baláš made no attempt to conceal his pique when he lashed out, "If she wants to write in Slovak why does she not move to Czechoslovakia where they don't write any English."[1] The irate author was in fact neither a nativist nor a youth alienated from his ethnic roots. Instead, he was a second-generation member of the National Slovak Society's Youth Circle (Kruh Mládeže) who was incensed by a letter recently published in its newsletter. His older sister, who was literate in Slovak, had translated the contents, which he "certainly didn't like." Not only had a fellow circle member, Julia Kramar, decried English-language articles in the official publication of a Slovak organization; she had branded parents who failed to teach their children to read and write Slovak as neglectful. Bristling at Kramar's reproaches, Baláš asserted: "I can't write in Slovak, but I am just as good a member of K.M. as she is, if not better."[2] The exchange occurred in the fall of 1931, the year there were so many Slovak Days that newspapers introduced special columns devoted to them. Neither Kramar nor Baláš indicated whether she or he had attended any Slovak Days, but, given their ardor, they certainly represented the youthful contingent that was not averse to participating in ethnic activities.

The newsletter in which the Kramar–Baláš missives appeared had been including English letters and articles for nearly a year. During the 1930s, English-language pages such as these became forums for young people to voice their opinions. The exchange between these youngsters was particularly significant because it indicates that, when it came to issues of ethnic identity, opposing positions did not merely reflect inter-generational differences between parents and children or between the "old" and the "young." Conflicting views existed within the second generation. So, like the older, foreign-born generation, this younger segment was by no means monolithic in its makeup or attitudes.

While the national leadership debated whether to incorporate English into Slovak publications, community activists were grappling with the everyday realities of drawing youths into the ethnic fold and keeping them there. Reflecting the same sensitivity that was shaping Slovak Day programs, local Slovaks turned to American popular culture, especially sports, as a way to lure young people and keep them involved in ethnic undertakings. Their objective was to link youths' leisure-time activities to ethnic organizations. By drawing Slovaks together into local webs of ethnically based teams, athletics helped foster a Slovak ethnic identity during the 1930s. The growing interest in American sports also aided the drive to include English in the Slovak print media. Aggressive efforts to accommodate both male and female youths and attract them to ethnic institutions further nurtured pockets of activism evident in the promotion of nationality days.

AT THE SAME TIME that national activists were campaigning to establish a Slovak Day in the 1920s, they were developing other tactics to perpetuate a Slovak ethnic identity. In particular, fraternal societies, with vested interests in group survival, initiated efforts to proselytize youths into "being Slovak." Reflecting on an upcoming 1926 convention, *Jednota* editorialized that one of the most important questions on the agenda would be "how to raise our children for our people." The future would be bleak if "our youth . . . will not be Slovak." The newspaper's Lutheran counterpart shared these sentiments. "Be Slovak, hold on to your national consciousness. Cultivate your language," one editorialist implored.[3] To make young people more "Slovak," activists channeled their energies into a strategy that relied on using Slovak-language materials to teach youths about their ancestral history and culture. The National Slovak Society compiled songs "all good for children" and published them in book form. Four-fifths of the collection consisted of Slovak songs; American patriotic hymns and a few English children's tunes made up the remainder.[4] Religious organizations adopted the same tactic. Lutheran spokespersons called for a youth magazine in which children could read Slovak literature. Being exposed to what, in their opinion, were beautiful works would cause young people to develop pride in the language that had produced them. The Slovak Evangelical Union's fourteenth convention authorized publications both for American- and foreign-born Lutherans.[5] Organizations also put together collections of poems, plays, and stories aimed at children and adolescents.[6] In an attempt to inspire youths, these materials portrayed Slovak "heroes," celebrated a national history characterized by repression and perseverance, and extolled supposedly ancient "Slovak" ideals.

During the years immediately following the 1924 immigration law, then, national activists put their faith into essentially educating people into "being Slovak." Wedded to the theory that ethnic survival hinged on maintaining the mother tongue, they preached language loyalty and forwarded their crusade by printing Slovak lessons in their publications. Although still concerned about refining the immigrant generation's sense of ethnic and religious identity, during the 1920s, activists increasingly aimed their cultural campaigns toward what was almost universally referred to as the "younger element." This contingent encompassed American-born persons as well as the generation and a half who, although technically immigrants, more closely resembled second-generation Slovaks.

When first launched, these undertakings by national organizations aroused enthusiasm at the grassroots level and, at the same time, were energized by local interest. Lodge officers appealed to national officials to furnish materials that would simultaneously entertain children and teach them Slovak history and culture. They also requested primers for language instruction. Organizations tried to accommodate these entreaties by publishing more materials.[7] *Kruh mládeže*, though, revealed a critical factor affecting language retention in 1926 when it introduced Slovak lessons in its February issue. Noting that some parents had asked for help in teaching their children to read and write Slovak, the editor explained that the paper would include a regular column devoted to language training. Another writer pointed to a premigration experience that was still influencing Slovak attitudes toward education. The reality was that the Hungarian government's policy of barring education in non-Hungarian languages meant that many parents, now in America, were unable to read or write fluently in their mother tongue. They cannot, *Kruh mládeže*'s columnist explained, teach their own children.[8]

By 1927, some activists were rethinking their approach and grudgingly coming to the realization that fostering ethnicity could not be achieved in the mother tongue alone. Desiring to keep young members from fleeing the fold as they matured and were "on their own," organizations increasingly had to bow to pressure to include English in some publications.[9] One by one, the major male and female fraternal societies introduced English items into their youth bulletins. Whether to add English, though, was often democratically decided at national conventions comprising rank-and-file representatives from local branches. Following the 1926 convention's decision to incorporate its youth publication, *Jaro,* into *Jednota* as a supplement with English-language articles, the editor explained with some resignation "that something must be done to keep up the interest of our young people in Slovak affairs, activities, doings, etc."[10] Other editors were equally forthcoming about explaining the reasoning behind similar decisions. Keeping "younger members" loyal was a paramount concern. Over the next few years, the remarks that inaugurated this bilingual edition became a common refrain in English-language pages, columns, and full supplements.

Tinged with acquiescence, the drive to include at least some English items pushed forward. By 1934, all the major societies had English-language sections in their publications. These segments reflected the age-based stratification within fraternal memberships, especially in adult lodges, where there were aging immigrants as well as younger American-born members. In addition, publications were adopting a bilingual format to accommodate not only the "'younger generation'... but all our members who are better versed in the English than in the Slovak language."[11] Demographic factors, especially variances within the first- and second-generation cohorts, affected acculturation rates and were significantly influencing convictions about language use.[12]

Not all Slovak organizations warmly embraced the notion of incorporating English into their literature. Stalwarts committed to the belief that language maintenance was vital to perpetuating group identity stood adamantly opposed. The idea sparked bitter exchanges between *Furdek,* a staunchly "Slovak-only" publication, and *Jaro,* published by a fraternal society anxious about youth membership. Chiding its critic, *Jaro's* editor claimed his organization was "better acquainted with the exact conditions among our people, and . . . with the present-day needs of our people and youth." Elaborating, he asserted, "There is an acute need for a publication in English about things Slovak." The paper wanted "to gain the good will of our young generation through things young people want, and we are willing to admit it."[13] In essence, the impetus for an English-language section had come from a pragmatic assessment of reality; it had not been imposed by an ideologically victorious or middle-class faction in the organization's higher echelons. The incentive sprang from the everyday experiences of nationally minded activists and ordinary members interested in preserving ethnic institutions. It is important to recognize that adopting English was an accommodation designed to secure the loyalty of second-generation persons who had already joined Slovak organizations. The pressure activists felt was thus spiraling upward from local communities, and the push was coming in part from existing young members whose fidelity enthusiasts wanted to secure.

The idea of employing English for "things Slovak" quickly gained momentum. When the nonaffiliated *Slovák v Amerike* introduced an English-language column, *Národné noviny* welcomed its editor "into the growing ranks of writers and journalists interested in Slovak affairs through the medium of the English language."[14] This commentator and others were vocalizing the shifting strategy for trying to win the younger generation's loyalty and for fostering ethnicity. They were aware that strong external forces as well as internal circumstances, especially parental ambivalence, were working against language maintenance. Sensing the growing futility of linking ethnic identity to the mother tongue, they moved toward employing English to turn youths into Slovaks. By 1930, even the ardent Slovak-only *Furdek* had capitulated and was including some English items. Over the next few years, a responsive second-generation readership helped transform Slovak societal organs from immigrant into ethnic newspapers.

Introducing English into Slovak publications did rankle more than a conservative faction active at the national level. Indeed, conflicting views could at times reflect generational differences. Putting it in combative terms, one columnist declared that some of the National Slovak Society's "older members" resented "the invasion of their newspaper by the English language." Opposition, however, was by no means the universal response of so-called old-timers. Reacting to what he considered a closed-minded stance, the commentator described the situation within the context of protest versus accommodation and at the same time acknowledged generational divisions. As he saw it, English was "the only means of communicating with younger members with whom the future of the organization rests," and old members therefore should be "adopting it warmly, [but] instead they only tolerate it."[15] Although the question of instituting English-language pages seemingly pitted identifiable categories (the elderly versus the young, the philosophically rigid against flexible accommodationists), the pages' contents— particularly, the ongoing discussion of English—reveal a more complex situation.

Youth supplements and English-language pages gave voice to differing viewpoints among the "younger element" in general. While editors experimented with different formats, and organizations vacillated between whether to publish supplements, pages, or merely columns in English, appeals to young members to submit letters remained a constant. To enliven the pages, readers were continually urged to express their views. Promising to publish correspondence, editors repeatedly insisted that they wished to know "just what our readers want in this section." Inaugurating its "English Page for Our Daughters" in 1929, *Dennica*'s editor pleaded, "Write about everything of interest. Send in your ideas." *Národné noviny* echoed the same invitation in 1934 when it established a "new English page, which will be . . . edited by an American born Slovak."[16] Filling the post with a second-generation representative demonstrated that the paper—and its parent fraternal organization—could attract committed young activists. Moreover, by selecting an American-born editor, fraternal decision makers were creating a second-generation role model and letting youths know that they were sensitive to their interests.

The invitations elicited responses. During the early 1930s, letters to the editor revealed that language-related matters did interest young Slovaks, especially those who joined ethnic organizations. They also show that disagreements over language retention cannot be placed solely within the parameters of intergenerational tensions. The 1931 Baláš–Kramar correspondence, for example, poignantly demonstrated the opposing views that had developed among Slovak youths. Kramar certainly declared a strong commitment to language preservation, and Sylvia Jalovecky "fully agreed" with her. Jalovecky did not attend a Slovak school but opined that, if people hungered to do something such as become literate in Slovak, they would find a way.[17] Fourteen-year-old Maria Duga regretted that so few of her fellow members sent Slovak letters to *Kruh mládeže*. She revealingly explained that she read the English material by herself; however, the Slovak correspondence became a shared family experience because she read those out loud to her parents.[18] The implication was that her parents were not well educated in Slovak, but she was. Another youth welcomed fraternal publications into his home because he used them for self-instruction in Slovak.[19]

Other members had a different opinion. Vexed because there were items in *Jaro* that he could not read, "J.K.," a young Slovak in Clairton, Pennsylvania, noted that those literate in Slovak could read *Jednota*, the adults' newspaper. Opposing *Jaro*'s bilingual format, he wanted the youth supplement to be "strictly an English publication" and be expanded from the current eight to between fifty and seventy pages.[20] Rudolph Albert no doubt thrilled sokol officials when he proclaimed that "ever since the English Section became a part of our official organ, I have been an ardent reader of all contributions."[21] This was the response they had hoped for. The bilingual approach seemed to ensure that this present member would remain a faithful adherent.

The youths who chose to become involved in the language debate revealed that it was not simply a contest between parents and children. Indeed, the public dialogue about English shows how language had evolved in households and the ramifications of this evolution for the larger community. Duga took pride in the fact that she could read Slovak communications to her family members. Baláš, who was illiterate in Slovak, was apparently not battling his parents over ethnic identity. His intense reaction to Kramar's reproaches was shaped in part by his own situation: his older sister could read Slovak, but he could not. He represented that contingent of younger siblings whose families had drifted toward using English. The exchange therefore exposed the different degrees of acculturation within immigrant families. Older brothers and sisters might have become literate in their parents' language, but as this elder component learned English, it became the regular medium of exchange, especially among siblings.[22] Baláš did not indicate how his sister had been trained, but clearly his parents were not committed to a Slovak education for all their children.

Other contemporaries highlighted the fact that many among the younger element could speak but were illiterate in Slovak.[23] One irked youth told *Jaro's* readers that his parents had taught him to speak Slovak but not to read or write it; therefore, using "numerous Slovak publications around the house," he had taught himself. He complained about parents who failed to make their children fluent in Slovak and went on to criticize those who, instead of Slovak, spoke "poor English" in their homes. Implicitly reproaching parents, presumably including his own, this zealous youth called on older people to "stimulate an interest in Slovak among their children."[24] Mary Martinis shared his sentiments. Because she could neither read nor write Slovak, this Kruh Mládeže member requested a primer so she could teach herself as well as her younger brother and sister.[25] Clearly, in terms of traditional models of intergenerational clashes over language maintenance, these "American" youths turned the debate on its head. Taken as a whole, the differing opinions expressed by youths in the English-language pages offer a fresh perspective on the traditional view that the fight to save the mother tongue was a battle only between resolute foreign-born parents and their recalcitrant American-born offspring.

Published discussions acknowledged that a substantial portion of youths could converse in at least rudimentary Slovak. Conversational abilities without similar reading and writing capabilities represented the real crux of the matter. The task, therefore, was to teach Slovak-speaking youngsters how to read and write the mother tongue. Obstacles to this goal, however, arose out of more than youth antipathy. Since the end of the Great War, activists battling Czechoslovakism had been grappling with the ramifications of a low Slovak literacy rate. Although nationalist campaigns and the availability of Slovak-language publications in the United States had apparently inspired some immigrants to become more literate in their native tongue, this did not evolve into a widespread enthusiasm to educate their children in Slovak. Instead, the evidence indicates that parental commitment to language maintenance varied. While speaking Slovak was essential for communication within families, literacy was not; thus, many parents did not exert tremendous efforts to teach their children to read the language. Schools did not offer an efficacious antidote to parental apathy. A contemporary study found that, in 1930, there were 115 Slovak elementary schools with only 25,085 pupils. This meant a vast majority of Slovak children were probably attending public or non-Slovak institutions. Moreover, it does not appear that Slovak schools, which were overwhelmingly Catholic, were necessarily committed to Slovak-language instruction.[26]

Individuals who engaged in public discussions about language issues offered another reason for weak parental interest. A Uniontown, Pennsylvania, resident admitted that some parents did not teach their children Slovak because they did not want them to be subjected to the same ridicule they had suffered.[27] Whether this was his own opinion, he did not say, but his observation stemmed from firsthand knowledge about sentiments within his community. New immigrants were well aware of the anti-foreign-language attitude pervading American society. The foreign born had lived through the excesses of wartime patriotism and had been conscious of the English-language sword figuratively hanging over people's jobs. They had encountered Americanization in the workplace, perhaps even promoted in their own pay envelopes. In their communities, residents personally witnessed the nativism that carried over into the 1920s. The hostility and stigmatization embodied in the country's 1924 immigration law were themes hammered in the ethnic press and by articulate Slovak critics. Immigrants' attitudes toward language retention thus could not escape the circumstances that had touched everyday life in wartime and then postwar America. When it came to language maintenance, premigration experiences combined with new-world circumstances to undermine parental resolve to teach bilingual children how to read and write in Slovak.

As language questions continued to capture interest, the ongoing dialogue revealed some harmony between the first and second generations. Both immigrants and their offspring agreed that functionalism had to outweigh symbolism. Across age and ideological lines, Slovak activists were united by a hard-headed acceptance of the reality that fluency in English was indispensable. According to one first-generation columnist, the matter was one of "Cold Logic versus Blind Idealism." Asserting that only a portion of the "half million Slovaks in America" could read Slovak, he queried: which language would a young person logically want to learn? While he applauded those competent in both languages, he proclaimed that "to insist upon training the youngster in Slovak to the detriment of his English is nonsensical." Inevitably, he asserted, "the future of the Slovak language in America is doomed"; therefore, a publication "cannot afford to be sentimental. It must look at matters stripped of all their rosy illusion and empty idealism." It stood to reason that "if you write . . . in a language they [young people] don't understand it is useless to try to interest them."[28]

Some rank-and-file immigrants shared this pragmatic view. Describing himself as "old," a local man represented the realistic element among the elderly when he admonished fellow fraternalists to "wake up to the fact that we cannot go on and succeed by harping on Slovak language and literature and holding our sons and daughters to our language." While it is "well to live as a Slovak . . . that is not getting us anywhere." He reminded fellow immigrants that "we old-timers will not live forever . . . [and] without them ['young folks'] we cannot survive." So, he concluded, give the young folks opportunities to participate "in the language they understand" and be proud of children who "take up the good work in English."[29] Clearly, this elderly immigrant did not see an inherent correlation between maintaining the mother tongue and ethnic identity.

Fears that carping might unleash a backlash among youths spurred some commentators figuratively to raise a cautionary hand. Warnings that endless criticisms might drive young people away appeared in the dialogue about language. For example, a foreign-born columnist who was literate in Slovak took up the younger generation's cause by pointedly admonishing people to quit complaining about the youths and, furthermore, to stop nagging them.[30] Offering "A Defense of the American Slovak Youth," one spokesperson warned critics that they were only irritating young people and implied that continual disapprobation risked driving away those who did belong to ethnic societies. Going to the crux of the issue, he reminded grumblers who were moaning, "The language, the language, what will become of the mother tongue?" that "we are considering the AMERICAN SLOVAK YOUTH not the EUROPEAN Slovak youth." Fluency in English, not Slovak, was what was required for "American Slovaks." This passionate defender opined that "sentimental bickerings are of no advantage. . . . [L]et us face realities."[31] Apparently relying on his own experiences, he declared that the American Slovak youth "admits his nationality and is proud of his foreign parents." This assertion reflected a growing shift in the early 1930s toward replacing language maintenance with "pride in ancestry." The author exuded frustration and resentment that probably were also being felt by young people like Baláš who were associating with ethnic institutions. They had not forsaken their ancestral heritage, but they also refused to conform to rigid criteria for determining what constituted Slovak consciousness. These young enthusiasts wanted to help set the terms.

Pragmatism did not obliterate deeply felt sentiments about preserving the mother tongue. Indeed, a contingent of hard-core believers remained adamantly committed to tethering ethnicity to language. The ongoing ambiguities created by language issues were tellingly revealed in the pages of *Kruh mládeže*. Introducing a "Handy Grammar" section in December 1932, the publishers proclaimed: "teach a child good English in the cradle and he will speak good English to the grave." The series focused on pronunciation and proper usage. A month later, the supplement began publishing its previously announced Slovak-language instruction, titled "For Lovers of Our Mother Tongue." Almost symbolically, the paper ran the two series on facing pages until June, when the Slovak instruction was discontinued. Admitting that a "lack of interest" had forced the abandonment of these particular lessons, the paper continued urging people to read Slovak literature. And even as the English-language instruction continued until December 1933, the paper provided titles of Slovak books suitable for youths and adults.[32] In the 1930s, some people continued to use English columns to promote bilingualism. For example, applauding the enthusiastic response to appeals for letters, *Kruh mládeže*'s editor turned his praise into an opportunity to try subtly to influence young readers to seek language instruction. Treading ever so gingerly into the discussion, he assured the paper's readership that the editorial staff was "not against the English language" but nevertheless wanted "to have the feeling that all members . . . are able to speak and write both languages."[33]

The clashes between preservationists, who were actually supporting bilingualism, and the champions of English reflected significant differences among the younger element. It is possible, as some scholars have concluded, that the second-generation individuals who joined ethnic societies did view their parents' native tongue more favorably.[34] In the 1920s and 1930s, however, there was not necessarily a direct correlation between language competency and participation in Slovak organizations or community-level activities. In short, feeble language skills did not deter young people from becoming involved in ethnic activities. The English sections of Slovak publications, especially the correspondence and articles discussing language issues, show that, among their second-generation memberships, organizations boasted both enthusiasts philosophically committed to language maintenance and equally ardent disparagers. Significantly, these sparring factions, especially those who had rejected their parents' language, comprised individuals who nevertheless had demonstrated loyalty to their group and an interest in maintaining ties to ethnically defined institutions. Rather than yield to pressure or simply abandon Slovak organizations, some youths forced changes by exploiting the fact that institutional survival depended on their allegiance. Thus, young Slovaks disposed to ally themselves with ethnic organizations were redefining the criteria for gauging ethnicity. For an especially articulate segment of these joiners, language was not a crucial component. From their perspective, Slovak, like traditional costumes and folk dances, became quaint. It was the language of ancestral heritage, not of their modern society.

During the early 1930s, both the rhetoric and strategy for fostering a Slovak consciousness shifted. Passionate defenses of the "youthful element," coupled with rebukes for idealists anchored to the language standard, demonstrated a move away from trying to make youths into "Slovaks" and toward trying to instill a "pride in ancestry." As early as 1930, an item in *Národné noviny* reflected this shift: a columnist, stating that "we [in the United States] are all Americans," went on to declare the difference is that "we are Americans of Slovak descent (or birth) while our next-door neighbors may be of Irish origin."[35]

More and more, spokespersons for both religious and secular organizations referred to "Americans of Slovak descent" or "ancestry." With equal regularity they started beseeching youths to take "pride in your Slovak ancestry" or "origin."[36] In 1933, a sokol president reflected the subtle yet significant philosophical change taking place. Pointing to the adverse effects of restrictive immigration laws as well as the impact that American culture was having on youths, he proclaimed his willingness "to accommodate those [members] who have been brought up in this country." He called them "the younger Americanized members of our organization." The newly inaugurated English-language section of the annual almanac gave him his "first opportunity to meet them on something of their own ground." This did not mean, however, that he thought they should reject their ancestral heritage. Instead, reaffirming the potential for using English to teach things Slovak, he asserted that "it is not difficult to be a thorough Slovak, and at the same time an upright American." He urged people to "be true to your nativity" and always to "be a Slovak" when dealing with others. And, he reasoned that "newer things . . . need not supplant the *old traditional feelings.*"[37] This address revealed the contradictory feelings—and, indeed, the dilemma—people grappling with the knotty "youth" problem faced. Clearly torn between the need to secure young people's interest and his own desire to perpetuate a Slovak consciousness, he resorted to emotional appeals rooted in pride. In much the same way as they had stressed Americanism in the Great War and afterward, he and other articulate enthusiasts insisted that maintaining an ethnic identity need not dilute one's "Americanness." But the emphasis was changing. "Be proud of your ancestors . . . you are [also] free-born American citizens," an English-language columnist admonished young Lutheran readers.[38] Accentuating *pride* in origin instead of insisting that they *be* Slovak offered a viable avenue for keeping second-generation youths involved in Slovak affairs and securing their long-term devotion.

Introducing English did help reinforce the loyalty of existing members; however, for ethnic societies, it was equally necessary to continue increasing their memberships. During the early part of the century, most Slovak organizations had established youth divisions, but enrolling young people had remained a somewhat secondary concern. From the national perspective, the 1924 immigration quota law altered the situation. Vocal activists left no doubt that they realized the new legislation could have a strong negative impact on group identity, and ultimately on ethnic institutions. Fraternal insurance societies faced a "dangerous enemy," one editorialist declared in 1926, and "that enemy is restrictive immigration." It used to be "quite easy to prevail on any good Slovak man or woman to join" a society, another columnist stated, but now "the immigration laws and time have changed all this. . . . The only field from which we can gain new members now (outside of the Young Folks Circle), IS THE YOUNGER GENERATION."[39] He knew the task was twofold: to keep existing members while attracting new ones. Rank-and-file members also understood the gravity of the situation. Going to the heart of the matter, one particularly astute fraternalist summarized the root causes and the thorny predicament facing ethnic institutions when he declared that there were "no new immigrants to provide new blood." Something had to be done, he warned, to make younger Slovaks "feel as one of us."[40] The laments and warnings went on. In the aftermath of the 1924 immigration legislation, increasing the number of young members evolved into an all-out objective that dramatically reshaped fraternal activities, especially in local communities.

In the mid-1920s, national organizations stepped up efforts to establish more youth branches where adult lodges already existed.[41] Like the fraternal organizations' campaign to educate youths into being Slovak, winning over young people depended on energetic commitment at the local level. Thus, national officers were undoubtedly gratified when their initiative sparked interest in Slovak enclaves. It was clear that ordinary members also believed that membership numbers could be higher than the approximately 100,000 who belonged to Slovak "youth orders" in the mid-1920s.[42] Venting his frustration in *Národné noviny*, a Connellsville, Pennsylvania, man decried the fact that some children in his community did not belong to any Slovak society.[43] Responding to the national offices' appeals, some lodges aggressively sought instructions on how to organize youth branches.[44]

Because the chief responsibility for enlisting young children rested with mothers and fathers, promoters targeted parents who had failed to enroll their sons and daughters in a Slovak mutual aid society. Some enthusiasts advanced the ethnically charged argument that parents had an obligation to instill a Slovak consciousness in children. If inspired at a tender age, these sentiments would likely endure as youngsters matured.[45] Most often, however, advocates appealed to parents' practical leanings by reminding them of the insurance benefits fraternal membership afforded. "Are you sleeping well?" one columnist accusingly asked mothers and fathers who had not insured their children. They could die suddenly in an accident, he warned.[46] Publicists also placed the issue squarely in the parents' own interest. They pointed out that an organization's survival—and, hence, its capacity to pay future benefits, which obviously affected current adult members—rested on increasing the youth rolls.[47]

With national officers bringing relentless pressure to organize youth lodges, some local members felt compelled to unleash frustrations and bring these promoters in touch with reality. Early on, a Patton, Pennsylvania, man spoke for small-town lodges as well as those with aging memberships when he related that most members of his assembly were too old to have sons and daughters eligible for youth branches. He explained that among members' families there were perhaps only two or three qualified children, certainly not enough for the lodge to start an affiliated circle. Although he did not address the issue, his letter carried the implication that some middle-aged immigrants who might still have adolescent children had not been joining the adult lodges.[48] People also could have been joining another Slovak fraternal organization.

Circumstances beyond their control could work against parents eager to enroll their young offspring in a Slovak society. An Akron man, who had no money to pay his children's dues because he was on strike, turned in desperation to the elder of the National Slovak Society's youth division. He wanted to keep his children from being expelled from the young people's circle. Clearly sympathizing with the man's plight, Michal Laučik could only reluctantly inform him that the society's bylaws had no provisions to handle the situation.[49] The man's predicament, which tellingly exposed ethnic organizations' vulnerability to economic downturns, demonstrated the basic fact that youth membership depended on parental willingness *and* ability to pay the dues. In this instance, at least, factors beyond his control hampered a parent's desire to keep his children within the Slovak institutional fold.

As the 1920s gave way to the 1930s, activists realized that they could not rely solely on adults to recruit young people into Slovak institutional life. Thus, in addition to pressuring local lodges to establish youth branches, the nationals launched massive campaigns aimed directly at youths.[50] "We must," one national fraternal officer reasoned, "approach the younger generation through [our] younger . . . members."[51] Hoping to energize its current membership, the National Slovak Society instituted a contest complete with prizes for persons who recruited new members. Although youths were exerting efforts on behalf of an ethnic organization, their potential rewards were decidedly nonethnic in nature. Individuals who persuaded 100 people to join the society would receive a radio; the prize for 75 new members was a bicycle; awards for 50 down to 5 new members ranged from wristwatches to cameras to fountain pens.[52] Nationally organized drives, together with badgering parents, produced mixed results. With varying degrees of success, the youth divisions of the major Slovak men's and women's organizations did grow in the late 1920s.[53] The economic calamity of the 1930s would undermine these successes, especially when parents could not pay children's dues. Nevertheless, despite the adverse impact of the Great Depression, efforts under way to shore up youth involvement in ethnic activities, particularly in local communities, not only continued but expanded.

In the 1920s when national organizations were promoting ethnicity through education and rhetoric or trying to bribe young recruiters with radios, wristwatches, and fountain pens, local members were developing a different approach for attracting youths. Reflecting the same strategy evident in Slovak Day programs, their strategy entailed capitalizing on American popular culture. The experience of everyday life in Slovak communities seemingly made them more attuned to young people's tastes. As early as 1919 a Trenton, New Jersey, man was counseling that young people "do not want to belong to an association where the only activity is required attendance at a meeting." He urged the First Catholic Slovak Union to follow the sokols' example and organize baseball teams and boxing clubs.[54] People in other communities apparently shared these views. In 1920, a Gary, Indiana, Slovak club formed a baseball team. By 1922, Youngstown, Ohio, also had a Slovak team. That year, the club went eight-and-two playing eight games against non-Slovak teams in the metropolitan area and two games with a Slovak church club in Cleveland. Since each club traveled to its opponent's ballpark, the intercity encounters helped make team membership an adventure for the athletes.[55]

Baseball teams sprang up in other small towns.[56] In 1924, clubs in eastern Pennsylvania's Lackawanna region formed a "Slovak Baseball League." Young athletes from the area's tiny industrial towns, such as Jessup, Olyphant, Throop, Dunmore, and Taylor, as well as from Scranton, could spend their summers involved in amateur but nevertheless organized sports.[57] The next year, Slovaks in Clarksburg, West Virginia, established what would remain the state's only Slovak baseball team until 1931.[58] Grasping the appeal that "this great American pastime is finding ... among the children of foreign immigrants," local parishes formed baseball teams. In 1928, a particularly vigorous Gary, Indiana, pastor directed the Midwest Slovak League, while one of the city's "social and gymnastic clubs" created a baseball team.[59] For some nervous enthusiasts, sports teams were not spreading quickly enough. Why are young people joining non-Slovak organizations? queried one exasperated man. He answered his own question: they offer sports.[60] Attracting youths to Slovak organizations and churches was an overriding objective of local activists. Thus, as national societies compiled books, debated about English-language publications, and sponsored membership campaigns, rank-and-file Slovaks focused on exploiting young people's leisure-time interests.

In the late 1920s, local branches began advancing the notion that national societies not only should encourage athletics but they should help coordinate recreational activities among geographically dispersed Slovak communities. Concluding that the "future of the Slovak people in America" required a unified effort, the National Slovak Society's Pittsburgh lodges took matters into their own hands in 1929 by calling for an idea-sharing meeting. Participants proposed that the society's assemblies create a single regionwide association to arrange plays, lectures, and other entertainment. One representative stressed the necessity of forming sports clubs to entice youths.[61] A year later, the elder of a Catholic youth branch enunciated the same point: "the best means of keeping youths is through sports."[62] When it came to the younger element, local activists demonstrated a better grasp of reality than national fraternal officers.

National activists were not oblivious to the powerful impact athletics were having on the popular imagination. Trying to inspire support for a membership drive, one fraternal organization's English publicity proclaimed that, working together, members could "put it [the campaign] over with a Babe Ruth Bang for a record Home Run."[63] Even without the rising popularity of "American" sports to open their eyes, national activists in the late 1920s had to confront the reality that the inspirational approach to attracting the younger element needed reassessment. Their own members were telling them as much in letters to English-language columns. A spokesman "From One of the Younger Group" put it plainly. He said that, when asked, young people explained that dull meetings centering on Old Country politics and collecting dues discouraged them from joining Slovak organizations. Elaborating his point, he continued: "the only social activity is possibly one dance and a long-winded banquet each year."[64] Emphasizing the need to broaden their purpose, another commentator warned that it was necessary for each fraternal society to be more than "merely an insurance company."[65] "How about a Junior League?" yet another columnist eagerly urged. It would be an excellent way to recruit people who would then move on to adult lodges.[66] Under pressure from local enthusiasts, in the late 1920s national organizations began moving from a primarily hortatory strategy to one fostering athletic activities. This tactic, which complemented what local activists were doing to transform Slovak Days, relied on encouraging community-level and regionwide involvement. The objective became to appropriate favorite American-style recreational activities and fasten them—and, coincidentally, young people—to ethnic institutions.

Initially, fraternal organizations viewed sports within the context of their membership campaigns. The First Catholic Slovak Union revealed this tendency when it announced in *Jaro's* English section that everything would be done to make "the younger members—feel perfectly at home."[67] Besides organizing their own chapters, they could introduce sports if they felt uncomfortable at regular adult lodge meetings. Revealing underlying motives, the announcement exclaimed that the fraternal society wanted Slovak youths happily to "spend their leisure time under the guidance of an immense national organization." The nationals, though, treaded step by step toward fostering athletics. They started by using their English-language pages to publicize Slovak sports activities and celebrate Slovak athletes. In its first "Sports Column," *Slovenský hlásnik* featured a boxer who was a member of a local Slovak Evangelical Union lodge.[68] *Jednota's* inclusion of a sports page sparked a revealing small-scale turf war between its editor and *Jaro*, the youth paper. "He knows," *Jaro's* editor complained, that "the only reason some persons read *Jaro* is to get the sports."[69] Clearly, he feared that, since it was a monthly supplement, *Jaro* could not compete with a weekly publication, which would have more up-to-date information. Adding sports columns to the adult organs of both religious and secular organizations was aimed at the younger element, most likely people between age eighteen and their mid-twenties who had graduated from youth to adult orders. Since younger English-speaking members of youth divisions could obviously also read adult newspapers, sports pages served as a link between the age-based branches.

In the late 1920s, English sports columns were capitalizing on Slovak teams that, spawned by local initiative, had sprung up in America's communities. Their expansion revealed the same copycat effect fueling Slovak Days. Local promoters trumpeted team successes, which in turn inspired other communities to imitate them by creating their own clubs. Newspapers, for example, reproduced photos of teams attired in smart uniforms. In 1928, junior leaguers from tiny Osceola Mills, Pennsylvania, saw themselves pictured on page one and held up as examples worthy of emulating. The next year, the new team in Yukon, Pennsylvania, called on other clubs in this region dotted with grim mining towns to organize so they could have worthy opponents. Although in 1931, Nanty Glo's Slovak team was not having a good first season in the local league, the reporter was confident that these young athletes would do better. The lodge could boast one achievement, though: since it had organized a baseball team, this Pennsylvania branch had received twenty-two new members.[70] A promoter in Mount Carmel, Pennsylvania, reported that the town's young Slovaks had promised to join the lodge if it established a baseball team. The branch took the promise seriously. The team, which was subsequently organized, merited high-profile coverage in the fraternal newspaper.[71] While baseball was the commonly promoted sport, Lutherans frequently founded basketball teams. By 1929, teams in Cleveland were playing opponents in Duquesne and Pittsburgh.[72] Basketball enjoyed the same front-page treatment in Lutheran papers that Catholic and secular publications afforded baseball teams. Protestants also were advocating mushball as a less strenuous alternative to baseball.[73]

By the late 1920s, local Slovak clubs were working to expand their athletic programs. For example, six baseball teams affiliated with small-town First Catholic Slovak Union lodges in western Pennsylvania coalesced into a league so young people could "participate in American sports." The Western Pennsylvania Jednota Baseball League had a grand purpose in mind: to advance an "athletic relationship among lodges" in the region and ultimately to expand and include all types of sports.[74] With a schedule spanning four-and-a-half warm-weather months, baseball teams from a sixty-mile area regularly played each other. Lodges elsewhere were also coming together to form leagues comprising teams from several small towns.[75] The flurry of activity was not lost on people at national headquarters. In 1931, the First Catholic Slovak Union sponsored a "National Elimination" in which winners of playoffs among Pennsylvania's four Slovak leagues competed for a title. At the time, there were twenty-two teams in the union's Pennsylvania leagues.[76] Zeal for nationally coordinated athletic programs, however, was tempered by fears about costs. In general, associations limited their actions to calling on local branches to organize athletic clubs and baseball teams.[77]

The continued interest in American sports and the burgeoning number of teams finally pushed national organizations to establish athletic programs. Taking advantage of existing clubs, the nationals adopted measures to draw together local teams and put them under a single ethnic tent. The Slovak Evangelical Union, which focused on basketball,

was the first fraternal society to establish a formal structure incorporating local groups into a single body. The 1929 "Constitution and By-
laws of the Slovak Evangelical Union Basketball League of America"
most likely influenced constitutions framed by other organizations.[78]
Three years later, the First Catholic Slovak Union took steps to consol-
idate numerous clubs, primarily baseball teams, already organized by
its local lodges. In addition to creating the office of sports director to
coordinate activities, the union's 1931 convention established a youth
fund to finance athletic groups. It also divided the United States into athletic districts. National Slovak Society branches cooperated to form the
"Western Pennsylvania N.S.S. Baseball League," whose two divisions
spanning three counties and including ten teams opened their inaugural season on Decoration Day in 1933.[79] Fraternal programs targeted
"young" people in all of the organizations' local lodges. Usually they
had two categories of athletes: "senior" players, who were young people belonging to adult lodges, and "junior" players, who were adolescents and teenagers in youth branches (Illustration 6).

Local vigor and national support fueled a spurt of new lodge-
sponsored teams. In 1935, the First Catholic Slovak Union boasted seven
senior and four junior leagues that, all told, comprised fifty-four teams
and 848 players. Teams from New York to St. Louis played regular
schedules and chased pennants in their quest to compete in the union's
national tournament. Another 138 athletes belonged to eleven independent teams sponsored by First Catholic Slovak Union lodges but
not affiliated with its leagues.[80] Cleveland's Indoor Baseball League had
eight teams and 119 players.[81] For Catholics, baseball remained the most
popular sport, whereas Protestants, primarily Lutherans, continued to
fancy basketball because it required smaller and more easily obtainable
facilities and fewer players. By 1930, the Slovak Evangelical Union's
recently pioneered league claimed three districts, and despite bad economic times, the number of participants increased from approximately
100 to 150. The Slovak Evangelical Union also held championships.[82]

Once they began sponsoring programs, national organizations helped
further the development of ethnically defined community groups.
Despite favoring a particular sport, the nationals, hoping to encourage
more young people to "maintain a common interest" in their local
branches, expanded and diversified their athletic programs.[83] The goal
became to forge a year-long tie between recreational activities and their
organizations. In the mid-1930s, therefore, besides its baseball divisions,
the First Catholic Slovak Union had thirty-one affiliated and independent basketball teams with nearly 300 registered players. During

ILLUSTRATION 6. Participating in team sports appealed to boys who belonged to youth branches of Slovak organizations as well as to those young adults who belonged to the senior lodges. *Upper:* Photograph of junior softball champs from *Kalendár Jednota,* 1939, 231. Courtesy of the Immigration History Research Center, University of Minnesota. *Lower:* Picture of adult baseball team of a western Pennsylvania First Catholic Slovak Union lodge from *Kalendár Jednota,* 1933, 88. Courtesy of the Immigration History Research Center, University of Minnesota.

the next five years, both Catholic and Protestant organizations incorporated softball, mushball, and bowling teams into their geographically based athletic districts.[84]

Bowling in particular could connect leisure time year-round to Slovak institutions. From the standpoint of activists committed to reinforcing ethnicity by strengthening it at the household level, this sport had a good chance of becoming a family and dual-gender activity. Raving about bowling's potential benefits, one zealous supporter asserted that it attracted "older as well as younger" persons and, moreover, that it appealed to married people and individuals who had matured beyond team sports. This enthusiast was convinced that, since individuals could participate until they were ninety, bowling clearly held out the possibility of long-term attachments to Slovak leagues.[85] As the 1930s progressed, national organizations constantly broadened their horizons when it came to supporting ethnically sponsored athletics. In 1939, the Slovak Evangelical Union proclaimed yet "another milestone" when it announced that "golf enthusiasts" from five areas would vie for its national golf championship.[86]

Proponents also speculated about the positive impact sports could have on Slovaks as a group. Establishing leagues where young boys could hone their talents might result someday in a "Slovak Babe Ruth," one visionary declared. The benefits sports could shower on Slovaks did not necessarily have to wait for a superstar to rise from the ranks. Organized leagues with teams playing regular schedules would merit coverage in American newspapers. "What fine publicity it would give to our nationality," he exclaimed.[87] Enthusiasts believed that the reports about Slovak teams would advance "the good name" of the Slovak people.[88] "Let's show our fellow American citizens that the descendants of immigrants are equal in all ways to the descendants of great and educated peoples," another zealous backer challenged.[89] From the perspective of some advocates, the success of "Slavic" players would have a positive ripple effect for all "Slavic persons." Their fame would demonstrate that children "of recent immigrants, descendants of peasants and humble laborers, are taking part in America as Americans with the best of the best."[90] Achieving such recognition rested on keeping nationality classifications. Therefore, the same "other nationalities" theme that typified contemporary Slovak Day campaigns, especially the publicity generated by local organizers for their community events, revealed itself in grassroots efforts to promote sports. In a spurt of typical hyperbole, a Pennsylvania man appealed to all area lodges to estab-

lish teams because, he maintained, organized sports provided opportunities to demonstrate that the Slovak is "as talented, fit, diligent, and
outstanding as any other nationality."[91] Community activists seemed
determined to stamp out negative attitudes they knew existed toward
new immigrants. At heart, both they and national activists viewed
American recreational activities as a way to achieve this end and, simultaneously, to cultivate Slovak ethnicity.

Competitive athletics did foster a Slovak consciousness. Organized
sports had the practical effect of encouraging individuals to participate
in clearly defined ethnic undertakings. Geographically scattered teams
were joined together into "Slovak" leagues. Community-based clubs
met other Slovak teams in regular season play; they vied for Slovak
championships. Their activities were publicized in Slovak publications.
From a young age, those involved in fraternal and parish-based sports
engaged in friendly competition with "other nationalities" and "Americans." In some regions, Slovak sokols, which regularly played non-
Slovak groups, enjoyed the reputation of fielding particularly strong
squads.[92] By playing under a "nationality" aegis, teams, even those
claiming only a small percentage of the local population, helped perpetuate ethnic rivalries and awareness in communities. Thus, both
interethnic and intraethnic games in their own way reinforced the ethnic identity of the players.

The zeal for ethnic teams and the enthusiasm some spokespersons
expressed for institutionally sponsored athletic programs were by no
means precise measures of actual grassroots involvement. During the
1930s, only a small percentage of people eligible to join probably did.[93]
Moreover, commitment among the rank-and-file fluctuated. Local promoters occasionally fretted about lack of interest in forming or joining
teams; some grumbled about sparse attendance at games.[94] Commentators, though, blamed hard economic times, not mere apathy, for the problems. The nationals did establish a dues or a per-person allotment system to finance local sports. People unable to pay the fees obviously could
not join a team.[95] Even the allotment plans, which provided money from
a national fund to subsidize local clubs, had shortcomings. Following the
inception of its assistance program in 1932, the First Catholic Slovak
Union headquarters was inundated with letters from disgruntled lodges.
Time and again, local officers complained that they had created teams,
based on the promise of financial assistance, but they either had not
received the promised funding or the money provided was inadequate
to cover expenses. Insufficient resources handicapped some efforts to

promote sports and also compelled some clubs to disband.[96] Still, as with professional sports, the number of players or teams is not an accurate measure of the more encompassing effect competitive athletics could have. While no doubt exaggerating when he proclaimed that "either as participants or spectators" members "thrived on athletics," one exuberant commentator was not totally off the mark when he asserted that Slovak teams had an impact that went well beyond the players.[97] Cleveland Slovaks demonstrated this point when they sponsored a basketball game and dance. At the social following the game, the out-of-town visiting team would be "welcomed by a group of young ladies" who represented parishes throughout the area.[98]

Cultivating ethnicity through athletics was a strategy aimed decidedly at males rather than females. National fraternal organizations with dual-gender memberships made only weak-willed gestures toward developing programs for younger female members. Of course, national Slovak sokols, which were dedicated to promoting healthy bodies through physical training, had female members, but these organization typically stressed gymnastic-style exercises for girls.[99] Reflecting established attitudes limiting girls and young women to such traditional activities, the newly elected head of the First Catholic Slovak Union's sokol division recommended in 1931 that funds be specified so young female members could begin training for gymnastic competitions.[100] The First Catholic Slovak Ladies Union reflected this turn of mind when it decided to encourage its local lodges to create drill teams; other sports were not mentioned.[101] While national sokol and fraternal organization officers preferred gymnastics, calisthenics, and precision-drill activities, a few local affiliates organized team sports. In 1930, female basketball players from a Milwaukee sokol won a midwestern championship.[102] In 1934, after the First Catholic Slovak Union's junior membership had recorded a two-year decline, the president of a Canonsburg, Pennsylvania, lodge advised fellow fraternalists to organize sports programs for both boys and girls.[103]

The Slovak Evangelical Union was the only national fraternal organization to promote female team sports aggressively. Its programs both encouraged and reflected local initiatives. By October 1929, the fraternal society's president was calling for boys and girls to form athletic clubs. A week later, one Cleveland Lutheran congregation announced that, because the church's male basketball team had decided to join the Slovak Evangelical Union's district league, it would continue supporting sports by creating a girls' basketball team. Into the 1930s, both at the national and local levels, Lutherans sustained an interest in forwarding female athletics. In 1936, a Pittsburgh Lutheran lodge appointed a committee of three men and one woman to explore the possibility of establishing male and female basketball teams in the region. More than any other sport, though, bowling seemed to hold the greatest potential for attracting females. Toward the end of the 1930s, Lutherans in particular were capitalizing on its dual-gender appeal. By 1941, bowling was so popular among men and women that Lutherans arranged a National Open Bowling Tournament of the Slovak Evangelical Union and stressed that both sexes would be allowed to participate.[104] Overall, though, where there were successful efforts to organize Slovak female teams in the 1930s, they seemingly reflected parochial interests growing out of distinct local circumstances.

In general, conventional beliefs about women's proper sphere shaped organizations' efforts to attract young women and girls. Activists at both the local and national levels typically viewed socials instead of sports as ways to make Slovak organizations appealing to young women. They called for more dances and other dual-gender activities. Whether in English or Slovak, the sporadic women's pages focused on domestic, culinary, and etiquette-related topics.[105] Some women, though, apparently viewed the sections as social or political forums. The official organ of the National Slovak Society acknowledged as much when it initiated a women's section in 1931. *Národné noviny*'s editor explained that he was responding to a member's appeal that the paper include items especially interesting to women, such as articles on domestic arts as well as on "the women's movement and involvement in social and political life."[106] *Slovenský hlásnik* began its first women's page by acknowledging that women had been neglected and by appealing to its female members to write letters about anything. When one woman submitted a letter blatantly denouncing what she described as male attitudes and essentially calling on women to assert themselves, the paper published it.[107] This was the exception, though, not the rule, for the kinds of items that appeared in the women's sections. Overall, the English publications targeting girls and women revealed a typical mindset about women's roles.

Societies seemed most prone to rely on membership drives to draw females into the ethnic fold. At the same time, during the 1930s these campaigns came to depend heavily on the organizations' young female members. Recruitment efforts by young women had been so outstanding that in its 1938 membership drive the National Slovak Society decided to establish "special prizes" for them. Developing a formula similar to that for determining Slovak Day queens, the society gave points for each new recruit. The individual who accumulated the most points would become queen of the National Slovak Society and, with all expenses paid, travel to Pittsburgh to be crowned at the society's 1939 national day.[108] The contest, which relied on the same type of intangible rewards as Slovak Day competitions, encouraged young women to become ethnic activists. Indeed, the society's scheme both grew out of and supported the growing tradition of women going out into the community and working for Slovak causes. Slovak organizations reached out to young women, then, by affording them special recognition for participating in ethnically defined endeavors. Thus, while the economic chaos created by the Great Depression was seemingly threatening the existence of ethnic organizations, at the community level the 1930s saw an expansion of activities that helped shape social lives and nurtured ethnic activism.

TRYING TO PROMOTE group survival, ethnic activists naturally reached out to young people during the 1930s. Observers characteristically called them "our Americanized youths" or the "younger element." An examination of the literature generated by and about this "younger element" reveals that, by the mid-1930s, "Americanized" had generally become a neutral concept describing American-born youths. Of course, it distressed activists that for some youths becoming Americanized did indeed mean shedding their ethnic identity. Nevertheless, rather than a derisive label, the term became one that typically acknowledged reality with neither animosity nor favor. The young people who joined Slovak organizations or engaged in public discussions about "Slovak" issues were routinely referred to as "our Americanized" members. By all accounts, they fit the standard image of the second generation. They spoke English, embraced America's civic principles, and most likely preferred its mainstream culture. The campaigns by both local and nationally oriented activists to ethnicize youths were built on the premise that individuals could be Americanized while still embracing their ethnic heritage. No doubt expressing hope as much as acknowledging reality, a columnist for *Slovenský hlásnik* personified the activist spirit when he exclaimed that the "American Slovak Lutheran youth . . . is highly American but tingles with ideals of our Slovak ancestry."[109] Throughout the interwar era, the emphasis on the compatibility of preserving one's ethnic identity and being "American" never wavered.

The battle to perpetuate some sense of ethnic consciousness in Americanized youths was waged at two levels: the national and the local. Incorporating English into official publications represented an accommodation by national organizations to an ethnically conscious segment of the second generation. The ongoing drive to ethnicize the young people ultimately compelled a reassessment of the notion that language and ethnicity were inextricably linked. No longer asserting a correlation between ethnic identity and the "mother tongue," ethnic preservationists changed their focus to instilling pride in ancestral origin. Contributions to English-language pages subtly exposed the complex nature of preserving mother tongues in America. They revealed that, when it came to questions of language maintenance, there could be just as much disagreement within the first and second generations as between them. This was not simply an intergenerational debate dividing immigrants and their American-born children, separating "the old" who wanted to remember from "the young" who wanted to forget.

While national officials were weighing the pros and cons of including English in official organs, enthusiasts in communities were also trying to figure out ways to attract youths to ethnic institutions. From their standpoint, competitive activities, especially athletics, could spark this interest. When they created sports divisions, national organizations helped draw isolated teams into coordinated networks that furthered interaction among widespread Slovak enclaves and advanced ethnically based activities. Local activists, however, promoted "Slovak" sports in part by resorting to the same "other nationalities" battle cry they were using to publicize local Slovak Days. This ethnic emphasis reflected the everyday experiences of Slovaks living in heterogeneous communities. The "other nationalities" appeal again demonstrates how immigrants and their children were viewing their world and that perceived rivalries could help fuel ethnic activism. It also, incidentally, reveals that other ethnic groups were involved in the same undertakings as Slovaks. Furthermore, by resorting to an ethnically charged plea—show the "other nationalities" and "Americans"—articulate local people once again revealed that countering negative attitudes toward new immigrants and fostering pride in origins were not exercises limited to a nationally minded elite.

The evidence shows there were youthful contingents that did not run away from their ancestral heritage. Young Slovaks, like other new immigrant youths, were active in ethnic organizations and participated in leisure-time activities in local communities. They were at least sufficiently interested in ethnic affairs to read their ethnic newspapers and concerned enough to write letters. At the same time, they considered themselves Americanized. The durability of athletic teams in the 1930s, despite the potentially crippling effects of the Great Depression, bears testimony to the fact that ethnically based pastimes did attract younger Americanized persons. Young women working among cohabitants of their community to promote Slovak organizations offer additional evidence of ethnic devotion. Participating in ethnically defined activities was perhaps only "occasion provoked" and consequently limited primarily to leisure-time, familial, or other narrowly defined events. Nevertheless, the energetic segment of second-generation males and females who became involved presented fertile soil for cultivating a Slovak consciousness in particular, and ethnic activism in general.

Certainly, a significant segment of the second generation did not join in sports or other ethnically based activities. Enthusiasts, critics, and commentators seemingly of all ages and philosophical persuasions also recognized that some youths were uninterested in their ancestry and in preserving ethnic institutions. The term "estranged" was common in discussions about "youths and the future," which regularly appeared in the Slovak print media of the 1920s and 1930s. However, a columnist for one English-language page poignantly articulated the dreams of the ethnically committed when, admitting that there were "Americans of Slovak descent" who had lost their "Slovak feeling," he declared: "deep down in their hearts they still have that spark of interest in their own people" that will cause them "to feel the glow of pride upon hearing of any unusual accomplishment by another American of Slovak descent."[110] Recognizing that some second-generation youths were openly ambivalent, activists placed their hopes on pricking torpid ethnic sentiments.

While nervous activists were reworking and expanding programs to cater to the younger element, one sober-minded critic cautioned against a lopsided emphasis on recreational activities. Making team membership essentially a "benefit" was inadvisable, he warned, because once their "play[ing] days" had ended, people would quit. To survive over the long term, fraternal organizations should not forget their mutual-benefit roots and, hence, should stress traditional advantages, including providing death and disability benefits. This admonition reflected a reality: the flurry of activities promoting sports and refashioning newspapers to pander to the younger element was taking place during the Great Depression. It would take more than coordinating athletic leagues, promoting entertainment, and publishing in English to sustain ethnic institutions through these devastating times. Despite all the rhetoric, losing the "younger element" was not the only threat to institutional durability. Generational issues had complicated, far-reaching implications that extended beyond divisions grounded in age differences or place of birth. Faced with unprecedented economic dislocations, ethnic institutions needed to focus on keeping "the old" almost as much as winning over "the young." To do this, Slovaks, like other ethnic groups, had to engage in collective actions that would have an impact beyond the boundaries of their particular nationality and benefit society as a whole.

7   Beyond the Generations
Ethnic Activism and Class Interest in the 1930s

THE SKY OVER Braddock, Pennsylvania, "had never been so clear and blue," Thomas Bell remarks as he takes readers of his powerful novel to a mill town during the Great Depression. This meant that nationality days, baseball games, and community events were occurring under pleasant conditions. Ironically, though, the blue skies symbolized the tragedy consuming people's lives. That "the mills lay silent month after month" was the ugly side of this beauty.[1] Town residents were free of the smoke and dust that had made everyday life uncomfortable, but this freedom had come only because they were victims of a national economic calamity. The Depression of the 1930s interrupted people's lives and threatened their futures.

Unemployment robbed people who had joined ethnic mutual benefit associations of the financial safeguards fraternal membership had provided. Paradoxically, as they carried out massive membership campaigns and creatively expanded their recruitment strategies, ethnic organizations were actually being forced to expel members. Most expulsions had nothing to do with intergenerational conflicts; they had everything to do with the inability to pay regular dues. Moreover, the departure of people who were ejected or who quit voluntarily did not necessarily reflect an estrangement from their ancestral heritage or ethnic institutions. It often had little or nothing to do with ethnic sentiments; it had everything to do with personal circumstances. Expelled for nonpayment of dues, jobless and elderly Slovaks were not willing to sit by idly; they appealed for clemency. Their entreaties revealed how present adversity was combining with fears about the future to shape sociopolitical attitudes among the new immigrant generations.

As the Depression worsened, leaders of national Slovak mutual aid societies realized that protecting Slovaks from economic disaster required more than providing death benefits or short-term relief. A growing commitment to insulating people against the vicissitudes of American capitalism and the elderly from destitution in their post-productive years prompted Slovak organizations to back "social insurance" legislation to provide unemployment compensation and old-age pensions. By the mid-1930s, national Slovak societies were promoting working-class interests to help preserve Slovak institutions and simultaneously using ethnicity to protect the long-term welfare of the country's laborers and elderly. In essence, they engaged in an activism that was galvanized along nationality lines but had objectives that reached beyond ethnic boundaries.

When it came to advancing the welfare of American workers, the rhetoric of nationally oriented activists clearly meshed with the real needs of ordinary Slovak immigrants and their children. Consequently, the same networks of lodges, parishes, and community groups that were collaborating on local Slovak Days and regional athletics also provided a basis for mobilizing people behind legislation viewed as favorable to workers. Their activities added a dimension to the ethnic working-class activism of the 1930s that goes beyond the workplace or union activities.

FOR ALL THE EMPHASIS on a distinct, ancient culture, class consciousness also filtered into the rhetoric championing a Slovak identity in America. Since the Great War, immigrant spokespersons had been almost perennially involved in countering negative attitudes toward new immigrants. This counteraction entailed a two-pronged effort to alter Americans' perceptions of Slavic groups while concurrently thwarting the adverse impact that unsavory popular opinions could have on the Slovak "younger element." Reshaping societal attitudes and swaying the second generation often rested on the same strategy and rhetoric. In addition to denouncing bigotry and theories about racial superiority, activists throughout the 1920s and 1930s hammered on the twin themes of the compatibility of the Slovak character with "American" principles and the staunch Americanism of Slovaks. While defenders claimed that analogous pasts rooted in struggles against a dominant power had bred shared principles, they could not assert that Slovaks—either through individual contributions or collective efforts—had participated in America's historical moments or contributed to the evolution of American democracy. Even the most single-minded rummaging though U.S. history could not unearth one august personage of putative Slovak ancestry. There was no Pulaski, Kosciuszko, or Columbus for Slovaks to vaunt for collective gratification. American history provided precious little ground to cultivate Slovak filiopietism.

Determined champions, however, were not willing meekly to accept suppositions that Slovaks and other new immigrants had not contributed to the American nation. Instead, they developed a class-based argument to demonstrate that these groups had had a beneficial effect on the country's past. Defenders essentially held that, while their ancestors might not have fought in the American Revolution or helped the country achieve its manifest destiny, Slovaks, together with other new immigrants, had been vital to the industrialization of the United States. Addressing the issue, one writer put it in a nutshell when he asserted that "Slovak immigrants . . . have done their goodly share of building America to her present position among the nations of the world."[2] Generalities would not suffice; he, like others, chose to elaborate. Slovaks, he declared, had advanced the country's greatness "by building railroads, working in the mines, steel mills, in the cultivation of land, and in every work or industry that America undertook to build." They had therefore helped to provide the labor supply that industries had needed to expand quickly at the turn of the century and to continue flourishing during succeeding decades. The persistent, underlying premise was that Slovak immigrants were working-class people, and their effect on United States history had been as a working-class people.

Placing emphasis on America's rise to a leading industrial nation gave new immigrants a legitimate claim to having played an indispensable role in the country's history and progress. Commentators employed this reasoning as a challenge to the "undesirable" label and the enduring stigma it carried. They in essence tried to offset disparagement by exalting a positive class-based impact. Thus, instead of shunning their working-class status, articulate activists built arguments encouraging Slovaks to embrace it. While there was no dearth of claims alleging that Slovaks, especially the second generation, had advanced on the socioeconomic scale, an acute awareness of the Slovak working-class status was embedded in the rhetoric proclaiming that Slovak contributions had come not through individual accomplishments but through the collective labor of ordinary laborers. In the 1920s, therefore, a complex Slovak identity was being forged. On one hand, promoters strove to present Slovak culture as ancient and refined and characterized by both a cultivated intellectual heritage and folk traditions. On the other, they endeavored to emphasize class by underscoring the fact that most Slovak immigrants had been miners and industrial laborers. Just as activists advocated pride in ancestry, they promoted pride in being working class.

Identifying Slovaks as working class persisted into the 1930s. Hollywood reinforced this idea among Slovaks themselves when Warner

Brothers produced *Black Fury,* which depicted life and labor struggles in a coal-mining town. The movie did not present a flattering picture of first- or second-generation Slovaks. It portrayed Joe Radek, a Slovak miner, as a lummox manipulated by an agent of a strike-breaking security firm.[3] Besides being a hardworking, jocund simpleton, Radek was fond of drinking, a habit that contributed to his unwittingly creating strife within the local union. In the end, he heroically expiates his misdeed by single-handedly forcing the company to capitulate to the workers' demands.

Despite the negative stereotypes embodied in the Radek character, the Slovak media welcomed the film. Months before its scheduled release, some Slovaks knew about the movie. Aiming at the second generation, an English-language report in *Jednota* alerted people about the forthcoming production.[4] Using prose that meshed pride in ancestry with class consciousness, the author urged all Slovaks to see it. Previewing the film, the commentator was elated that Warner Brothers had chosen to make the lead character a Slovak miner. He was thrilled that the famous Paul Muni would play the role of Joe Radek; he rhapsodized over the fact that Slovak songs would be sung and there would be dancing in a "Slovak hall." He gloried in the thought that audiences would hear an actor of Muni's stature speaking and singing in Slovak. Instead of recoiling at the working-class image the movie reinforced, he rejoiced in it. Through Radek's character, people would see "the average Slovak arrival to America who plodded on in [his] daily routine with no apparent break in the unvarying monotony of his existence." The film would let Slovaks "boast of the fact that the early struggles of their life in America will be made known to the rest of the world."

This report augured the enthusiastic response *Black Fury* received when it premiered in April 1935. Looking to the abstract benefits, *Jednota* praised it as the first film about Slovak life and again lauded the use of Slovak songs and dances. While *Jednota*'s reporter only alluded to the class-based themes of the movie, the *Slovenský hlásnik* commentator combined class and ethnic pride. He recommended the film not merely because people would be delighted with the Slovak songs, but also because the movie graphically described the suffering that miners endured at the hands of cruel companies. Urging Slovaks to see *Black Fury, Národné noviny* focused on the mistreatment of miners and asserted that the movie showed why Slovaks had a duty to advance workers' rights.[5] Embroiled in the current push for federal legislation to protect workers, society spokespersons considered the movie's portrayal of labor struggles and the vicious treatment of miners as an opportunity to draw Slovak workers to the cause.

Although *Black Fury* reinforced popular, unflattering stereotypes, articulate Slovaks with their own agendas apparently chose to ignore them. From their perspective, the movie bestowed a collective honor, for, in a heterogeneous society, it highlighted the Slovak experience and culture. If they happened to read the *New York Times* review, those people so gratified about the film's implicit tribute to Slovaks could not have been pleased when the reviewer described Muni's character as a "Hunky miner."[6] How many Slovaks in the United States actually saw *Black Fury* and how they felt about it—especially about the naive, oafish Radek—are questions history cannot answer. However, some immigrants and their children did see the movie. As part of the program, for example, the organizers of western Pennsylvania's 1935 Slovak Day arranged to show *Black Fury*.[7] Regardless of how people responded to it, the film did reinforce the close link between ethnicity and class, between being Slovak and being working class. For Slovaks, even with its flaws, the movie blended pride in ancestry and pride in class.

While the literature seeking to endow Slovaks with an estimable place in United States history ennobled the Slovak working class, everyday experiences and the struggles so poignantly described in *Black Fury* underscored the reality of what it meant to be a laborer in America. Coping with the crises of working-class life, however, was something that went beyond the trials of ordinary people; it affected Slovak institutions as well. In the postwar decades, Slovak mutual aid societies could not escape the fact that the overwhelming majority of first- and second-generation Slovaks were manual laborers. As a result, despite their concern with preserving a Slovak consciousness, fraternal societies were working-class organizations. Moreover, they had been founded to help immigrants, especially workers, deal with the uncertainties of life in industrial America. As a consequence, although activists in the years following the Armistice were seemingly consumed with issues concerning the newly created Czechoslovakia and with forging a Slovak national identity, they did not completely ignore the interests of working-class Slovaks in the United States. The major Slovak secular, Catholic, and Lutheran organizations, for example, supported the nationwide steel strike of 1919. The First Catholic Slovak Union and the Slovak Evangelical Union did warn Slovaks not to become involved in violent activities; nevertheless, spokespersons left little doubt that they wanted "justice for the workers."[8]

This sanctioning of strikes continued during the 1920s as Slovaks participated in work stoppages in the United States.[9] A symbiotic relationship developed between national officers and members, especially as local people relied on the fraternal network to support workers' actions. The 1928–1929 miners' strike in West Virginia and western Pennsylvania, which involved a large number of Slovaks, graphically illustrated how extensively fraternal organizations and their institutional resources nourished ethnic working-class activism. As the strike dragged on for months, the newspapers of the First Catholic Slovak Union, the National Slovak Society, and the Slovak Evangelical Union routinely printed favorable reports and commentary supporting it. They published letters from Slovak miners who pleaded the strikers' case. The First Catholic Slovak Union's *Jednota* regularly carried appeals for money to help the strikers and published the names of Slovaks who donated "toward alleviating the misery of thousands of suffering souls."[10] The Slovak Evangelical Union and National Slovak Society did the same. *Národné noviny* publicized the aggressive campaign by the Slovak League of America to help the strikers.[11] The First Catholic Slovak Union created a "Welfare Committee" and charged it with organizing district committees to collect "money and other necessities" for "our striking brothers."[12] *Jednota* published pictures of First Catholic Slovak Union officers preparing donated clothes to be sent to strikers and their families.[13] This strategy no doubt encouraged sympathy as well as additional charitable donations. In a move that underlined the more far-reaching negative impact unemployment could have on ordinary Slovaks and ethnic institutions, some of the money collected by the committee went toward paying strikers' fraternal dues. This protected already distressed members from the additional misfortune of being expelled and, hence, losing insurance benefits; it also, not coincidentally, shielded the mutual benefit society against membership losses.

Fraternal organizations' support for strikes in the 1920s was not grounded in ideology. It signified neither a rebuff of capitalism nor an embracing of left-wing radicalism; it reflected reality. The very nature of ethnic fraternal societies—their working-class composition—unavoidably required fraternalists to maintain a keen interest in and, perhaps, a watchful eye over working-class issues and activities. As one priest astutely editorialized in *Jednota*, the fact was that the First Catholic Slovak Union's membership was "overwhelmingly working class."[14] This point was amplified by another writer when he asserted that the issues being raised in the miners' strike were "working-class questions that hang over all Slovaks."[15] A spokesperson for the National Slovak Society perhaps explained it best when he asserted that, because workers made up 98 percent of the membership, the organization had a "moral obligation" to carry news about the "working world" and reports that would benefit laborers. The society had to provide information "so that the Slovak worker will not always be the lowest."[16] Whether they wanted to or not, Slovak fraternal organizations could not ignore matters that touched the lives of so many members. The language of class consciousness thus permeated both the rhetoric extolling Slovak contributions to American history and the literature depicting the real-life existence of ordinary people.

While national organizations took steps to help strikers, these endeavors depended on the web of local lodges and on members willing to cooperate to assist fellow Slovak workers. Coordinated activities therefore helped fortify existing regional networks and strengthen local activism on behalf of Slovak miners, in particular, and by extension mineworkers in general. Efforts executed by both national and local activists, though, were purposely designed to help fellow "Slovaks," not other nationalities on the picket lines. Nevertheless, in the 1920s, the interactive efforts by national organizations and ordinary members to support strikes helped reinforce both an image and a reality: Slovaks were overwhelmingly working class. Their interests were inextricably linked to those of America's other laborers.

When it came to labor activities, working-class issues in the 1920s superseded generational differences. Grumbles decrying or even alleging divisions between the "old" and the "young," the foreign versus the American born did not creep into the promotional literature about class-based contributions or published articles about labor-related activities. Workers' interests spanned the age spectrum as both "old-timers" and the second generation found themselves on picket lines or collecting donations for Slovak strikers. However, as the foreign-born population grew older, a vexing age-based issue was surfacing. By the late 1920s, while local activists were promoting athletic teams and sponsoring queen contests to attract the "younger element" at one end of the demographic scale, the dilemma of an aging population was growing at the other end. With few pension systems for industrial laborers, Slovaks could not look forward to retirement. Many would be compelled to work until they were no longer physically able, and then, left with no regular income, they faced the possibility of becoming dependent on family benevolence. They could not look to ethnic mutual aid societies.

These organizations were designed to help workers weather short-term unemployment and to help families deal with the loss of a breadwinner. They disbursed monetary payments to persons temporarily out of work due to illness; they provided lump sums to workers injured or disabled in work-related accidents; and they paid death benefits to surviving beneficiaries. But there were no provisions in the fraternal system to assist elderly people who were too old to continue working.

By the late 1920s, with their working-class composition and a mission rooted in providing insurance, fraternal organizations could no longer ignore the other generational problem, namely the increasing number of elderly members. The large societies began discussing the possibility of building old-age homes. This topic was mentioned at the 1926 convention of the First Catholic Slovak Union. In 1927, its female counterpart, the First Catholic Slovak Ladies Union, announced it was considering opening a home for the aged. Calling this a "beautiful idea," *Jednota* raised the prospect of a "common" home. It was unrealistic, the paper editorialized, for every Slovak organization to have a separate old-age facility. The National Slovak Society was also reportedly weighing plans for a home.[17] As the decade wore on, it was clear the fraternal institutions were growing not only increasingly cognizant of but sympathetic to the plight of the elderly. After all, many of these older people had been loyal members for decades. Leaving sentiment aside, an impoverished older population posed a dual threat: it seriously reduced the likelihood that elderly people could remain members in good standing, and it meant that their families would not receive any death benefits when they passed away. Beyond these practical considerations, abandoning the elderly to their own resources ran counter to the humanitarian spirit of ethnic fraternalism.

No coordinated effort to establish an old-age home materialized in the late 1920s, and none was built. Just as it shattered the lives of so many, the stock-market collapse in October 1929 dashed any immediate dreams of founding a humane refuge for the Slovak elderly. The tribulations brought about by the Great Depression, however, accentuated common interests that overlapped generational differences. Unemployment forced young and old alike into the same dire financial predicament. Moreover, coping with the present intensified a growing awareness of the economic insecurity that could torment old age. For Slovak fraternalists of all ages, the breakdown of the American economy in the 1930s struck a particularly cruel blow. Fraternal organizations had successfully cultivated enough ethnic identity for their memberships to grow in the 1920s. The economic disaster of the 1930s compelled mutual benefit societies to face the stark reality that they were never meant to deal with problems of the magnitude created by the Great Depression, when one-fourth or more of the workforce was unemployed.[18] As the Depression deepened, ethnic organizations, committed to increasing their memberships, actually found themselves expelling people instead.

Although fraternal societies had always executed the bylaws stipulating expulsion for nonpayment of dues, the situation they faced in the 1930s had no comparable antecedent. The strikes and recessions of the 1920s had affected only segments of the Slovak working-class population. Thus, throughout the decade, Slovak fraternal organizations had been able to help their members weather intermittent crises. Local lodges and, as a last resort, the national treasury typically were able to extend credit that permitted striking members to pay fraternal fees. In past times, therefore, people involved in strikes or who faced temporary joblessness did not usually see their good standing or insurance benefits sacrificed. The calamity of the 1930s was a different matter. Five years after the stock market crashed, steady membership declines continued; every major Slovak mutual aid society ended 1934 with fewer adult and youth members than in 1933.[19] Official newspapers published the names as well as statistics on the number of persons ejected, so readers glancing through fraternal publications knew what was happening.[20]

People were being forced out of organizations because they could not pay their dues. Unemployment had left workers without the wherewithal to purchase basic necessities; they certainly lacked the resources to meet incidental expenses such as fraternal fees. In desperation, unemployed and elderly workers turned to their local and national officers. As a consequence, by 1932 lodges and members were flooding national headquarters with an unprecedented deluge of appeals for leniency or assistance. Letters came from small and midsize towns as well as from major cities. Since Slovaks were concentrated in the Mid-Atlantic and midwestern states, most letters were from those regions, but appeals flowed from areas such as Maine, where only a small number of Slovaks resided. Often seeking some bending of the rules so they would not be expelled, petitions from ordinary members also poignantly related experiences influencing grassroots attitudes.

Penned appeals to fraternal organizations revealed the distress that Slovaks were coping with. Some sought out-and-out charity, often paltry amounts from the organizations' poor funds. A farmer in Ino, Wisconsin, who had lost "his barn, cow, hay, and tools" in a fire and could not find any work asked "for any amount like 50 cents or $1.00."[21] An unemployed father of six children most likely had a larger sum in mind when he turned to national officers for help in 1933. The family had no money to pay for operations that one son needed. Now, since they did not have $3 for each visit, the doctor refused even to examine the boy.[22] One father with tuberculosis probably reflected the thinking of others when he reasoned that it would be advantageous for his family to be supported now, before his death.[23]

While desperation induced personal entreaties for charitable assistance, a compassionate spirit spurred some local officials to act on behalf of others. Branch officers seemed particularly willing to seek benevolence for wives of deceased members. The widow and six children of a lodge organizer "have nothing," lamented the officers who were soliciting financial aid for her.[24] For the sake of five widows, a Minersville, Pennsylvania, lodge officer applied to the First Catholic Slovak Union's poor fund; two of the women had been married to lodge founders and another to a long-time member.[25] Seeing their everyday struggle to survive, lodges clearly felt a sense of obligation to the families of departed brothers, especially those who had helped found branches decades earlier.

Although many petitions requested outright charity, the largest number by far came from expelled members or those facing ejection for nonpayment of dues. Some sought rebates for their own or their children's dues; others demanded recompense when fraternal societies ejected them and thus voided their insurance polices.[26] Individuals did write directly to national officials, but most organizations expected members to filter fraternal-related business through local officers. Thus, as the Depression worsened, lodge personnel found themselves spending more and more time composing appeals and pleading cases.

Employing strikingly similar language and logic, petitioners from Slovak communities far and wide made their arguments. Although they came from places as distant and distinct as Milwaukee and Peckville, Pennsylvania, correspondents, almost without exception, dwelled on local conditions and especially the length of time people in their own area had been out of work. Writers could not resist lecturing national officers about the ripple effects of widespread, continual unemployment. Many laid emphasis on the fact that the simultaneous decrease in membership and increase in unemployment put lodges in a precarious situation. Begging forbearance for his entire lodge, which was in arrears, a Mammoth, Pennsylvania, man summed up the universal situation. Without work for years, people here "have nothing," he moaned. By distributing "clothes, flour, and coffee," county relief helped families "live from day to day." Otherwise, "people would die of hunger," he declared.[27] Charity in kind, though, obviously did not give people self-purchasing power, and it certainly did not provide the means to pay fraternal dues. Entire lodges faced the possibility of having to dissolve. Some fraternal branches saw their accounts vanish when local banks failed. Again and again, they lamented that dwindling local treasuries meant they could no longer assume the dues of hard-pressed members. Moreover, the resources to provide sick benefits had been critically drained so that people fortunate enough to have jobs could not be accommodated if they became ill. The adverse effects radiated even farther when unemployed parents could no longer pay their children's membership fees. Youth branches, especially in one-industry towns, were being decimated.[28]

Desperation echoed through the letters as local officers sought both assistance and advice from national headquarters. What should they do about delinquent members? The appeals showed a painful reluctance to discharge persons who did not want to sever ties with a Slovak organization. Representatives of one lodge advised national officers that "we need to take into consideration those members who, through no fault of their own but because of the current depression, have lost everything they had." Please discuss this issue at the national officers' upcoming meeting, they begged. Remember, they pleaded, these people "want to remain members."[29] The same sad refrains—"want to remain members" and "through no fault of their own"—were sounded over and over.[30] The appeals were so passionate in part because the failing was not the delinquents', and lodge officers knew it. Until they were forced into joblessness and left without resources, these people had faithfully fulfilled their fraternal obligations. Even many still fortunate enough to have jobs were subsisting on starvation wages. Overall, the petitioners were attempting to generate an understanding that would let involuntary defaulters remain members and maintain their insurance benefits.

Women's organizations heard the same pleas. People called on officers to develop plans to prevent their sisters from losing membership. Some had been members for twenty years—since their youths, one younger woman noted. Today "when they are old and need the society the most ... they are being expelled because, due to the depression, they cannot pay dues." Reaching to put it in heartbreaking terms, this local member described a touching scene of a woman tearfully offering to give her "last dollar" toward her fraternal assessment and asking her lodge sisters to be patient until she could obtain the remainder. Do something for sisters in need, she entreated, "because we see in them today what awaits us tomorrow."[31]

Distress in search of understanding characterized letters seeking some easing of membership rules for the jobless. The sundry petitions on behalf of the aged, however, pleaded for outright compassion. The expulsion of the elderly seemed particularly cruel because, as one lodge secretary wrote, "Our old members . . . don't even have a place to earn .05 for a loaf of bread," they cannot pay their dues.[32] Letters like this one, written in English, demonstrated the sympathy younger people felt for the "old-timers." But whether in English or Slovak, petition after petition voiced the plight of the aged and expressed dismay at their treatment after having been faithful fraternalists for decades. "When they were young, they helped their brothers but now they cannot even pay their own dues," Detroiters lamented.[33] Using astonishingly similar language, officers from tiny Natrona, Pennsylvania, made precisely the same points. "When they were young, they [our old members] helped their brothers. . . . Are we to leave them to themselves or help them as they helped others?" they asked. The fact that "they want to be members" heightened the pain.[34] Petitioners also used the ethnic press to emphasize the magnitude of the problem. In some lodges, one writer pointed out, nearly the entire membership consisted of elderly people, and "many of them do not work because of their age."[35]

Expelling lodge founders was even more agonizing. A Barnsboro, Pennsylvania, man had helped organize two lodges—the first in 1893, and the second in 1905, when he went to another town. During his life, he had moved several times, but he had never, even temporarily, dropped his fraternal membership. "So, if possible," lodge officers beseeched, "please exonerate" this seventy-seven-year-old man from his dues. Signed by two officers, but written in English, this particular appeal was also most likely being made by at least one person who belonged to the oft-referred-to younger element.[36] Again, both English and Slovak letters conveyed a sense of respect by younger people, who chose to affiliate with fraternals, for the old-timers who had long served as the lodges' mainstay. In late December 1932, three branch officers crafted a lengthy appeal that blended compassion with practical considerations. They implored: "if you have a tiny bit of mercy in your heart for our offspring and the founders of our lodge . . . do not ever allow our old members to be expelled . . . but show them mercy so that they can feel that for the long time that they paid [fraternal dues] . . . there will now be aid and [thus] make this burden lighter for them."[37] Mindful of the current efforts to attract younger Slovaks, other petitioners tried to cajole fraternal chiefs by reminding them that the children of older members would assess how the organization treated their parents. When they see how well the society was dealing with the elderly, one letter signed by two officers cleverly noted, they would realize they could rely on it to show similar benevolence in their old age.[38]

Although petitions on behalf of the aged rang a tragic note, the most heartrending letters came from the elderly immigrants themselves. Pleading their case, they graphically expressed their own anguish while simultaneously articulating the general bewilderment induced by the elderlys' particular state of affairs. Employing emotional language, writers regularly described themselves as "destitute" and repeatedly referred to their "old age." In typical style, "I am destitute, merely existing," wrote a seventy-two-year-old man who had been a fraternalist for thirty-eight years.[39] People fused their old age with long-standing devotion. "I am old, but I am a good Jednotar," one forty-two-year loyalist asserted.[40] Another implored, "I came to America in 1878 . . . and was a member of the first lodge in Hazleton . . . and helped organize another, . . . now [at seventy-six] I am old and ask for help."[41] Combining age with service, one man who had been a delegate to "several conventions" expressed a common theme of frustration running through the letters. For more than forty years he had paid his fraternal dues, and now, when he had lost everything, there were no benefits for him.[42] Long-time members raised the point that their assessed contributions over the years totaled a large sum of money. Now facing poverty, they reasoned that, because they had been laying out money for benefits but had never used them, they merited a bending of the rules.[43] Some petitioners resorted to scare tactics to persuade national officers to respond favorably to their request. Acting on his own behalf, one man minced no words when he queried: "what kind of example is this to the youth when they see large numbers of old members being expelled?" They will, he concluded, wonder why they should remain faithful to the organization.[44]

Letters citing how loyalty was reaping no benefits typically carried a tone of bewilderment, not anger. Rather than lashing out at the fraternal organizations, the jobless and elderly, as well as those speaking on their behalf, for the most part were constructing arguments to evoke mercy. They did not blame the organizations for enforcing the bylaws.

Instead, they acknowledged the officers' right to abide by the rules, but they sought forbearance and, in many cases, a revision of them.

While the elderly and delinquent members mentally calculated what they had personally spent for their policies, those still in good standing focused on what lost revenues meant to them. Self-interest prompted some members to express concern that disbursing money to assist the elderly or to cover unpaid dues jeopardized lodge treasuries. There might not be sufficient funds for fraternalists who remained in good standing should they become sick.[45] At the same time, coming face to face with the current situation of the elderly spawned fears for their own future security. People came to realize that mutual benefit organizations needed to establish procedures so that helpless members, both the elderly and the involuntarily unemployed, would not lose their protection and be forced from the fold. Officers from the small town of Nemacolin, Pennsylvania, expressed the sentiments of many when, concluding an elaborate petition seeking leniency for the destitute, they vowed enduring loyalty to their society "so that we will always be there to assist one another."[46] An undercurrent flowing steadily through correspondence was the fear that the plight of the elderly and jobless signaled what the future could hold for others.

The appeals by and on behalf of the unemployed and "old-timers" revealed anxieties haunting Slovak working-class people and institutions in the 1930s. A two-pronged attack was being made on their security and on that of their families. Not only had the Depression caused the loss of jobs, but the type of security that some had long enjoyed through fraternal membership was being threatened. Within the broader context of the Depression, loss of fraternal benefits was one more crisis in the onslaught of misfortunes, but it was one that directly touched people, young and old alike, who belonged to fraternal societies. Whether individuals had joined these organizations out of ethnic sentiment or purely for the insurance benefits, there was a sense of injustice that something they had so long invested in was so quickly gone. Their predicaments were not of their making. The Depression, with its widespread unemployment, was the villain.

Letters from ordinary members to national fraternal officers revealed circumstances shaping the views of working-class immigrants and their children. The tragedy of lost savings, home evictions, and bankrupt businesses visited the small towns and cities where new immigrants lived. Their communities saw the same bread lines, queues of the unemployed, workers loitering at factory gates, and peddlers on the streets that Americans everywhere saw. The malnutrition, disease, and psychological impact on individuals were similarly present. But for ethnic groups with long-established self-help institutions, there was yet another dimension to this adversity. There were the personal experiences of lodge officers forced to submit expulsion forms or write impassioned letters on behalf of desperate members; the experience of individuals compelled to watch fellow fraternalists or friends lose protection they had counted on; and the experience of seeing elderly people being forced out of local lodges they had long shown devotion to and perhaps had even helped found. All this grief stemmed from involuntary unemployment or the inevitability of old age, and all too often a combination of both. Whether old or jobless, misfortunates were victims of societal conditions beyond their control.[47] No one seemingly could escape the potentially devastating effects of periodic economic downturns, temporary layoffs, reduced working hours, or loss of the ability to work because of sickness or injury. Of course, the insecurity of old age loomed over everyone. Industrial America, it seemed, had failed them, and fears grounded in present circumstances were magnifying anxieties about the future.

Despite the energy lodges spent on behalf of members, the elderly, and impoverished families of deceased fraternalists, by and large Slovaks did not promote charitable activities in their own communities. Letters to mutual aid societies implicitly explained why they did not. In many places, the area's entire workforce was adversely affected by the Depression; some workers had been laid off while others were barely getting by on severely reduced wages. Families that could not make their own ends meet certainly had nothing to give away to charity. Even Slovak Days, which had evolved into money-making events, typically did not funnel receipts to the Slovak poor. Publicists for some Slovak Days took pains to stress that, due to the hard times, there would be no admission charges; the majority, though, either imposed modest entrance fees or sold refreshments and souvenirs. Revenues from the Slovak Days controlled by Catholics continued to go to religious institutions. Sponsors of Chicago's Slovak Catholic Day, who, like the organizers of the city's "national" day, had an established tradition of donating proceeds to a philanthropic association dedicated to assisting needy Slovaks upheld that practice in the 1930s. Chicago's Slovaks, however, were atypical.[48] Cleveland Slovaks did respond to the Depression by creating a charitable organization to help their own. This legally incorporated body aimed to assist all needy Slovaks, irrespective of religious affiliation, in the metropolitan area.[49] The Slovak League of America sponsored the only concerted effort to solicit contributions of money and goods for the Slovak indigent. Its efforts, together with grants from existing fraternal "poor funds," provided some assistance but could not mitigate the financial crises gripping individuals and their families. In the summer of 1933, as it published the names of nearly 2,600 recipients of small allotments from its Indigent Fund, the National Slovak Society and other organizations were bracing themselves to face the fifth winter of the Great Depression.[50]

Slovaks, like other Americans, clung to the hope that newly elected President Franklin D. Roosevelt would lead the country out of the calamity. During 1933, the nation did witness energetic, even innovative, attempts to combat the Great Depression, but as the New Deal moved into its second year, no end to hard times was in sight. Instead, for some workers the situation arguably took a turn for the worse. In January 1934, Roosevelt decided that at the end of March, the Civil Works Administration (CWA), which had employed more than 4 million people during the previous winter, would be terminated. Instead of relief in kind, this short-lived jobs program had paid wages and thus allowed workers to purchase goods and meet financial obligations. After their temporary elevation out of the ranks of the unemployed, laborers who had gone onto the government payroll found themselves again reduced to the jobless category. The Federal Emergency Relief Administration (FERA) did complete already started CWA projects and continued to disburse means-tested assistance. Devised as part of the New Deal's immediate relief effort, though, neither the CWA nor the FERA was designed to provide lasting protection against economic misfortune. Lacking a nationwide system of unemployment compensation, even those with CWA or FERA jobs had never really left the ranks of the insecure. Roosevelt would not openly address the issues of national unemployment compensation or pensions for the elderly until early summer; meanwhile, other forces in the country were confronting these matters.[51]

By the winter of 1934, some members of Congress were turning their attention to questions of long-term security for American workers and the elderly. In January 1934, congressional committees were considering proposed legislation that fell under the heading of "social insurance." Senators Robert Wagner and David J. Lewis co-sponsored a bill to establish unemployment compensation. While the Wagner–Lewis legislation was undergoing scrutiny, the Dill–Connery old-age-pension bill, which had been introduced two years earlier and been passed by the House, finally received a favorable report from the Senate Pensions

Committee. Together, these independent bills embodied the core of what constituted social insurance: unemployment compensation and old-age pensions. As committees studied proposals that coped separately with unemployment insurance and pensions, the House Committee on Labor was given a comprehensive bill encompassing both. Representative Ernest Lundeen of Minnesota had proposed a system of old-age pensions and broadly defined unemployment compensation.[52] At the same time that these bills were winding their way through committees, the Communist Party and Dr. Francis Townsend were rousing popular sentiment in favor of their own social-insurance measures. Townsend in particular was mobilizing elderly Americans behind a plan touted as the panacea for their peculiar woes and one that, he argued, would simultaneously propel the country toward recovery. As winter turned into spring, Townsend's scheme was evolving into a crusade and attracting an increasingly aggressive following among the elderly.[53]

While visionaries hawked their elixirs and the nation continued grappling with the ravages of the Depression, ethnic organizations still had to struggle with their own problems.[54] In April 1934, the National Slovak Society was forced to call a special convention to act on alleged financial misconduct by officers. In addition to dealing with the infractions, the meeting adopted measures to keep people from being expelled from the society. It established a system that let members draw on their insurance policies to pay regular dues.[55] The meeting's action addressed but did not solve the difficulties its members were facing. Moreover, as unemployment spread in the early 1930s, fraternal societies continually confronted a basic truth: ethnic loyalty was irrelevant if individuals could not pay their dues and remain members. This reality underscored the need to support legislative measures both to bring about an economic recovery and to mitigate the impact of future economic catastrophes or cyclical unemployment. Thus, despite its major order of business, the convention could not avoid addressing the more sweeping issues devastating its members' lives.

Obviously aware that Congress was weighing social-insurance bills, the convention passed a resolution declaring that the National Slovak Society, with a membership of more than 45,000 people, "wholeheartedly supports and endorses all pending legislation the object of which is unemployment insurance and old age pensions." The participants did not single out any particular bill but merely said that they were acting on the principle that the nation has a "sacred obligation toward its unemployed and its aged." By sending their resolution to state legislatures in session, as well as to Congress, they were joining "the humane and sacred movement" to help relieve the "dire distress" of the elderly and the unemployed.[56] The resolution called on all the society's members "to support EVERY ACTION" in their communities to promote universal social insurance. Clarifying what they were aiming for, an editorial announcing the convention's decisions described social insurance as including compensation during unemployment or periods of reduced working time as well as old-age pensions.

Both the resolution and the editorial placed the convention's actions within the context of the National Slovak Society's interests. The resolution was introduced with a clause deploring the vast unemployment wrought by the Depression and proclaiming that, because they had been out of work, members could not afford to pay fraternal dues. The editorial calling on members to rally behind social reforms was not limited to expounding organizational concerns. Instead, clothed in class rhetoric, it dwelled on the wide-ranging ramifications of social insurance. Emphasizing both class and ethnic concerns, *Národné noviny* declared that enacting social-insurance legislation was "in the interest of our Slovak working people." Trying no doubt to justify this intense promotion of social insurance, the editorial accentuated the National Slovak Society's socioeconomic makeup. Proclaiming the society a "100 percent working-class organization," it called members to action. Lodges were asked to discuss the special convention's resolution at their local meetings and to disseminate both Slovak- and English-language versions of it. Reiterating ethnic and class interests, the editorialist urged members actively to strive "for a better future for themselves, their organization, and their people." The resolution and editorial brought the society squarely down on the side of "social insurance" in general. At the same time, although it did not mention the Lundeen bill, the resolution, together with the commentary, clearly implied support for that particular legislation.[57]

Over the next months, Slovak organizations continued the gloomy task of wading through appeals from dispirited members. On June 6, the National Slovak Society's Committee to Review Requests, Petitions, and Grievances published its recommendations on sixty more appeals. *Národné noviny* also carried a particularly strident editorial reminding members again about the special convention's resolution "to support EVERY ACTION" and calling them to arms in the fight for social insurance. Having emphasized the organization's working-class makeup and interests, national spokespersons were now asking local members to attend all gatherings concerning social insurance that were held in their communities. They believed the topic should not be limited to lodge meetings.[58] Two days later, Roosevelt, who had long favored some type of protective system for the unemployed and elderly and had been mulling over his course of action, finally sent Congress a message calling for "furthering . . . security . . . through social insurance." Informing representatives and senators readying for summer adjournment that he was searching for a solid program "to provide at once security against the great disturbing factors of life—especially those which relate to unemployment and old age," he promised to have a plan ready for the Seventy-fourth Congress, which would begin its first session in January 1935. Finally, on June 29, he issued Executive Order No. 6757 creating the Committee on Economic Security. Chaired by Secretary of Labor Frances Perkins, the committee had five months to "study problems relating to the economic security of individuals." Its recommendations were due by December 1, 1934.[59]

The stepped-up activities on behalf of social insurance by Slovak activists and the Roosevelt administration in the spring of 1934 were taking place in parallel, not in tandem. Nevertheless, viewed side by side, they present a split portrait of what was happening simultaneously at the ethnic-community and federal levels as forces were gearing up behind some type of national plan to help shield individuals against the adverse effects of unemployment and the inevitability of old age. Giving voice to current anguish while subtly rousing fears about the future, the supplicatory letters Slovaks dispatched to fraternal officers vividly enhance this portrait. The misery of the present was nurturing fears about the yet-to-come. Slovaks, like many Americans, felt themselves blameless, and there was a growing sentiment that the solution to their problems lay beyond them and their communities.

As the Committee on Economic Security busied itself with developing recommendations and Congress recessed for the summer, life in Slovak communities in many ways went on as before. Local arrangement committees were getting ready for Slovak Day 1934. Slovaks in Ironwood, Michigan, were sponsoring their first annual day, while in western Pennsylvania locals were planning their eleventh. Some affairs would be held on July 4; others would take place throughout the summer and into the early fall. Announcements might refer to having fun despite the "hard times," or, acknowledging "the times," promise inexpensive entertainment and no solicitations for special causes. People surveying the program for the 1934 Slovak National Day in Detroit, however, learned that that year's planners were including a speech about the "social insurance" bill that Lundeen had crafted. Although other items on the program had only cryptic descriptions, the anticipated talk on legislation merited extended hype, which was explicitly designed to draw an audience. While the address would enlighten people about the necessity of social insurance, the speaker's primary purpose undoubtedly would be to garner popular support for the bill authored by Representative Lundeen.[60]

Lundeen had introduced his "workers' unemployment, old-age, and social insurance act" on February 2, 1934. Assigned to the House Committee on Labor as H.R. 7598, the bill had been under consideration for thirty legislative days when Lundeen filed a motion to have it discharged. He reintroduced the same bill, which was designated H.R. 2827, in January 1935. Although he was not a member, Lundeen's bill was essentially a Communist Party production.[61] Since 1930, the party had been calling for a nationwide unemployment insurance program, and in 1933, with a slightly revised draft of an earlier proposal, it had renewed its drive to get legislation enacted. With only minor changes, H.R. 2827 was the 1933 version of the party's social-insurance bill.[62] It reflected communist ideology and contained provisions that, if executed, could potentially advance the party.

Although short, the Lundeen bill proposed a comprehensive plan. Rather than focusing on a single component of social insurance, as other bills had, Lundeen's proposal dealt with unemployment, reduced working hours, disability, and old-age pensions.[63] Moreover, with benefits designated for farmers as well as all for industrial, agricultural, domestic, office, and professional workers, the bill covered the broad spectrum of America's working and middle classes. Placing only a lower age limit on eligibility meant that all persons over eighteen years old who through no fault of their own had been laid off or forced to work fewer hours qualified for compensation. In effect, it promised to shield workers' purchasing power and ensure a minimum standard of living by stipulating that unemployment compensation had to equal prevailing local wages, and "in no case" could a person's income be less than "10.00 per week plus 3.00 for each dependent." Individuals reduced to part-time work also would receive subsidies that would raise their earnings to the local average full-time pay. By building in cost-of-living increases and placing no time limit on benefits, the bill incorporated further safeguards against long-term unemployment. From the standpoint of Slovak and other workers forcibly idled by the Depression, this legislation provided real security against economic forces beyond their control. If enacted, the Lundeen bill would solve their current predicament and offer out-and-out protection from the devastating effects of future temporary or permanent unemployment.

Besides shielding victims of the country's economic vicissitudes, the proposed legislation extended coverage to people who might encounter personal catastrophes even in good times. The same promise to ensure a minimum standard of living characterized Lundeen's nationwide plan for the disabled and elderly. In effect, it instituted a system of benefits for the temporarily and permanently incapacitated. Using the same prevailing wages and cost-of-living provisos contained in the unemployment clause, it would allow compensation to persons unable to work due to sickness, maternity, old age, industrial injury, or any other disability. Maternity, an obviously temporary condition, was the only "disability" given a time limit. Divided into two eight-week segments—one before and another after childbirth—women could take a total of sixteen weeks of paid time off. Since it placed no limitations on compensation for old age, this legislation would effectively create a permanent pension system.

The Lundeen plan to pay for this comprehensive social-insurance system reflected the bill's radical nature. Instead of a self-sustaining plan dependent on reserves built up through payroll taxes, moneys would be derived from taxes on inheritances, gifts, and individual and corporate incomes of more than $5,000. Workers' incomes would not be reduced even slightly to fund this nationwide system. This was definitely a "soak-the-rich" approach, but from the workers' perspective it could be interpreted differently. They were faultless victims. Those believed responsible for the country's economic collapse, as well as those with the financial resources, would pay for the social-insurance program.

In theory, the Lundeen bill would give workers an input into managing the program, and one that implied they could influence decisions about prevailing wages. It specified that the system, including setting minimum compensation, would be administered by local commissions comprising people elected by workers' and farmers' organizations. The proposed legislation made no attempt to identify qualified groups or provide guidelines for determining legitimacy. The Communist Party surely would have striven mightily to establish its Unemployment Councils as legitimate organizations or, at least, to secure their influence in locally elected commissions. Whether Slovak or other workers realized it, the funding plan, together with this nebulous system for administering social-insurance programs, signified not only the bill's class bias but also its communist radix.

Without a doubt, the Communist Party and left-wing radicals viewed the Lundeen bill with an eye to advancing their own ideological interests. Casting aspersions on its origins or underlying ideology, however, cannot negate its practical appeal to the elderly and the jobless. Working-class Slovaks, especially those who had been affiliated with mutual aid societies, saw the measure through the lens of their own experiences. One by one, the clauses of the Lundeen bill addressed the predicaments described in appeals flooding local Slovak lodges and their national headquarters. It would help the farmer whose barn had burned and who could not find work in his region, the father with tuberculosis whose illness made him unable to work, and parents who could no longer pay either their own or their children's membership dues. Of course, a wealth of experiences fashioned the viewpoints of the elderly long faithful to their lodges but now threatened with having their ties torn asunder. Regardless of the particular fraternal-related claim, joblessness was the taproot of their problem. In addition, apprehensions about future security being undermined by recurring economic downturns or advancing age were ever present. From these standpoints, the Lundeen bill looked like the answer to present tribulations and a guarantee of future security. It was a solution, not an ideology. Moreover, restoring workers' solvency would plug a leak that was draining fraternal memberships and thus would help fortify the viability of Slovak ethnic organizations.

During the summer and fall of 1934, when the Roosevelt administration's actions were limited to an exploratory committee and a promise, there was no viable alternative to the Lundeen proposal. While the Committee on Economic Security was devising a plan for Roosevelt to submit to Congress, proponents of the Lundeen bill were rallying grassroots support for this already constructed legislation. Some Slovaks gave their efforts a warm reception. As the National Slovak Society's special convention demonstrated, by early spring of 1934 the social-insurance idea was stirring emotions. The evidence suggests it was the Lundeen bill that was animating this interest among Slovaks and consequently generating a small groundswell of activity. In a July 1934 English-language article, the National Slovak Society called on all members to pressure Roosevelt for social-insurance legislation.[64] Slovaks formed regional associations to promote the Minnesota congressman's proposals. It was an officer of the Federation of Slovak Societies in

Detroit, for example, who gave the speech about social insurance and the Lundeen bill at Detroit's 1934 Slovak Day. While Detroit publicists were using the Slovak Day address to heighten interest, advocates in Milwaukee Slovak societies were urging Slovak societies in their area to create their own united alliance to promote social insurance. Proponents elsewhere worked to draw existing Slovak organizations into a united body on behalf of social-insurance legislation. As the summer progressed, federations comprising local Slovak societies sprang up in Pittsburgh, Chicago, Cleveland, and other areas, including hard-hit industrial and mining towns.[65]

Local Slovak groups committed to getting the Lundeen measure passed typically sponsored meetings to mobilize the public behind it. Activists played on fears that transcended generational differences. The Cleveland Action Committee, for instance, unabashedly conjured up the range of anxieties lurking in people's inner thoughts. "In each of our hearts," it declared, "there is at least a secret fear about what will become of us when we grow old, when we are thrown out of our work, when we become disabled or sick." While these potential afflictions represented the perennial reality hanging over the heads of workers, the present "crisis has gobbled up our hope for our old days, our savings, a little house." In addition to playing on underlying apprehensions, the publicity for these gatherings deftly blended class and ethnic issues together with personal and institutional interests. Because people cannot pay their dues, Cleveland promoters observed, "Our organizations, which are as much social as cultural centers of American Slovaks" are facing annihilation. "Unemployment threatens all our futures"; therefore, the next session of Congress must enact this workers' legislation.[66]

Social-insurance proponents in Milwaukee believed the same, and its Slovak action committee put it in even plainer language. Reflecting the subtle impact that New Deal legislation was having on transforming popular attitudes about the role of government, its summons to a public meeting proclaimed: "if manufacturers jointly with the government cannot provide employment to jobless millions, the law of humanity says the government must take care of all those who through no fault of their own were thrown out of work into hunger, want, and despair." So that the unemployed do not die from hunger, "We must collectively work for the enactment of legislation before congress, H.R. 7598."[67] The committee was implicitly pointing out that the New Deal's federal jobs program had made no substantial dents in unemployment. Anxieties, then, centered as much on the future as on the present, and it was felt by Slovak workers and Slovak organizations as well as by the American working class in general. From the vantage point of desperate people, in the summer and fall of 1934, the Lundeen bill was the best—indeed, the only—legislative plan for addressing workers' current afflictions and laying down lasting safeguards against economic hazards.[68]

The well-crafted publicity and coordinated efforts reaped results. In several cities, local branches of different Slovak organizations responded favorably by sending representatives to general meetings. More than 400 people attended an October 1934 gathering called by the United Slovak Societies of Pittsburgh, a collaborative group organized to secure the "future of our Slovak working people" by pushing for social-insurance legislation.[69] In addition to interested people, the assembly included designated representatives from fifteen separate Slovak organizations, thirty-nine lodges, and four newspapers. According to reporters, participants at the meeting collectively agreed that, while the United States was the richest country in the world, it had the "most backward" system of social insurance. It seems that one man with more radical views tried to inject class warfare into the oratory. The representative of the Slovak division of the International Workers Order (IWO) probably came closest to a tirade when he asserted that workers could never rely on the wealthy to give poor people what rightfully belonged to them.

The meeting, however, did not evolve into a unilateral attack on the country's socioeconomic system. Instead, ardent proponents, the heretofore minimally informed, and the merely curious were treated to a succession of speeches about the Lundeen bill. Speakers represented the range of Slovak organizations. Some national officers announced their association's endorsement of Lundeen's proposed legislation. The National Slovak Society and the Slovak League of America went on record in support of the Lundeen measure. Although no national representative of the male-dominated First Catholic Slovak Union attended, the vice-president of its women's counterpart, the First Catholic Slovak Ladies Union, gave what was described as a moving speech asking God's blessing for passage of the Lundeen bill. She also said that the Ladies Union endorsed it. Another speaker claiming to be acting on behalf of both Živena, a female mutual aid society, and the (Slovak) Progressive Union declared they backed the legislation. The meeting reportedly voted unanimously to endorse the Lundeen bill.[70]

Participants initiated plans to turn words into deeds when they capped off the day's speeches with a challenge to action. Every Slovak lodge in the Pittsburgh region would be asked to elect two persons to represent its membership on the general action committee for social insurance. Adopting a three-part resolution, they called on all Slovaks to work on behalf of the Lundeen bill and to join with Slavs as well as other groups to promote it. In addition, the Pittsburgh action committee was instructed to determine each political candidate's position on the Lundeen bill and to back only those who indicated that, if elected, they would vote for the legislation and other measures that would benefit workers. Finally, the resolution promised an energetic effort to arrange a national conference of American Slovak men and women to rally support for social insurance and to establish ways "to help our Slovak working people."[71] This Pittsburgh meeting probably typified what was happening at the interfraternal and public meetings taking place in other cities. The objectives were the same: to convince Slovaks to help advance their intertwined class and ethnic interests by supporting federal legislation covering old-age pensions and unemployment compensation.[72]

By early December, when the Committee on Economic Security submitted its recommendations to Roosevelt, Slovaks had already organized pockets of zealous support for the Lundeen bill. This fervor received an additional boost around mid-December, when calls went out urging Slovak organizations and their local affiliates to select representatives to a National Congress for Unemployment and Social Insurance scheduled for January 5–7 in Washington, D.C. Neither the announcements nor the published minutes of local meetings mentioned that the Communist Party was behind the upcoming congress. The publicity dwelled on Slovaks doing their part to help Slovak workers in particular, and the working class in general. The frenzy to get Slovak delegates for the conference reflected the growing rank-and-file momentum for the Lundeen bill. In Detroit, Slovak and Czech organizations cooperated to identify representatives and raise the money necessary to send them to Washington. In conjunction with the upcoming conference, local activists collected signatures on a petition to present to U.S. congressional representatives.[73] The National Slovak Society sent Congressman Lundeen official confirmation that 400 of its local assemblies had voted to endorse his bill. The society's national headquarters announced it was sponsoring delegates to attend the Washington conference and asked members to donate toward their expenses.[74]

The National Congress on social insurance had a radiating effect. In an exuberant front-page report on the Washington meeting, the Slovak Evangelical Union lauded the Lundeen bill as the way to help workers now and to ensure a safer future for all working people. Calling the conference only part of an ongoing endeavor, the union's official organ promised to keep members fully informed about the social-insurance movement. The union also threw open the doors of its national headquarters in Pittsburgh to a regionwide meeting about the recently concluded national congress.[75] During the following months, Slovaks far and wide heard reports from delegates to the January conference. People residing in towns near metropolitan areas such as Chicago and Pittsburgh learned from lodge representatives who carried information from general meetings back to their regions. Industrial laborers in Charleroi, Pennsylvania, and miners in Livingston, Taylor Springs, Mount Olive, and surrounding areas in Illinois, as well as from nearby East St. Louis, also got firsthand accounts at regional conclaves. As Slovak supporters of the Lundeen bill were basking in the enthusiasm roused by the national conference, President Roosevelt was hammering out the final details of his own economic security bill. On January 17, 1935, he submitted his proposed legislation. Lundeen also reintroduced his "workers' unemployment, old-age, and social insurance act," which was designated H.R. 2827.[76]

As these rival bills were being considered in Congress, national Slovak organizations and local lodges accelerated their activities. Building on the already active fraternal and interorganizational network, Slovak efforts promoting the Lundeen bill intensified at both the national and local levels. By March 1935, at least four national Slovak organizations had publicly endorsed the resubmitted Lundeen bill. National Slovak associations encouraged cooperation among different societies and continued pushing locals networks to remain actively involved. Cliques committed to the Lundeen bill had nursed an early activism among Slovaks, but now with two competing measures on Congress's 1935 agenda, local committees seemed even more disposed to lobby as well as arrange public meetings. In April, people in Charleroi, Pennsylvania, gathered to discuss the Lundeen bill.[77] More than 600 men and women, mostly Slovak miners and their wives from small towns, attended a Sunday afternoon meeting hosted by Slovaks in Livingston, Illinois. Representatives from nearby East St. Louis also traveled to what was later described as the "largest Slovak assembly in the [southern Illinois] area." By evening, when the number had increased to more than one thousand, activities were moved to a larger facility. After hearing from a series of Slovak speakers representing secular and Catholic organizations as well as the International Workers Order, the meeting named an action com-mittee to contact all lodges throughout the region, solicit their partici-pation, and coordinate efforts on behalf of the Lundeen bill.[78] During the spring, Slovak activists in Chicago, Detroit, Pittsburgh, Philadel-phia, and New York arranged gatherings to rally support for H.R. 2827.[79]

In addition to public events designed to muster grassroots backing for the Lundeen bill, activists tried to lobby congressional representa-tives. Concluding that H.R. 2827 was the "most favorable and most salutary" legislation for the working class, delegates to the Nineteenth Convention of the Slovak League passed a resolution affirming their organization's solid support. It was forwarded to the House of Repre-sentatives and to the Senate. On behalf of the entire organization, the National Slovak Society's officers sent resolutions to members of Con-gress. Admitting that they hoped to "flood" Congress with petitions favoring H.R. 2827, they also called on local branches to send tele-grams.[80] These officers were not out of step with sentiments at the com-munity level. Indeed, local zeal for pressuring lawmakers sometimes surpassed that of national proponents. Attempting to rouse fellow lodges to copy its action, one Yukon, Pennsylvania, assembly called on all National Slovak Society affiliates to forward resolutions supporting the Lundeen legislation to their congressional representatives. More-over, members of this particularly zealous lodge believed that the national officers were not aggressive enough. In an open letter they chided them for not doing more to promote the Lundeen bill; they wanted the society to dispatch resolutions to President Roosevelt as well as to *all* members of Congress.[81] Throughout the entire period that legislation was pending in Congress, no local or national Slovak efforts resembling those on behalf of Lundeen's bill ever developed for the social security act supported by the Roosevelt administration.

This flurry of activity continued as Congress deliberated through the spring and into the summer of 1935. On March 15, the Lundeen bill was favorably reported out of the House Committee on Labor, but it never reached the floor of the House. In early April, the Ways and Means Committee, which had been considering the Roosevelt administration's social security act, sent an amended draft to the House. In early May, the Senate Finance Committee began its executive sessions, and the full Senate finally took up the bill on June 14. In early August, a House and Senate conference committee settled on a version, which Roosevelt signed on August 14.[82] For more than a year afterward, activists in some cities continued working for "social insurance" and for the Lundeen-style program. Some local committees advertised in fraternal publications, but their efforts were not as closely tied as before to fraternal networks. Instead, they were nurtured by still committed left-wing vestiges of the campaign for the Lundeen bill.[83] Once the Social Security Act passed, interest in social insurance among Slovaks at the national and community levels declined.[84]

Although Slovak religious and secular fraternal organizations in general had supported some type of social-insurance legislation, their involvement in efforts to get it enacted varied. The First Catholic Slovak Union, for example, did not thrust itself into the early campaign for social insurance. Officers of that mutual aid society were not opposed to calling attention to the plight of the working class, especially "Slovak workers," and asking for just treatment. *Jednota* published a few Slovak League appeals as well as endorsements of the Lundeen bill, including one titled, "To Victory in the Fight for Bread and Justice."[85] The newspaper, though, threw its support behind the more conservative social security act. And the First Catholic Slovak Union quietly lobbied on behalf of Roosevelt's plan. In a cover letter to the chairs of Senate and House Committees, national officers explained that, "mindful of the well-being of our membership," they were backing "the National Program which provides for social legislation, to better secure the future welfare of our members." The officers' concern went beyond their own organization. Expressing a "desire to promote the welfare and the greater future of social security, not only of its own [First Catholic Slovak Union] membership, . . . but of the American people," the accompanying resolution formally declared the national officers' endorsement of the system recommended by the Committee on Economic Security.[86] They grasped the relationship between promoting working-class interests and bolstering the survival of ethnic institutions, but religious philosophy molded their views and limited their activities. This Catholic fraternal society condemned "all communist and bolshevistic movements," and the whiff of Communist Party advocacy hanging over the Lundeen bill would be more than the organization could endure.[87] So, given the union's position, it would be foolish simply to conclude that being associated with the Communist Party had no adverse impact on attitudes toward the legislation.

The Slovak Evangelical Union was less constrained by religious ideology. When it finally took a stand in favor of the Lundeen bill, the organization was prompted in large part by a desire to enact legislation promising economic security for workers and the elderly. At the same time, the National Slovak Society's advocacy on behalf of workers blended pragmatism and class tensions. Together with its other dire effects, massive joblessness meant that efforts to perpetuate fraternal loyalty among youths were being jeopardized. Making a particularly astute observation, the author of a 1935 *Kalendár* article pointed out that running membership campaigns and forming sports teams were useless if youths were leaving their communities in search of work. Reporters reminded people that unemployment compensation would let them pay their fraternal dues.[88] The society's commentary on the Depression and its calls for passing social-insurance legislation, however, were laced with the language of class conflict. Although they did not openly embrace anti-capitalist ideologies, articulate spokespersons did not give radical organizations a total cold shoulder. In 1934, for instance, the editors of *Národné noviny* only feebly distanced themselves from a blatantly pro-socialist article by a second-generation member. Moreover, the National Slovak Society took a benign view of Unemployment Councils and left-wing organizations that became involved in local relief efforts. The society's official organ editorialized that such groups were assisting helpless people who had been callously denied a livelihood.[89] Taken on the whole, the National Slovak Society's support for the Lundeen bill, as well as its reliance on the language of class antagonism, reflected sympathy for the plight of the working class, which unquestionably made up nearly its entire membership. It was a compassion that reached back to the society's origins. After all, publicity for a 1935 membership campaign explained: the founders had workers in mind when they created the organization.[90]

Intertwining class and ethnic interests also spurred the Slovak Evangelical Ladies Union to come out in support of the Lundeen bill. Declaring that unemployment had inflicted "massive want" on Slovak homes, and that it had disastrously affected women in particular, national officers of this mutual benefit society called to arms its 7,000 members in the "fight for social insurance." They envisioned women as standing beside men in the battle to pass this working-class legislation, but the women's role went beyond mere collaboration. The union's national committee believed that women entering the fray would inspire leaders of Slovak fraternal societies that had stayed out of the fight for unemployment insurance and old-age pensions to join.[91] In their view, women could help fuel activism and move people to action.

For Slovaks, working on behalf of social-insurance legislation was part of a cooperative effort between national organizations and lodges, but grassroots involvement was influenced by a combination of local circumstances and personal experiences. Some particularly energetic Slovak federations emerged in cities where the Communist Party was notably active, and the party's Unemployment Councils no doubt had a hand in churning local enthusiasm for social insurance.[92] During the crusade for the Lundeen bill, however, it was the International Workers Order that focused on uniting local ethnic institutions behind the legislation. A mutual benefit organization whose membership consisted primarily of foreign-born persons, the IWO had nationality divisions and was therefore structured along ethnic lines. Although it was not formally affiliated, the IWO did not conceal the fact that it endorsed the Communist Party. As the historian Harvey Klehr has demonstrated, however, ordinary workers who belonged to the IWO typically were not communists. Instead, most people probably joined either because they wished to affiliate with a "progressive" organization but not with the Communist Party or because they wanted the low-cost insurance the IWO provided. The Slovaks who entered the IWO thus were affiliating with a workers' organization that coincidentally reinforced ethnic identities. At the same time, Slovak IWO members cooperated with long-standing networks of Slovak organizations as well as with other nationalities.[93] Hence, for all the clang of class-consciousness rhetoric, grassroots drives for the Lundeen plan resembled in part the established practice of nationalities participating as distinct groups in multi-ethnic undertakings.

Even as Slovaks promoted class interests, interethnic competition in local communities did not dissipate. Slovaks in western Pennsylvania subtly exhibited this ongoing rivalry with "other nationalities" in July 1933 when Secretary of Labor Perkins included the town of Homestead in her fact-finding mission designed to reassure steelworkers that the administration had their interests at heart.[94] Sensitive to the fact that the secretary's visit was not intended to pay homage to Slovaks, local enthusiasts nevertheless used her presence to do just that. Reports in the Slovak press placed Perkins's mission within a combined ethnic and class context when they explained that she had come to Homestead to learn what "toiling steel workers, a large percentage of whom are Slovaks," wanted. Ethnicity eclipsed class, however, when Pittsburgh's Bishop Boyle arranged for Perkins to use the Slovak Catholic church in Munhall for a public meeting. Local Slovak Catholics were overjoyed. Their rapture prompted the area's Slovak Catholic lodges to dispatch resolutions of thanks both to the bishop and to President Roosevelt. Figuratively sticking their tongue out at other nationalities, in the resolution to Roosevelt the Slovaks twice mentioned "the signal recognition and honor" that this visit by a cabinet member to a Slovak Catholic church bestowed "on all people of Slovak birth."[95] While Slovaks went to the meeting as working-class people pleading the case of steelworkers, the Perkins visit symbolized a converging of ethnic and class interests. The proclamations made by local Slovaks following the secretary's trip once again demonstrated the persistent, underlying competition with other nationalities and the ongoing quest for respectability.

Perhaps only a fraction of Slovaks or other nationalities got involved in campaigns promoting social insurance and workers' interests in the 1930s, but their efforts added another dimension to the ethnic activism that flowed through the decade. The Lundeen bill grew out of an ideology critical of American capitalism and, more specifically, of its failures in the 1930s. Slovak support, however, was animated by the personal experiences of ordinary people living in communities. Political rhetoric notwithstanding, in the midst of the Depression, distraught workers logically would have been drawn to class-based language that spoke to their own ordeals. Based on letters that poured into national headquarters, strong resentment existed among Slovaks for having been thrust into a wretched situation they knew was not their fault. Time and again, petitioners voiced this realization on their own behalf and that of fellow fraternalists or their families. The same thing was happening in organizations serving other nationalities. Overall, pragmatism, not ideology, fueled Slovak support for seemingly radical social-insurance legislation.

Despite the class overtones, Slovaks drawing together on behalf of a social-insurance plan was an example of ethnic mobilization. As the Depression deepened, ethnic interests hinged in some respects on promoting class issues, and conversely, promoting class welfare gained momentum by mobilizing ethnic organizations. By recognizing their own limitations and expanding their activities to become lobbyists on behalf of all American laborers, mutual benefit societies remained true to both their ethnic and working-class roots. During the 1930s, then, ethnic interests became a rallying force and a force to rally behind.

Since the mid-1920s, ethnic activists had been focusing on issues important to new immigrants and their children in the United States.

With no national or international events sparking concerted action, ethnic activism had ebbed into an undertow moved by a devotion to perpetuating a presence in America's heterogeneous society, a desire to attain respectability, and a concern about the welfare of the working class. At the community level, activities and perspectives on issues had often been shaped by local circumstances. Competition with "other nationalities" was a constant, energizing theme. Throughout the era, a few articulate Slovaks pounded on homeland issues, but that drumbeat was muted by other concerns. In the late 1930s, though, events in Europe were once again seizing the attention of Slovak immigrants, and now their children. As a consequence, Slovak activism would surface once again to take on national and international objectives.

8   The Triumph of Principles

*National Unity and Ethnic Activism
in World War II*

ON SUNDAY, AUGUST 2, 1942, Chicago Slovaks attended their
fourteenth annual Slovak National Day. Less than a week earlier, Slovaks in Detroit had held their sixteenth yearly celebration. Slovaks elsewhere also continued to arrange their once-a-year events. The programs
contained what, over the past decade and a half, had become standard
features for these ethnic celebrations. Despite carrying on established
traditions, the 1942 events featured aspects that were tellingly different.
These festivities, after all, were taking place in wartime America. Following Chicago's long-standing practice, profits would be given to a
philanthropic association that assisted the area's needy Slovaks, but the
1942 proceeds were also designated for "unfortunate Slovak families,
widows, orphans, and mothers" of men who were serving "Uncle Sam."
Detroit Slovaks would donate their returns to the American Red Cross.
Instead of a Slovak queen competition, Chicago held a "Miss Victory
Contest." Organizers hoped to send the winner, together with other
contestants, to the White House as a delegation to express personally
the support of Chicago Slovaks for President Roosevelt and the war.[1]
Trying to patch bitter divisions that were splitting Slovak Americans,
publicists promoted Slovak Day under the slogan, "Unity for American
Victory." Like ethnic affairs during the Great War, Slovak Days reflected
the reality of the times.

Nationality days were not the only opportunities for immigrants and
their "Americanized" offspring to join in group activities that blended
patriotism and ethnicity. People who attended these days in 1942 probably also participated in the "I Am an American Day" celebrations held
in 1941 and during the war.[2] The United States was still a society bent
on using public, collective actions to gauge group loyalty, so in scenes
reminiscent of the Great War, Slovaks came together to show "others"
that they were loyal Americans. The wartime activities of Slovaks—
and, indeed, of other nationality groups—demonstrate that nativism

was not the only sentiment that could boil to the surface in times of national crisis. Ethnicity could burst forth as well. Once again, linking exhibitions of patriotism and displays of ethnicity became a leitmotif of wartime America.

In fundamental ways, the home front in World War II differed from the situation a quarter-century earlier. In particular, the makeup of the "ethnic America" that faced World War II contrasted dramatically with that of the previous conflict. Based on a computation of "mother tongue" data in the 1940 census, the second generation now accounted for nearly 59 percent of the Slovak stock. The addition of third-generation individuals who acknowledged their Slovak heritage on the census form raised the proportion of native born to nearly 65 percent.[3] Immigrants thus accounted for just slightly more than one-third of the total Slovak American population. From the standpoint of nationality groups, World War I had been an immigrant ordeal; the generation that faced World War II was largely American born. By 1941, a significant segment of the second generation had matured beyond the reaches of educational and promotional campaigns aimed at inculcating ethnic consciousness and overcoming the effects of the "undesirable" stigma. It was time to see how successful endeavors aimed at ethnicization, which had seen the goal of preserving the mother tongue give way to stressing pride in ancestry, had been. The war raised the basic question of whether the second-generation new immigrants could be counted on to acknowledge their ethnicity or whether, given the opportunity, they would run away from it and seek shelter in an amorphous American identity. Before Slovak Americans began confronting these questions, though, the fate of the homeland was generating a resurgence of Slovak activism. As a result, before the United States went to war against totalitarianism, grappling with Old World political issues was already causing Slovaks to reaffirm their adherence to American principles.

EVEN AS CONDITIONS in America demanded their attention in the 1920s and 1930s, Slovaks still glanced across the ocean sometimes to see what was happening in the Old World. In the late 1930s, though, Germany's machinations were fast turning occasional glimpses into piercing stares. Since the end of the Great War, interest in Czechoslovakia had centered on Czech–Slovak relations and, more specifically, on the relationship between Slovakia and the central government in Prague. But it was the Sudetenland, where the country's large German minority was concentrated, that prompted this renewed attention. First- and second-

generation Slovaks watched from afar as the ultranationalism Adolf
Hitler was stirring up in Germany found fertile ground in the Sudetenland, a slim, horseshoe-shaped region curving north to south around
Czechoslovakia's western border.[4] Some Slovak Americans let out a collective gasp when the French and British governments appeased Hitler's
aggressive demands and German troops began occupying the Sudetenland on October 1, 1938. Others, especially Catholic spokespersons,
viewed events as a singularly Czech misfortune. It was a case of the
Czechs finally having to sample what betrayal tasted like and, hence,
what Slovaks had been swallowing for twenty years.[5] Emotions remained mixed when, five days later, weakened by the Munich Agreement and fearful of Slovak secession, the Prague government bowed to
the Žilina Accord, a plan that gave Slovakia legislative autonomy within
the joint state. Monsignor Jozef Tiso, a Catholic priest who had become
leader of the Slovak People's Party after Andrej Hlinka's death in
August 1938, became Slovakia's prime minister.[6]

Despite his asseverations to the contrary, Hitler's plans did include
ultimately gobbling up all the Czech lands, but he was willing to let Slovakia remain a separate state. At a March 13 meeting in Berlin with
Hitler, Tiso caved in to threats that declaring independence was the
region's only alternative to being partitioned or annexed by Hungary.
Although Tiso was no longer Slovakia's prime minister, on March 14,
1939, the Slovak Provincial Assembly followed his advice and proclaimed Slovakia independent. The next day, while German troops
occupied the Czech lands and reduced them to a protectorate of the
Third Reich, Hitler recognized Slovakia. Czechoslovakia ceased to exist,
and Tiso became the head of the independent Slovak state. Nine days
after declaring sovereignty, the government of the so-called independent country signed agreements placing Slovakia under Germany's "protection." Slovakia did not survive Hitler's aggression with its territory
intact, though. In the fall of 1938, Czechoslovakia's boundaries had been
redrawn; southern and eastern sections of Slovakia were given to Hungary while a small northern portion went to Poland. In March, with
Hitler's blessing, Hungary laid claim to additional territory and occupied areas in Slovakia.[7] When they looked across the ocean in the late
1930s, then, this was what Americans of Slovak birth and ancestry saw.

As events rapidly unfolded in Czechoslovakia, reports filled the
pages of the Slovak press in the United States. At no time since the rati-
fication of the country's 1920 constitution had interest in the Old World
been so intense. Instead, from the mid-1920s onward, homeland issues

had attracted the attention of a hard-core contingent, and, depending on the political questions at any given time in Czechoslovakia, even this attention had waxed and waned.[8] There was one constant: when it came to homeland politics, Slovaks typically divided along religious lines. Catholic activists supported the Slovak People's Party while Protestants strongly opposed both the party and its clerical leader. Slovak Protestants were far less critical of Czechs and the Prague government than their Catholic counterparts were. Protestants counseled cooperation with the central administration and usually supported political parties that opposed the Slovak People's Party. Some were centralists clearly against an autonomous Slovakia, while others saw implementation of the Pittsburgh Agreement as the ultimate objective but still believed that Slovaks were not ready for self-government. Protestants, primarily Lutherans, could not shake a long-standing apprehension that an autonomous Slovakia governed by a clergy-dominated party would once again come under the Catholic, Hungarian yoke. Adding to their trepidation was the concern that Protestants would suffer discrimination in a Slovakia whose legislative body would be controlled by a Catholic-led party.[9]

As Slovaks gazed from a distance, the events of 1938–1939 represented both the dreams and nightmares of passionate activists in the United States. The Slovak League of America and spokespersons for Catholic institutions praised the Žilina Accord as the realization of the Pittsburgh Agreement. The only reservations these Catholics initially had were concerns that the Czechs would find a way to undermine the accord.[10] The secular National Slovak Society, with a religiously diverse membership, warmly welcomed autonomy; its commentators nevertheless were somewhat uneasy about what policies the controlling party would put in place. Officials of Protestant organizations greeted the newly established Slovak autonomy with implacable hostility. Even the official organ of the Slovak Evangelical Ladies Union, which had tended to shy away from political issues, expressed fears about Germany's designs on Czechoslovakia and weighed into the debate on the side opposing Slovak autonomy.[11] The redrawn borders only intensified fears about Hungarian designs on Slovakia.

When Slovakia proclaimed independence in March 1939, the reaction of American Slovaks varied to the extreme. The Slovak League was jubilant. Catholic spokespersons were also pleased, but the First Catholic Slovak Union, at least, remained circumspect and voiced its delight only by printing favorable reports on Slovakia and permitting ardent supporters to use its newspaper to express their views. In June, *Jednota* carried a message from Tiso to American Slovaks; a few months later, it published the new state's constitution.[12] No doubt targeting its second-generation readership and attempting to reach the American public as well, both the editorials and columns in *Jednota*'s English-language sections bluntly defended the independent state.[13] Recoiling from a country voluntarily allied with Hitler's Germany, the National Slovak Society opposed independence and wanted Czechoslovakia restored to the federated structure created by the Žilina Accord. The day after Slovakia declared independence, the front-page headline in *Národné noviny* announced, "The Traitors Have Completed the Deed." The English-language section proclaimed, "Slovakia Betrayed." Lutheran commentators took the same position. Reporting on Slovakia's declaration and Hungary's subsequent territorial moves, *Slovenský hlásnik* titled its lead story, "Tiso Sold Out Czechoslovakia to the Nazis. Now He Is Selling Out Slovakia to the Magyars [Hungarians]."[14] Neither Protestants nor secular organizations such as the National Slovak Society could accept Slovakia's affiliation with Hitler, a situation they repeatedly maintained constituted the enslavement, not the liberation, of the Slovak people. For Slovaks in America, then, Slovakia's autonomy following the Munich Agreement; Germany's subsequent invasion of Czechoslovakia; and finally, the creation of the independent state were seismic events. This succession of upheavals demonstrated that the homeland could still evoke powerful emotions and spawn reactions across a broad spectrum of the Slovak American population.[15]

For two and a half years following the creation of the independent Slovak state, Slovaks in the United States engaged in a vitriolic battle of words. Looking at the homeland situation through the prism of their own religious or political views, Slovaks developed unyielding, contrary stances. Following the breakup of Czechoslovakia, Catholic spokespersons seemingly went out of their way to assert a fundamental antagonism between Catholicism and Protestantism. They incessantly attacked the "Protestant" character of the former Czechoslovak government and alleged that it had been repugnant to Slovaks.[16] For their part, Protestants, ever wary about Catholic control, kept insisting that non-Catholic denominations were being mistreated in Slovakia.[17] As the debate intensified, supporters of the independent state revived themes implicitly linking the Slovak national identity to Roman Catholicism. Vociferously averring their own "Slovakness," Lutherans continued fighting the notion that all true Slovaks were Catholic. Publications highlighted the fact that Lutherans had been in the vanguard of the Slovak national awakening in the nineteenth century. Not only had a Lutheran codified the Slovak language; Lutherans had written much of the work that made up the body of Slovak nationalist literature. Asserting their legitimacy as spokespersons,[18] these Protestants, who staunchly proclaimed themselves Slovaks by birth or ancestry, rejected as ludicrous the claim that independent Slovakia was free.

Public discussion degenerated into name-calling. Critics of Slovakia could find themselves labeled communists.[19] "Czechoslovak" took on a more encompassing and odious meaning than it already had. When used to deny a unique Slovak national identity, the term had always carried an offensive connotation. Following the 1939 creation of Slovakia, its opprobrium expanded to besmirch those calling for the restoration of Czechoslovakia. Transforming a political position into an ascribed ethnic identity, "Czechoslovak" became a negative epithet for those who, regardless of the depth of their own Slovak consciousness, opposed the breakup of Czechoslovakia. Critics allowed for no distinction between supporting a reunified country and retaining one's Slovak identity. In effect, Catholic and Protestants alike who called for the reunification of Slovakia and the Czech lands were vilified as "Czechoslovaks."[20]

For Slovak Americans, the wrangling over Slovakia became more than a battle between opposing political positions or antagonistic views of Slovak nationalism. As the fight raged, combatants framed the issues within the context of "American" democratic principles. For each side, it became a matter of Americanism and of the supposed democratic values embedded in the American, as well as the Slovak, character. On one hand, proponents of an independent Slovakia exerted tremendous effort trying to legitimize its creation. Spokespersons for Catholic organizations, together with the Slovak League of America, presented Slovakia as the embodiment of American principles. From their perspective, the newly established state represented Wilsonian self-determination and the same freedom from domination symbolized by the American Revolution. Czechoslovakia's government had not been grounded in democratic ideals, they maintained. Be "On Guard," one English-language editorial warned, against attempts by the former president, Eduard Beneš, to claim that Czechoslovakia had been a democratic country. "There is no harmony" between the terms "democracy" and "Beneš," this second-generation Slovak man declared.[21]

For Slovak Protestants, on the other hand, independent Slovakia symbolized neither the ideal of self-determination nor democracy. No country allied with Nazi Germany could credibly claim it was free. In addition, commentators alleged, Lutherans and Jews in Slovakia were suffering discrimination at the hands of the new government. Thus, they charged, democratic principles were not being upheld in Slovakia; instead, the new state was an affront to American ideals. Beginning in November 1940, the Lutheran *Slovenský hlásnik* carried a statement on its masthead in bold capital letters proclaiming its support for the restoration of Czechoslovakia. Lutherans were not alone in seeking the reunification of the Czech and Slovak lands. The view that Slovakia was neither a sovereign nor a democratically governed country reverberated through the National Slovak Society's publications as well.[22]

Slovak organizations waged a seemingly incessant battle in the media. Advocates on opposing sides of the independence debate hurled epithets and vilified one another, but the most serious invective was reserved for the leaders of Slovakia's government. If, from the perspective of antagonistic factions, independent Slovakia represented a nightmare versus a dream come true, for these same factions Tiso was either a traitor or a savior. Supporters showered praise on Tiso as a hero and defender of Slovakia. Detractors excoriated him. Defenders maintained that under his leadership, Slovakia had been spared the fate of the Czech lands and, moreover, Slovakia was independent for the first time in its history. Critics countered that Slovakia was merely a puppet state whose government was collaborating with Hitler's heinous Third Reich. They spared no acrimony in their denunciation of the president. His actions were labeled treasonous, and he was routinely referred to as a "traitor to the Slovak people," a "renegade."[23] Regardless of their position, few commentators could mention Tiso without affixing an appositive.

The passion aroused by Tiso and the depth of the bitterness toward him were ingeniously expressed in an English-language editorial that appeared eight days after the breakup of Czechoslovakia. Published in *Národné noviny* under the headline, "Slovakia Betrayed," the editorial proclaimed that Judas Iscariot, Lajos Kossuth, and Benedict Arnold "have tossed in an extra shovel of coal while stocking [*sic*] the fires in happy anticipation of the new member." According to this analyst, Tiso had "submitted his application for membership to this infamous group of betrayers, traitors, and renegades" when he cooperated with "Hitler, the mad dog of Europe."[24] By linking Tiso to this troika, the commentator shrewdly put him in company with three notorious traitors. In this astute public-relations maneuver, he placed the new president in a group containing villains of Christianity, of Slovak nationalism, and of

U.S. history. The editorialist was thus implicitly and adroitly conjuring up the putative historical foundations of contemporary democratic and religious values. Within these parameters, Tiso became an affront to the traditions and principles that were believed inherent in the Slovak and American characters.

Cleverly going beyond mere harangue, the editorialist maligned Tiso even more by making him a weakling, a leader who chose cowardice over principle. The critic expressed understanding for the "terrific pressure" that had been exerted on Tiso and that "he was on the spot, and that it might even have been a matter of life and death for him." Yes, he understood that. However, in his judgment, "even if this be true, it still does not justify his traitorous action. There are some things worse than death." Certainly for this commentator and those who felt as passionately, Tiso had failed a test of principle. There was no question that the homeland and its leader not only triggered fierce emotions among Slovak Americans, but that, on the eve of World War II, they were perceiving these issues within the context of American ideals.

While organizational leaders and newspaper editors were turning ethnic publications into battlefields, local activists were going to work at the grassroots level. Ads for local events revealed that Hitler's designs on Czechoslovakia were clearly stirring an interest in European matters among rank-and-file Slovaks. They arranged demonstrations to rally public support for or against independent Slovakia.[25] Old World issues began to figure prominently once again in local Slovak Days. Harking back to the politically oriented days held in the early 1920s, the speech segments got heightened pre-event publicity, and based on published reports, more time was devoted to public addresses.

The fact that 1938 marked the twenty-year anniversary of both the Pittsburgh Agreement and the birth of Czechoslovakia fanned the flames of an already flickering interest in Old World affairs. Homeland themes—or, perhaps more accurately, political positions trumpeted by community activists in 1938—reflected underlying disagreements already splintering Slovaks in America and augured the bitter fights that would openly erupt during the next year. Organizers of Chicago's 1938 Slovak National Day dedicated that year's affair to celebrating the twentieth anniversary of Czechoslovakia's birth. They used it as an opportunity to remind people of America's long-standing support for the joint state. The English-language ads described the "hard-won independence of Czechoslovakia" and the "good will of the American people" toward that country. Keeping with this theme but going a step further, one particularly long column about the upcoming function mentioned the significant contributions Chicago Slovaks had made both to the wartime effort and to the creation of Czechoslovakia.[26] Slovaks elsewhere were showing the same conspicuous interest in Czechoslovakia. Publicists for Slovak Day in the Ohio Valley, as well as those arranging the event in nearby western Pennsylvania, used the opportunity to demand that the Czechoslovak government finally implement the Pittsburgh Agreement. Activities at both days included passing a resolution calling on Czechoslovakia's president to effect the agreement. The resolutions were reportedly forwarded to President Beneš.[27] One zealous local reporter surely overstated the case when he declared that people had gone to Kennywood Park "to demonstrate for democracy and freedom for Slovakia." Undoubtedly a variety of motives caused the estimated 35,000 to 40,000 participants to travel to that Slovak Day in late July 1938. Nevertheless, Old World matters were clearly sifting into publicity for local days, and people were conceptualizing issues within the framework of American democratic principles.

Because Roman Catholic organizations had taken over most Slovak Days, publicity for the summer 1939 events generally reflected the Catholic position supporting the Slovak Republic. Promoters in the Philadelphia area told Slovaks that "the victory of our dear ones in Slovakia" provided an excellent reason for people to join that year's celebration. They also implicitly acknowledged that disagreements about Slovakia were exacerbating divisions in the community.[28] Reports on Youngstown's day presented it as an occasion when people who had not been deceived by the "enemies" of the Slovak nation had come together. Individuals allegedly had shared in a collective pleasure over Slovakia's independence and got news about conditions there. Listeners heard one speaker assert that "misleading" stories were being circulated. Addressing twin criticisms of the new state, he told the crowd that Slovakia was free from interference by both the Germans and the Hungarians.[29] Planners of the Catholic day in Chicago were also interested in the homeland. Their program featured someone who had just returned from Slovakia and would report on the situation. Even people in Lake County, Indiana, were treated to a firsthand account by a recent visitor to the Old Country.[30] Participants at western Pennsylvania's historically well-attended day reportedly expressed their admiration for Tiso. He was praised as a "great leader" who had obtained a right for Slovaks that had long been denied to them.[31] By adopting the language of derision, local rhetoric mirrored the invective characterizing exchanges in the

Slovak national media. Publicists for Detroit's Slovak Catholic Day, for example, indiscriminately tarred those in that city who supported the reunification of the Czech and Slovak states as "Czechoslovaks."[32]

Rather than welcoming Slovak independence and lauding the clerical leader who had helped make it happen, Slovak Days in a few communities became occasions to decry what had taken place. In 1939, Chicago Slovaks continued the nearly decade-old habit of holding rival events. Detroit did the same. While the Catholic days in these cities celebrated the new state, publicity for the secular affairs referred to the "sad" events of the past year.[33] Like the organizers of the national days in Chicago and Detroit, planners in Danbury, Connecticut, expressed dismay over what had occurred in Czechoslovakia. Planners invited people to come, enjoy themselves, and support actions that would lead to the "revival of Czecho-Slovakia." Using the hyphenated spelling suggested that the people arranging Slovak Day in Danbury wanted to return to the system that had existed under the Žilina Accord, which had given Slovakia legislative autonomy in a common state.[34] The hyphenation also suggested that local activists were knowledgeable about the political, even symbolic, issues at stake. Local days sponsored by Slovak Lutherans also became forums for Old World politics. Promising a program of amusements, dancing, baseball, and contests, Cleveland's local Slovak Evangelical Union assemblies advertised their 1939 day as an opportunity to get the world to listen and "not stop fighting for the freedom of our homeland from Hitler." People in Akron viewed the upcoming Slovak Lutheran Day as a chance for Lutherans, who were "proud of being Slovak," to demonstrate their abiding hope that Slovakia would be freed.[35] Annual fraternal days organized by National Slovak Society lodges echoed the same theme of liberation. Assemblies in Johnstown, Pennsylvania, dedicated their 1939 day to "freeing Czechs and Slovaks" in Europe.[36]

While snide, often vague, references to "enemies" flowed freely in ads for the 1938 and 1939 Slovak Days, the longer, analytical announcements articulated more varied, complex themes. Focusing on the homeland, local activists tried to turn upcoming Slovak Days into demonstrations of the mutuality between Americanism and Slovak consciousness. For instance, in an English-language appeal exclaiming that Czechoslovakia, "the home of our fathers," needed support and encouragement, organizers of Chicago's 1938 national day pleaded with Slovaks to attend "so that our fellow Americans as well as our brothers across the sea will realize that we, loyal Americans that we are, have not forgotten our Slovak heritage."[37] Using practically the same terminology, Johnstown's publicity committee echoed these thoughts a year later.[38] References to "citizens" and "citizenship" abounded. As local activists stressed the "citizenship" makeup of the Slovak American population—which, incidentally, included foreign- and American-born Slovaks—they were implicitly defending their involvement in matters related to the homeland. "Let the Americans see that we are a people who love freedom and who also want other peoples to enjoy freedom," a Johnstown committee proclaimed. This type of publicity was part of a long-time but, in the midst of crises in the Old World, stepped-up tendency by Slovaks publicly to affirm their commitment to Americanism while simultaneously underscoring their ethnicity.

In addition to the usual recreational activities, Slovak Day programs contained traditional patriotic rituals. The festivities still typically opened or closed with an "American hymn," often the "The Star-Spangled Banner" or "America the Beautiful." In addition to American patriotic songs, the Slovak hymn "Hej Slováci" was regularly performed. The Catholic-sponsored events, however, were particularly prone to symbolic manifestations. Seemingly even more than in the recent past, reporters took pains to comment on flag displays. Readers learned that a huge American and Slovak flag waved as contestants competed in the afternoon games at the 1939 Slovak Day in Lake County, Indiana.[39] In several instances, local zealots went out of their way to feature the American and Slovak national emblems. Children marching in the parade for the 1939 Slovak Day in New Castle, Pennsylvania, carried an American flag in one hand and the Slovak flag in the other.[40] With people singing "America the Beautiful" and "Hej Slováci," Slovak Boy Scouts in Binghamton, New York, filed by with American and Slovak flags.[41] Having children carrying the flags was a particularly symbolic gesture. Only the youngsters themselves actually knew why they were participating in these parades, but marching through the streets, they personified the objectives that committed activists had been laboring to achieve since the late 1920s. Individual motivation notwithstanding, to Slovaks, Americans, and other nationalities alike, these young people—undoubtedly second-generation Slovaks—were exhibiting loyalty to America and pride in ancestry.

Jointly displaying the American and Slovak flags was more than a combined expression of patriotism and ethnic pride. Given the general penchant for viewing the American flag as symbolizing the country's democratic principles, this action was a declaration alleging harmonious ideological values. Having youths wave flags as they paraded through streets was an attempt to flaunt Americanism to legitimize their position on Slovakia. It is reasonable to conclude that supporters of independence were using the side-by-side display as a means of asserting that the Slovak national banner—and hence, the Slovak state—stood for the same democratic principles represented by the sacred symbol of the United States.

In addition to the Americanism theme flowing through the rhetoric and public displays, local supporters saw a mutually advantageous relationship between the independent Slovak state and Slovaks in America. Trying to motivate people to attend Slovak Day, Detroit's 1939 publicity committee presented it as an opportunity for Slovaks to show their "huge strength." Coming out in large numbers, however, was not presented as a way for Slovaks to flex muscle in local politics; instead, it was lobbying reminiscent of World War I demonstrations that publicists had in mind. The point was that this year's nationality day would let Americans see that the Slovak people are "worthy of freedom" and "deserve to be on the map of Europe as a free nation."[42] Encouraging people to attend western Pennsylvania's 1939 Slovak Day, a local promoter, jubilant over the "resurrection of our Slovak nation," went on to give his opinion about the positive impact this development was having. "Before Czechoslovakia was created in 1918, people knew us only as 'Hunkies' . . . and afterwards they called us Czechoslovaks," he told readers. But today, he went on, "they write about and call us Slovaks."[43] From his standpoint, a separate homeland was a gigantic leap forward in the ongoing effort to gain respectability and secure a distinctiveness in America's ethnically diverse society.

When the click of goose-stepping boots finally turned into the deafening rumble of an invading army that thrust Europe into World War II, Slovaks in America remained divided over the fate of Slovakia. Nevertheless, the onset of the European war in the fall of 1939 added another vexing dimension to the disagreement over the independent state: Slovakia was allied with Nazi Germany. This fact caused a noticeable shift in the publicity and activities scheduled for Slovak Days the following summer. Although communities continued to hold the days, fewer pre-event announcements were published in 1940. Moreover, in places where enthusiasts had been using these affairs to stir up moral and political support for independent Slovakia, publicity was muted. Promoters at least toned down their public cheering for the state. Slovak Day in western Pennsylvania did celebrate the one-year anniversary of the "independent Slovak state," and lodges participating in Chicago's Slovak Catholic Day announced plans to parade with both the American and Slovak flags.[44] But by and large, the notices that did appear in the summers of 1940 and 1941 contained information only about the program, date, time, and location. In elaborating on objectives, publicists for the Fayette County, Pennsylvania, day in 1940 deviated from more common behavior. This deviation, however, took the form of proclaiming their Americanism. "Let us show that Slovaks are loyal citizens," the notice urged. "When all of Europe stands in fire . . . let us come in huge numbers so that everyone can see that Slovaks love and work for the ideals of democracy and of our dear United States."[45] How these promoters felt about independent Slovakia was not mentioned, but this passionate statement probably reflected a growing sense that they should impress others in the community with their patriotism and commitment to democratic principles.

The crises in Czechoslovakia in the late 1930s and, finally, Germany's dismemberment of the country energized the Slovak American population. These issues did more than merely fill the pages of the Slovak- and English-language sections of the ethnic press; they generated fierce debates in local communities. And it was both the first and second generations who engaged in the discussions. Thus, even before the United States entered World War II, turmoil in Europe had injected new life into Slovak consciousness in the United States. It was, however, an ethnic awareness that reflected the philosophy that being a true American— defined as a loyal citizen devoted to democratic principles—was not at odds with pride in Slovak origin. The ascendancy of this thought was evident in August 1941 when the annual convention of the National Slovak Society revised the motto for its Young Folks' Circle. Symbolizing the culmination of what Slovak activism had been about since the late 1920s, the long-time motto, "Our Nation Is Calling Us to Work," gave way to, "Loyalty to America, Pride in Our Ancestry."[46]

The National Slovak Society's legal counsel, John Willo, gave voice to current thinking about ethnicity and Americanism. No doubt fearing that a resurgence of anti-hyphenism and heightened patriotism might frighten Slovaks away from their ethnic ties, Willo, an American-born Slovak, went on the offensive. Speaking at different occasions in 1941, he asserted that there was nothing wrong when a "hyphen, on the part of second or third generation Americans, simply signifies respect for the land of their ancestors, simply signifies pride in their own blood and culture, without in the least interfering with their whole-hearted devotion to the land of their birth."[47] He maintained that "being loyal to America, and feeling the throb of love for Slovakia, involves no conflict on the part of Americans of Slovak ancestry." While not a designated spokesperson, Willo was nevertheless a second-generation voice. And he was one dedicated to the notion that, in his words, native-born Slovaks could simultaneously be "proud of our ancestry" and true Americans.

Willo's addresses also offered insight into how second-generation Slovaks had come to view the American flag. He proclaimed it "the most beautiful emblem ever raised for the adoration of any people." Within this context, the American flag was more than a national symbol; it became a sacred object. This was not surprising. For nearly a quarter-century, Slovak activists had been consecrating the Stars and Stripes in their rhetoric, and local promoters had made it intrinsic to Slovak activities. Both contemporary popular and ethnic thought ascribed a sacredness to the American flag, which endowed it with tremendous emotive power. On the eve of America's entry into the war, Willo embodied the commitment that would animate core activists and the sentiments that many Slovaks might be harboring.

The discomfort supporters of the Slovak state might have felt when war broke out in Europe was turned into anguish in late 1941. Defenders were confronted with the bitter reality that, when it came to foreign policy, at least, Slovakia did follow in lockstep behind Germany. On December 12, 1941, one day after Germany declared war on the United States, Slovakia followed suit.[48] Slovakia's action pulled the rug out from under the pro-Tiso faction in America. The Slovak League, which had been working to convince American policymakers to recognize the independent Slovak state and abandon the idea of restoring Czechoslovakia, was suddenly vulnerable to heightened criticism. In early 1942, a young female member of the National Slovak Society probably spoke for others when, rephrasing a venerable Slovak motto, she mocked the league's political activities on behalf of Slovakia. Instead of being proud, she declared, "I am ashamed that I am Slovak." She also recounted that she knew a woman who five years earlier had taken pride in her league membership but now was adamantly denying her former affiliation.[49] Of course, given the temper of the times, lobbyists for Slovakia could hardly have expected a widespread embrace by Slovak Americans. Even those who supported an independent Slovakia could not deny the logic—and, perhaps, even secretly shared the distress—of another distraught commentator. If Tiso had not cooperated with Hitler, Slovakia would have suffered the same fate as other countries that fell victim to

Nazi aggression, he acknowledged. However, he continued, at least in that case, Slovaks would be in the war on the side of the United States and its allies. Now Slovaks were dying for Germany, and the allied nations considered them enemies of democracy.[50]

Although the U.S. government dismissed Slovakia's declaration of war and did not categorize Slovaks as "enemy aliens," reports about the declaration mortified well-informed Slovak Americans. Both native- and foreign-born Slovaks felt the pain. A writer in *Národné noviny* put it plainly when he lamented that Slovakia's action "is quite funny to American citizens of other origins but not to citizens of Slovak origin. It is the greatest shame that we American Slovaks have experienced."[51] Expressing grassroots sentiment and leaving no doubt about their civic status or ethnic consciousness, lodge members in New Kensington, Pennsylvania, sent a letter to President Roosevelt. Identifying them- selves as "Americanized citizens of Slovak descent," they emphatically "reject[ed] the slander committed by the so-called Slovak government of Hitler's tyrants on everyone of Slovak blood when it declared war on our country." The message continued: "Americans of Slovak descent are determined to wipe this slander off the Slovak name by giving the utmost . . . labor . . . and sacrifice to the United States."[52]

The most immediate response by Slovak Americans to the war came in the form of resolutions. Although passions about the homeland had hardened into rigid divisions, in a display of harmony officials from Slo- vak societies and newspapers jointly composed memoranda affirming the unwavering loyalty of Slovak Americans to the nation and to an American victory. In the fall of 1942, the assembled representatives of fifty Slovak organizations signed a resolution proclaiming "in this crit- ical hour, . . . there can be but one call to every true American, to every disciple of democracy, and that is to consecrate everything . . . to the united war effort." The pronouncement, which was sent to President Roo- sevelt and both houses of Congress, further declared that the "societies and . . . cultural organizations of Americans of Slovak ancestry . . . pledge our whole-hearted and unconditional support of the President and the Congress . . . in their determination to protect the honor of America and its ideals of right . . . and . . . we dedicate our lives, our fortunes, our all to this great and holy cause." The Slovaks who attended the 1942 meet- ing were not satisfied with merely declaring their allegiance. They pledged action. After calling on "every member of . . . [Slovak] organi- zations, young and old, [to join] in this great war between the Forces of Freedom and the Forces of Slavery," the resolution ended with a promise that the delegates' organizations would continue to add to the $10 million in U.S. war bonds already "in their [collective] portfolios."[53]

Thus, even as antagonisms still festered, Slovak organizations banded together to support America's wartime mobilization. Sharing a joint objective, they wanted to project the respectable image that, collectively, people of Slovak birth and ancestry were good Americans. They were reiterating the twin themes of Slovak loyalty to America and American principles that had echoed through the literature and rhetoric since World War I. This and the Kensington, Pennsylvania, memorandum typified language that would be used in public discussions, formal statements, and publications by Slovak Americans throughout World War II.

These resolutions were in part preemptive strikes against potential nativist attacks. Despite a concern with worldwide issues, national officers and editors knew what ordinary Slovaks could encounter in their communities. They realized that highly charged patriotism could breed bigotry. Even before the United States entered the hostilities, Slovak organizations were readying for a possible onslaught of renewed superpatriotism. Warning of a potential resurgence of a "ku klux mentality," in August 1941, *Národné noviny* admonished Slovaks to "be 100 percent American . . . and public[ly] display that . . . [you] are good citizens and adherents of democracy."[54] A year earlier, the National Slovak Society's executive committee had passed a resolution requiring that, at every local assembly meeting, "be unfurled 'the stars and stripes,' the flag that stands for the priceless treasure America stands for."[55] In the English-language publication for its junior division, which consisted of second-generation children, the First Catholic Slovak Union warned, "Let's not do anything to be called foreigners."[56] The resurrection of "100 percent American," the World War I slogan that was no longer part of popular discourse, indicated that memories of that wartime experience and its aftermath lingered among Slovak Americans. Clearly, people worried that if a militant nationalism again gripped America, this time both native- and foreign-born Slovaks might be targeted.

Slovak activists were aware that popular opinion could influence policymakers, and they were equally cognizant of the volatility of the popular temper. Indeed, throughout the interwar era, they had monitored the national mood, especially in the 1930s when Congress made several unsuccessful attempts to pass legislation hostile to aliens. Reflecting contemporary intolerance for so-called un-American ideas, several of these failed bills targeted alleged subversives. Slovak organizations had vigorously lobbied against such legislative efforts. The

National Slovak Society had mounted campaigns calling on members to inform lawmakers about their opposition to proposed bills. In the climate of fear heightened by the European war, congressional diehards finally succeeded in enacting the Alien Registration Act in 1940. It was by no means the omnibus deportation bill that some xenophobes wanted, but in addition to criminalizing vaguely described "subversive" activity, it required all aliens age fourteen and older to register and be fingerprinted. Whether ordinary Slovaks knew about earlier efforts to enact anti-alien legislation in the 1930s is speculative, but the registration bill touched the lives of noncitizens as well as their families. The requirement that an individual—or, in the case of citizens, their nonnaturalized parents, relatives, or friends—actually go to register and be fingerprinted made them acutely aware of their precarious situation.[57]

The Alien Registration Act, with its implied hostility toward immigrants, was just one thing that may have evoked grim memories of the past. In some places, employers were apparently leaning toward reintroducing the World War I practice of discriminating against the foreign born, especially noncitizens. Immigrants who remembered the war years legitimately feared for their jobs. From the perspective of foreign-born persons, the temper of the day made demonstrating loyalty to the United States and American principles a wise move. Such apprehensions probably helped fuel the rise in naturalizations that occurred during the war years.[58] Patriotic actions, however, were not motivated by fear alone; sincerity moved people. For example, in all likelihood the New Kensington lodge members who openly declared their allegiance to America were articulating genuine sentiments; at the same time, they did not shy away from their ancestral heritage. Once the United States was at war, as they engaged in ethnically sponsored activities, first- and second-generation Slovaks contributed to the country's "Americans All" spirit.

Buying war bonds in Slovak-sponsored drives became a popular way for people of both native and foreign birth to support the war.[59] Faithful to their 1942 resolution, the various societies continued to purchase bonds, and they orchestrated campaigns to encourage their members to do the same. The Slovak League established a national committee to manage bond drives. Slovak Evangelical Union members were urged to obtain bonds because "we want to prove to the Government that we are doing things for our Country." National societies rewarded local members and lodges for their purchases by publishing their names in newspapers.[60] For their part, Slovak organizations received citations from official U.S. sources and even had accolades recorded in the *Con-*

gressional Record.[61] There was other symbolic but, certainly from an ethnic perspective, gratifying recognition. A $50,000 contribution by the Slovak Evangelical Union resulted in its president being made an honorary mayor of Pittsburgh. At the same ceremony, the president of the National Slovak Society was given a gold key to the city for his pledge of $150,000 on behalf of his organization.[62] Public acclaims singling out Slovak Americans for their patriotism and contributions to the war effort could not help but spawn additional support by Slovaks.

In addition to participating in nationwide efforts promoted by various Slovak organizations, Slovak Americans worked collectively on local bond drives. Many communities responded to the Treasury Department's program to promote sales among nationality groups. The Slovak War Bonds Committee in western Pennsylvania was a case in point. To make Slovaks part of a local multiethnic drive in 1942, the committee, chaired by a second-generation woman, established the "American Slovak Booth" in downtown Pittsburgh.[63] Advertising that "Slovaks" would get credit for the purchases, it launched a campaign calling on area Slovaks to buy bonds at that particular station.[64] Carrying out ethnically backed drives was not merely a big-city phenomenon. In the Third War Loan, which concluded in the fall of 1943, the Slovak community of Owosso, Michigan, invested $95,000; Slovaks in Endicott, New York, raised more than $175,000; those in the industrial town of Lansford, Pennsylvania, spent $430,000 on bonds. Communities elsewhere, large and small, displayed the same enthusiasm.[65] By January 1944, reports credited Slovak Americans with having purchased $30 million in war bonds. During just the Third War Loan campaign, more than $11 million was credited to them.[66] As time passed, financial support for the war effort escalated. In April 1944, western Pennsylvania's Slovak bonds committee reported sales of $3.5 million during the initial six months of the Fourth War Loan drive.[67] It is significant that, at the grassroots level, these bonds were purchased as part of campaigns carried out specifically among Slovak Americans. The millions of dollars' worth that they bought between 1942 and 1945 demonstrates that Slovak Americans were responsive to patriotic appeals linked to pride in ancestry.[68]

All this patriotic activity did not go unnoticed. Some local newspapers praised Slovak Americans for raising funds for the war.[69] Any favorable mention, especially in ethnically diverse regions, flattered the pride of the area's Slovak residents. The same "other nationalities" rivalry that had characterized Slovak undertakings and had been nurturing local activism since the early 1930s thus continued into wartime America. But throughout the war, gratification went beyond outdoing other ethnic groups, eliciting local accolades, or having names published in the ethnic press. The federal government rewarded, even promoted, this ethnically based activity.[70]

In recognition of contributions, the U.S. military subsequently named planes and naval vessels for prominent Slovak figures and communities. It did the same for other nationalities. Achieving such plaudits had been the objective of local Slovak bond drives. Organizers of Detroit's 1942 Slovak National Day advertised that money collected would be donated to the American Red Cross to procure an ambulance.[71] That same year, western Pennsylvania's Slovak bonds committee had resolved to sell enough bonds to purchase a bomber.[72] In the spring of 1943, as a tribute to Slovak Americans of western Pennsylvania for their bond subscriptions, *The American-Slovak*, a B-17, was dedicated. Better yet from the standpoint of enthusiasts promoting campaigns among Slovak Americans, a picture of the plane with its name prominently visible adorned the cover of *The Minute Man*, the newsletter of the Treasury Department's War Savings Staff (Illustration 7).[73] In 1944, Slovaks of northern Ohio received recognition when a plane was christened *The Greater Cleveland Slovaks*.[74] Other communities merited similar acknowledgment. The names *Slovaks of Wisconsin, Scranton Anthracite American Slovaks*, and *Slovaks of New York State* graced the sides of bombers. The Slovaks of Trenton, New Jersey, raised sufficient funds to have an ambulance airplane dedicated in their honor. And the Slovak League contributed enough money so that in May 1943 the Department of War credited it with having paid for three trainer planes. Eleanor Roosevelt surely delighted Slovak Americans when she mentioned that fact in one of her "My Day" columns.[75] The government also named four liberty ships after individuals who were probably obscure to American government officials but prominent in the eyes of zealous Slovak Americans. Three were Slovak immigrants, including Matthew Kocak, a U.S. Marine who had received both an Army and a Navy Medal of Honor in World War I. As another tribute to Slovak Americans for their contributions to the war effort, the military honored a sailor of Slovak descent, Jozef Durik, for heroics that cost him his life in March 1942. In 1943 the navy launched the USS *Durik*, a destroyer escort.[76]

Rewarding Slovak contributions by naming equipment for Slovak personages or communities was part of the government's ethnic-mobilization campaign, but, government-sponsored patriotism notwithstanding, people responded to ethnic appeals. Slovak publications car-

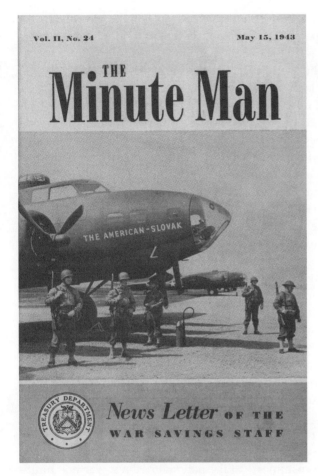

ILLUSTRATION 7.
The Minute Man,
15 May 1943.

ried claims that, by contributing to their own bond drives, Slovak Americans had actually bought these various planes and ships for the U.S. military. In addition, by investing in war bonds, Slovak Americans could take credit for financing the purchases of hospital beds, surgical equipment, and ambulances.[77] Slovak Americans, together with other nationality groups who sponsored drives, discovered that "Americans All" meant they could manifest patriotism by featuring their ethnicity. The quest for unity thus did not make ethnicity unacceptable as a basis for group action in wartime America; rather, stirring ethnic sentiments became one ploy government officials used to advance wartime mobilization.[78] It is significant that, despite government sponsorship, people were not subjected to the same heavy-handed pressure that had characterized World War I bond purchases. Hence, even though the bond campaigns perpetuated the notion that individuals could somehow purchase the right to be called patriotic Americans, voluntary participation fueled the World War II ethnic bond drives.

The success of local campaigns to raise money specifically to have ships, planes, and other vehicles named for Slovak communities suggests that friendly rivalries helped nurture these territorially based campaigns. Even if they did not openly compete with Slovaks elsewhere, the efforts reflected the same copycat phenomenon evident in the Slovak Day publicity and in the athletic competitions of the 1930s. Through the web of fraternal organizations, local institutions, and ethnic and American media, residents of one area were aware of what Slovak Americans in other places were doing. They continued to imitate or draw inspiration from their actions. Additionally, the boasting about the contributions of "Slovak Americans" reflected the same "other nationalities" theme that had helped nourish Slovak activism for the past decade. It was an activism, though, that was relying more and more on the second generation to sustain it.

Slovak women were particularly active in promoting ethnically oriented bond sales, especially at the local level. Visual evidence suggests that this was true not only for Slovaks but for other ethnic groups as well. Pictorial records in particular show that women were the most likely to don folk costumes to ensure that their nationalities were clearly represented in multiethnic bond campaigns. On one occasion, the War Savings Staff reported that "one of the many effective devices used to attract attention to the booth was to staff it with women of foreign origin in their native costumes."[79] Like nationality days, wartime multicultural undertakings became occasions when sporting traditional folk attire was acceptable. The distinctive festive garb set ethnic groups apart. In Pittsburgh, women, some dressed in ancestral apparel, staffed separate nationality booths intended to attract persons of particular ethnic backgrounds. Sometimes working with local clergymen, women also helped coordinate bond drives in Slovak communities and at Slovak Days held during the war.[80]

Slovak women played a prominent role in local bond campaigns in part because military service siphoned off the young male cohort. Similar to the general situation in society, this left women with the task of supporting the home-front efforts. However, the participation by Slovak women—and, more particularly, the second generation—in ethnic ventures reflected what had evolved into standard practice. During the 1930s, young women helped encourage involvement in nationality days. Even with lodge sponsorship, the popularity or queen contests depended on young women and teenage girls working to convince fellow Slovaks to support an ethnic event.

For women, then, vending in the community for a "Slovak" cause and participating in Slovak undertakings were hardly novel experiences. Rather than growing out of wartime imperatives, such activities represented a forged tradition. It was certainly a tradition for Margaret Kuzma, the woman who chaired Pittsburgh's Slovak American Bonds Committee. A second-generation Slovak, Kuzma had been involved in local parish and fraternal activities in Munhall, Pennsylvania, since childhood. When she was old enough, she transferred to the Senior Order of the First Catholic Slovak Ladies Union, and when she was elected to its Supreme Court in 1923, she became the first former Junior Order member ever to hold a national office in the Ladies Union. In the late 1930s, Kuzma served on the local arrangements committee for Slovak Days in western Pennsylvania. It seemed natural that, when the campaign to sell war bonds adopted a combined ethnic and patriotic objective, this long-time Slovak activist would press into the effort. Chairing the local Slovak War Bonds Committee, Kuzma helped organize Pittsburgh's Slovak booth and also conducted a bond campaign among Slovaks in her own small community. Seeing to it that Slovak events blended ethnic and patriotic objectives, she helped coordinate bond sales at Slovak Days in western Pennsylvania.[81] Unlike Kuzma, few Slovak women had attained national prominence in a mutual benefit society, but they had witnessed the tradition of female activism in their communities. The nationwide mobilization, which urged all women to do their part for the war effort, further encouraged Slovak women to become involved in bond drives. For these second-generation Slovaks, ethnicity and Americanism became mutually reinforcing impulses, and they worked to stir corresponding sentiments among fellow Slovak Americans.[82]

Historical records are exasperatingly silent about why individuals invested their hard-earned money in endeavors credited specifically to "Slovak Americans." Faint whispers suggesting a mix of motives, however, can be detected. Some Slovak Americans bought war bonds as a way to save money and rebuild financial security that had been devastated by the Great Depression. People embarrassed by Slovakia's declaration of war on the United States were moved by a desire to erase the stigma and thus do their part to demonstrate that Slovaks were loyal Americans. Those proud of their ancestry sincerely wanted to participate in efforts reflecting well on their ethnic group. There was also a touch of ethnic competition, especially in local communities where rivalries with "other nationalities" existed and had helped nourish Slovak activism.[83] The politically astute hoped that such contributions would translate into Slovak political power. At the same time, community or family pressures probably caused some otherwise disinclined individuals to participate in efforts identified as "Slovak." Finally, heartfelt patriotism, combined with a Slovak consciousness, prompted people to take part in ethnic campaigns.

The historical record is also silent about the demographic characteristics of people who responded to the ethnic bond drives.[84] Based on the sales credited to Slovak Americans, though, thousands of individuals did participate. Narrative accounts reveal that both native- and foreign-born people purchased bonds in the Slovak campaigns. In addition, the large number of sales, together with the generational makeup of the Slovak population in the United States, justifies the conclusion that the campaigns had to marshal the American-born children of immigrants—truly persons of Slovak descent. A significant segment of second-generation Slovaks in local communities thus accepted the message that there was no inherent conflict between being American and acknowledging their ancestral roots.

Ironically, amid all the ethnic activity—and, indeed, despite it—the war had a stronger detrimental impact on Slovak organizations than the Great Depression had had. During the last years of the 1930s, the major Slovak mutual benefit societies had actually experienced modest upswings in their senior lodge memberships. Seemingly, people were not as disillusioned with fraternal organizations as observers have often asserted; instead, with the return of good times, former members were apparently coming back.[85] The junior branches, though, did not enjoy similar increases. This was probably due both to a lack of interest and to age restrictions that typically forced persons older than sixteen to join senior lodges. Regardless, by 1939 it was evident that, while adversely affected and perhaps even weakened, Slovak fraternal organizations had survived the Depression of the 1930s.

For ethnic institutions, the onset of war posed fresh threats that required renewed activism by ordinary members. Even before the United States went to war, Slovak activists were becoming aware of their predicament. In the fall of 1940, a columnist for *Národné noviny*'s sports page wondered whether the imposition of the national draft would weigh negatively on fraternal athletic programs. Although in some organizations the number of teams had declined slightly, clubs had continued playing games and vying for tournament bids.[86] However, an announcement in November 1941 by Lutherans in Hazleton, Pennsylvania, that they were losing the young man who had managed sports activities in their area reflected what would soon be happening elsewhere. Admitting that the departure of this second-generation youth would create a keenly felt vacancy, people were nevertheless proud of him. By going into the army, he had adopted "the attitude of a good American citizen" and reportedly stated that he would "serve my country to the best of my ability."[87]

The outbreak of war had an immediate adverse effect on Slovak sports activities. Registration for the upcoming summer 1942 tournament was low because "most of our finest athletes . . . [are] in the services of Uncle Sam," one reporter concluded. A local official in Detroit described the general situation when he explained that "most of our young men are being drafted and others are working all odd hours."[88] Commentators were not complaining. Indeed, they took pains to clarify that they were merely pointing out the realities affecting Slovak activities in their communities. In addition, travel restrictions due to the war made it harder to schedule or attend games.[89] As a consequence, by the summer of 1942 sports coverage in fraternal newspapers had decreased significantly. The midsummer editions of *Národné noviny*, for example, needed just a portion of a single page for sports news. Some fall issues carried only brief sports items that more clearly resembled fillers than reports.

Losing young members to military service wreaked havoc on athletic programs and created mixed emotions among fraternal leaders. On one hand, enthusiasts regretted the damage to ethnic organizations, but on the other, they gushed at the fact that Slovak Americans were performing their civic duty. When mentioning members who were in military service, commentators throughout the war often resorted to the language of yeasty patriotism. The Slovak media, especially institutional publications, carried pictures and printed information about members who were in the military.[90] From an ethnic perspective, pictures of men in uniform represented "Slovak Americans'" patriotism and contributions to the war effort.

Pride and collective benefits notwithstanding, activists were concerned that members in the service might lose interest in ethnic institutions back home. Early on, therefore, organizations developed plans to swamp them with reminders. The National Slovak Society sent small gifts to servicemen. The *Národné noviny* column "Letters from our Members Serving our Country," which first appeared in mid-August 1942, published messages expressing thanks to their fraternal brothers and sisters for the presents and for remembering them.[91] From the perspective of Slovak fraternal officials, printing these letters had a three-fold purpose. First, from a practical standpoint, fraternal officers hoped to keep the young men attached to their organization while they were away. Second, they thought that publishing letters from members in the service might enliven interest in the organization. Finally, these communications from fellow Slovaks fighting in the war might inspire men and women left behind to support Slovak-sponsored efforts on the home front.

Slovak Evangelical Union officers took the idea of maintaining contact with servicemen a step further by trying to turn a fraternal activity into a patriotic duty. Concerned about the lack of articles for *Slovenský hlásnik*'s English page and fearful that people were becoming preoccupied with other pursuits, in the spring of 1942 officers inaugurated a pen-pal program. Dubbed "Adopt an SEU Yank," the plan was to recruit civilian members to send letters to servicemen. This program was aimed as much at young people remaining at home as those who went off to serve. Officers hoped that promoting communication with members in the military might keep individuals faithful to the Slovak Evangelical Union. Those masterminding the project reasoned that such personal interaction would make young people at home "sufficiently concerned" to stay in the union while "our boys are over there giving their all."[92] Thus, promoters gave fraternal membership a new twist by linking it to support for the war effort. As the plan evolved, its architects cleverly called it the "Keep 'em Happy Club" and advertised the program as a patriotic venture. Correspondents on the home front could help keep up morale. "Bear in mind," one notice proclaimed, that "every time you write to a soldier boy and send him a little gift, you're doing your part to help AMERICA." To excite interest, the designers turned the plan into a contest and encouraged lodges to establish their own chapter of the "Keep 'em Happy Club." Each local should adopt a name. Leaving little doubt that they expected most participants would be female, promoters offered "Hazleton Honies" and "Sharon Sweeties" as examples of the kind of possibilities clubs might consider.[93]

Whether any local chapters actually chose such fatuous, gender-imbued names is uncertain, but young women did heed the call to participate in the pen-pal program. In fact, the idea apparently enjoyed an enthusiastic response. A national officer facilitated the project by providing addresses of Slovak Evangelical Union members in the military. He also occasionally sent bundled letters to men in the service. Through the summer and early fall of 1942, items related to the "Keep 'em Happy Club" and letters from "Yanks" replaced *Slovenský hlásnik*'s sports section, which had essentially withered away.

Within six months after it began, the correspondence program came to a halt because of unanticipated obstacles. Fearing that enemy agents could infiltrate pen-pal clubs and obtain information from unsuspecting soldiers, by the fall of 1942 the War Department was discouraging military personnel from writing to strangers. Although it acknowledged the validity of the government's concern, the Slovak Evangelical Union's leadership was nevertheless disappointed. One commentator openly questioned whether members of a fraternal organization were truly "strangers" to one another. For a short time after *Slovenský hlásnik* reported the War Department's objections, union members displayed an ongoing interest in the club and continued to request soldiers' addresses. By January 1943, however, the fraternal organization had bowed to the War Department's wishes and abandoned the program.[94] Some members nevertheless probably kept corresponding with servicemen they had contacted before the union did away with the "Keep 'em Happy Club." Although this attempt to turn participating in a fraternal project into a patriotic act was short-lived, young Slovak women and teenage girls, who probably made up the majority of those who belonged to the club, did respond. It was a snag created by extraneous circumstances that wrecked this activism grounded in a combined ethnic and patriotic appeal.

RETURNING AFTER military service, Chuck Bednarik, a second-generation Slovak and soon-to-be football star, found that the war had not changed what he described as the "ethnic neighborhood system" in Bethlehem, Pennsylvania. This small industrial town still boasted the same melange of nationality sports clubs, which would continue competing with one another into the next decade.[95] Margaret Kuzma would not have been surprised by Bednarik's observation, since her particular involvement in America's united war effort had actually relied on the country's persistent ethnic diversity. While Kuzma worked at the community level, John Willo had tried to heighten ethnic consciousness by keeping up rhetoric that emphasized a fundamental harmony between Slovak ethnicity and Americanism.

John Willo and Margaret Kuzma were not unique. There were significant numbers of second-generation Slovaks who neither rejected their ancestral heritage nor were indifferent toward it. They belonged instead to that core of national and local activists who willingly devoted energy to rouse fellow Slovaks, of foreign and native birth, to ethnic causes. For these people, World War II was indeed a "moment" to feel "fully accepted as Americans." It must be understood that "Slovak Americans" as well as other nationalities realized this "historic moment" by emphasizing their ethnicity.[96] Indeed, Slovaks and other new immigrants had been readying for such a moment for more than two decades. Their participation as ethnic groups in home-front efforts such as the bond campaigns and in the "I Am an American" days was indebted to the activism that had flowed through the interwar era. These activities represented a continuation in a heightened, more visible form of what ethnic enthusiasts had been doing for a quarter-century.

It seems that the strategy of the 1930s to make youths loyal Americans, proud of their ancestry, paid dividends. During World War II, Slovak activists of all political and religious persuasions joined hands to demonstrate their American patriotism by highlighting their ethnic identity. It is significant that ethnically based wartime activities were not grounded in the same coercion that had characterized the Great War; instead, the second-generation individuals who chose to engage in these undertakings did so voluntarily. It is also important to remember that, unlike foreign-speaking individuals of the World War I era, the second generation who faced World War II could have much more easily hidden their ethnic roots and blended into the amorphous "American" identity. Some new immigrant Americans did choose that path; others did not.

The Slovak experience demonstrated that patriotic ideology was a powerful stimulant for ethnic activism. This ideology permeated the declarations of loyalty to America, spirited the ethnically driven bond campaigns, and rationalized attempts to transform fraternal activities into support for the war effort. In all these instances, promoters saw a reciprocal relationship between the country's national interests and their own ethnic interests. While it is certainly true that ethnocentrism had no acceptable place in wartime America, the activities of Americans of Slovak descent indicate that ethnic cohesion did have its place.[97] Indeed, the benign rivalries with "others," which immigrants and the younger element perceived in terms of nationality, actually nurtured ethnic activism. The multiethnic character of community-level bond drives suggests that the ongoing competition with "other nationalities" blended with public-spirited rhetoric to nurture patriotically based ethnic actions. What would happen to ethnic impulses in the postwar era as persons of new immigrant descent joined other "Americans" in the ideological battles of the Cold War is another chapter in the history of the country's ethnic groups. But during World War II, people of Slovak ancestry, as well as those of other descents, could be—and were—both proud ethnics and patriotic Americans.

Conclusion
Persistent Issues and New Perceptions

FOLLOWING WORLD WAR II, most Slovaks—as well as other nationalities, both foreign and native born—returned to their everyday lives. Even if they did not pursue illustrious professional football careers, some took the same course as Chuck Bednarik and left their hometowns. Bednarik's leaving did not entail severing ties with his community or rejecting his ancestral heritage. "There's no question in my mind," he later wrote, "that I'm primarily an American, but I'm a Slovak too, and I always will be." This second-generation American remained a loyal member of his Slovak fraternal organization. Every year, when he visited Bethlehem, he went to the Slovak Hall to pay his dues.[1] Another second-generation Slovak who also left the community in which he had grown up revealed a similar attachment to his ethnic roots. Commenting on his popular novel *Out of This Furnace*, Thomas Bell explained in a 1946 interview that he wrote the book about "his people" because he "wanted to tell the world that Slovaks with their blood and lives helped to build America. . . . It was also my aim to strengthen in the Slovaks their pride of their origin."[2] Bell let Dobie, a second-generation Slovak, sum up his views on ethnicity and Americanism. Reflecting on the diversity of union organizers as well as his own identity, Dobie proclaimed, "[If] anything I'm an American." What made one an American "wasn't where you were born or how you spelled your name or where your father had come from. It was the way you thought and felt about certain things. About freedom of speech and the equality of men."[3] Other people did what Margaret Kuzma did: she stayed in her small town and continued to work on behalf of Slovak interests and institutions in her area. And, of course, there was the contingent that followed John Willo's course and remained involved in national fraternal organizations, where they kept promoting group survival.[4] The life experience of these second-generation Slovaks varied, but they all reflected a common belief that being "American" was not at odds with pride in ancestry. They represented the ethnic pride and patriotism that had been cultivated in interwar America.

The picture that emerges from the interwar era is that new immigrants and their children sought to assert a presence in America's culturally diverse society and that ethnicity remained a relevant part of their lives. For some, ethnicity was expressed in a strident dedication to group survival. For others, ethnicity was grounded in torpid sentiments that were ordinarily irrelevant. And there is, of course, evidence that some American-born youths were estranged from their ancestral roots and sought to ignore their ethnic origin. To be sure, new immigrants as well as their offspring asserted their ethnicity in different ways, to different degrees, and at different times. Still, regardless of whether they engaged in lobbying for the homeland, joined sports teams, participated in nationality days, or put pen to paper to voice an opinion about a language-related issue, they were to some extent thinking about and acknowledging their ethnic identity. How accurately articulate activists at the national or local level expressed sentiments felt by their broader ethnic populations is beyond the historian's ability to determine with any degree of certainty. Taken together, however, words and deeds do show that there were people who were solidly committed to perpetuating ethnic identities in America's culturally diverse society while others harbored feelings that, when the situation presented itself, were vulnerable to ethnic appeals. What motivated new immigrant activists in particular during the era spanning the two world wars also defies easy explanation. Their commitment sprang from a variety of sources, ranging from self-interest to the philosophical to the pragmatic. In some instances, a blend of all three factors was at work.

A close investigation of the period reveals the ongoing emotional power of the "Old Country."[5] In the aftermath of World War I and the onset of World War II, we can see the capacity of what was for immigrants their native land and for the American born their ancestral homeland to spark passions. However, during the interwar era, ethnic activists, while not forgetting about the homeland, focused on group survival in the face of acute pressure to Americanize. Trying to perpetuate an ethnic consciousness, Slovaks as well as other new immigrants did not reject Americanization outright. They wanted instead to demonstrate that it had happened, but within parameters they had laid down. For many, Americanization was an odious concept *only* when it took the form of cultural aggression and debased ancestral pride. It was welcomed when it meant adherence to democratic ideals, which in their purest expression entailed tolerance and thus sanctioned pride in ancestry.

While Old World issues could ignite rank-and-file responses, at the local level ethnic activists in the main spent their energy trying to ensure a group presence in their communities. Haunted by the dual stigmas of being labeled "undesirable" and "inferior," they also sought respectability. Among the ways Slovaks worked to achieve these goals was to sponsor nationality days. Attuned to local circumstances, community activists resorted to appeals they believed would strike a responsive chord among fellow cohabitants. It was competition with "other nationalities" that they used the most. Throughout the 1930s, "showing other nationalities" and demonstrating that Slovaks merited respect were incessant themes woven into the rhetoric. Booster literature laced with references to "other nationalities" suggests that, in the local arena, rivalries helped nurture ethnic activism. The theme permeated publicity for Slovak Days, athletic teams, and later, collective wartime activities. This persistent usage reveals how first- and second-generation persons were coping with their multiethnic world. The lack of specificity that characterized the "others" motif is significant because it shows the universality of the situation. Regardless of where they lived, Slovaks as well as other ethnic groups competed with cultural minorities who were engaging in similar activities in the communities. At times, the competition could be bitter, and at times, benign.[6]

Community-level activities were influenced in part by personal experiences, lingering memories, and the everyday realities faced by ordinary immigrants. Depending on the times, the "others" that they were trying in some way to impress could embrace a wide range of people: employers, politicians, leery supernationalists, xenophobes, or even sympathetic supporters. Aware of the hostility toward new immigrants, local activists were moved in part by a desire to demonstrate the fundamental Americanism of both the foreign and the native born. Impressing others, however, also included forging an image that the second generation—the Americanized "younger element"—could identify with. National and local activists alike wanted to convince young people there was a basic compatibility between being American and maintaining pride in ancestry.

During the decades between the two world wars, America's nationalities thus employed an array of ethnically based activities to demonstrate that they were "American." The ongoing use of patriotic displays, a tradition that grew out of the World War I experience, reflected the world they lived in and yet became a strategy to attract youths by convincing them that ethnic activities were also inherently American. Slovaks in particular touted American historical figures as embodying principles that Slovaks in America championed or values that were supposedly at the core of the "Slovak" character. Their organizations even printed biographies of notable Americans in their publications to demonstrate their pride in their "adopted country" and to stress links between Slovak and American ideals. There is no evidence that Slovaks embraced American personages because they yearned for "'Nordic' ancestors" or, in the 1930s, saw Franklin Roosevelt as a "'Nordic father.'"[7] In fact, in the interwar era, the opposite occurred: the goal was to foster ethnic pride by fighting the "Nordic" ideal and the "superiority" label attached to this racial designation, not to legitimize it.

Ethnic groups did promote popular features of modern American culture such as sports, beauty pageants, modern dancing, and contemporary music. But they did this to accommodate young people and advance ethnic objectives. Obliging Americanized youths ultimately meant that rigid adherence to language retention as the benchmark of ethnicity had to give way to another criterion, one rooted in maintaining pride in ancestry. Differing attitudes toward language retention demonstrated that neither the first nor the second generation was monolithic in its makeup or attitudes. When it came to the sticky question of cultural preservation, it was not simply a matter of the children preferring to forget what parents wanted to remember. Foreign-born Slovaks were not unified on questions of language maintenance, and, equally significant, there were profound differences *within* the second generation. In addition, a sense of fair play not withstanding, the regard so poignantly uttered by young fraternalists for "old-timers" as they confronted the Great Depression together reflected an underlying respect for immigrants, and especially for their long-time devotion to Slovak organizations. The economic crisis of the 1930s exposed overlapping first- and second-generation concerns, while the drive for social-insurance legislation reflected the intertwining of intergenerational, class, and ethnic interests.

The fact that native-born youths openly became involved in ethnic activities and voluntarily allied themselves with ethnic institutions offers testimony to some success in inculcating a consciousness. The support by the American born for ethnically based patriotic activities during World War II is evidence that assimilation did not occur in linear fashion along generational lines. Moreover, as pride in ethnic ancestry became a legitimate sentiment, it seems that, for the second generation, the artifacts, dress, and symbols of ancestral cultures became quaint, nostalgic, and acceptable for display in particular circumstances. This was an attitude that clearly endured among nationality groups into World War II.

Placed within the context of the previous quarter-century, wartime ethnic activism was not shaped in the vortex of a national crisis. It was the culmination of what Slovaks and other nationalities had been striving for since World War I. For ethnic groups that had been trying to negotiate a place in America's heterogeneous society, World War II thus did not trigger a commitment to the ideological component of the American identity. In one way or another, ethnic activists had long been promoting its ideological dimensions and the idea that being American was grounded in principles. This concept of the national identity allowed ethnic pride and American patriotism to go hand in hand.[8]

Over the past decade, scholars investigating race, its complexities, and its complex influence on American history and culture have added yet another dimension to perceptions of the early twentieth century's new immigrants. Pointing to race as a social construction, the literature has gone a long way toward reminding us that contemporaries viewed new immigrants as "racial" groups. And, it is argued, racial attitudes among *whites* in America caused them to perceive new immigrants as "less than white."[9] Indeed, on America's racial scale, these newcomers and their offspring were placed between old-stock Nordics and persons categorized as "colored races" and thus were "inbetween peoples." Within this context, the immigrant and second-generation saga became a conscious pursuit, a search—indeed, a quest—to become white or Caucasian.[10] When trying to discern the salience of "whiteness," the issue must be as much about how new immigrants allegedly perceived themselves as how others perceived them.

Looking at contemporary society from a new immigrant perspective shows that their pre- and postmigration experiences reinforced a disposition to view themselves and their world through the lens of cultural diversity. Most Slavic peoples had come from heterogeneous lands and primarily from the Austro-Hungarian Empire, where they had been ruled by and could have lived with "other nationalities." Encountering in America an even greater range of diversity based on language and culture than they had known in their homelands reinforced this "nationalities" perspective. At the same time, there was precious little in their experience in the United States to make these Slavs doubt that they belonged to the "white" race. On the contrary, during the World War I era, their "whiteness" was reconfirmed by those who insisted that they could be Americanized. For all its cultural repression, the Americanization movement, even at its worst, held firm to the underlying premise that, like other white groups, new immigrants should—and, indeed, must—become citizens.[11] In addition, from the standpoint of new immigrants, arguments surrounding immigration laws in the early 1920s were framed within the context of nationalities. Even suppositions about Nordic superiority were set within the context of Germans, English-speaking peoples, and immigrants from northern Europe versus those from the southern and eastern regions. The battle over national origins was about a racial hierarchy, but this was a two-tiered system of superior versus inferior, desirable versus undesirable. From where new immigrants stood, there was nothing "inbetween" about the stakes they were fighting over.[12]

The racial aspects of the new immigrant saga, which have so captivated modern scholars, cannot negate the fact that, even if immigrants accepted the notion that their place on America's social scale was biologically derived, they viewed their ascribed inferiority as one tethered to their national origins. The ignominious slurs; the allegations of mental, biological, and cultural inferiority; and the assertions about their fundamental undesirability as Americans were all framed within the context of nationality. Superiority was based on the same yardstick. These criteria—geographic origin, language, or culture—fit both the definition and the language of ethnicity. No amount of scholarly finessing can alter the reality that, from the new immigrants' perspective, it was their nationality, not their ranking on a variegated color line, that was the root of their debasement and made them different from others. They were not trying to divert the topic from "whiteness to nationality and loyalty to American ideals." When they talked about "races," new immigrants *did* mean nationalities.[13]

Also, the perennial struggle to prevent the estrangement of the "younger element" was rooted in the fact that, once they spoke English, they could easily fit into—no, easily become lost in—American society. To prevent this from happening, new immigrants realized they had to fight a culturally derived insult, one that the second generation clearly saw as well. When thinking about their identity and place in American society, they did not conceptualize issues in terms of "whiteness"; they thought in terms of nationalities or, in more modern terminology, ethnicity. In the interwar era, for new immigrants and their children "becoming Caucasian" was a nonissue because in their minds they already were white.[14] Their struggle was taking place on the battlefield of ethnic diversity.

The literature on race and "whiteness" has indeed refined our understanding of American history and reminded us of the weaknesses of single approaches to complicated issues. However, the Slovak experience suggests that turning nationality-based epithets, contempt, and antipathies into a questioning of individual or group "whiteness" can distort the types of discrimination that the new immigrant generations coped with.[15] Commentators seemingly determined to run away as quickly as possible from ethnicity as an interpretive framework are, in their haste, adopting a course too narrow for the path they are trying to blaze. Failing to deal with racial attitudes and "whiteness" from the perspective of the new immigrants and their progeny risks stopping short of grasping the impact that ethnicity, based on descent, *as well as* race, characterized by physical markers, has had on American society, and why appeals to both work.

Despite distinctions based on ethnicity, a cultural characteristic that new immigrant generations shared with other "Americans" was a penchant for flag-waving and public displays of patriotism. This affinity for patriotic manifestations, which, one can credibly argue, has become part and parcel of American culture, stems to a degree from the interrelated experiences between the native and the foreign born. Since at least World War I, immigrants have used collective public avowals to salve the concerns of Americans who were ever suspect of foreigners in their midst. During that war, coercion, political aims, and heartfelt feelings motivated exhibitions of loyalty. In succeeding decades, what was a wartime necessity became a peacetime custom, especially as ethnic groups tried to use public displays to show others, including their own American-born offspring, that pride in ancestry and being American went hand in hand. During the era spanning the world wars, then, both old-stock Americans and new immigrants mutually nurtured a fondness for patriotic manifestations. This was an ethnic impulse that became more than a cultural tradition, it became "American."

Abbreviations

ORGANIZATIONS AND INSTITUTIONS

FCSU	First Catholic Slovak Union
IHRC	Immigration History Research Center, University of Minnesota
LPSCU	Ladies Pennsylvania Slovak Catholic Union
NSS	National Slovak Society
SCS	Slovak Catholic Sokol
SELU	Slovak Evangelical Ladies Union
SEU	Slovak Evangelical Union
SLA	Slovak League of America

COLLECTIONS

EFOHP	Ethnic Fraternal Organizations Oral History Project, Archives of Industrial Society, University of Pittsburgh
FCSU Records	First Catholic Slovak Union Records, IHRC
LPSCU Records	Ladies Pennsylvania Slovak Catholic Union Records, Balch Institute for Ethnic Studies, Philadelphia
NSS Records	National Slovak Society Records, IHRC
Podkrivacky Papers	Adam Podkrivacky Papers, IHRC

PUBLICATIONS

AHR	*American Historical Review*
IAR	*Immigrants in America Review*
JAEH	*Journal of American Ethnic History*
JAH	*Journal of American History*

KJ	*Kalendár Jednota* (FCSU)
KM	*Kruh mládeže* (NSS)
KŽ	*Kalendár živeny* (Živena)
NK	*Národný kalendár* (NSS)
NN	*Národné noviny* (NSS)
NYT	*New York Times*
SH	*Slovenský hlásnik* (SEU)
SvA	*Slovák v Amerike*

Bibliographical Note

I AM BEHOLDEN to many scholars for their research on topics covered in this book, and this debt to English- and foreign-language secondary sources is acknowledged in each chapter's endnotes, which follow this section. My purpose here is briefly to describe the primary sources that proved most valuable for gaining a new immigrant, or "inside," perspective of interwar America.

English-language sources helped establish the context for developing an immigrant perspective on World War I and the immediate postwar era. Among these sources were *Immigrants in America Review*, published papers and addresses of Woodrow Wilson, speeches and commentary by Theodore Roosevelt, the report by the Committee on Public Information, the proceedings of the 1919 Americanization Conference, and U.S. Bureau of the Census publications. Newspaper accounts of wartime parades and postwar anti-Klan activities, as well as anti-immigrant articles in the early 1920s popular media, were also illuminating.

The "inside" perspective comes from materials generated by Slovaks and, to a lesser extent, other ethnic groups. For national and international activities, the most significant sources were editorials, news reports, feature articles, resolutions, memoranda, and communications sent to members of government. Some late 1930s and World War II materials were in manuscript collections, but many were published in Slovak newspapers and sometimes were reprinted in more than one. For local activities, letters to the editor and community-event letters written by local people were invaluable. With each newspaper publishing items from local people, hundreds of submissions could appear every year. The range of topics seemed endless as writers debated political and fraternal matters, commented on feature materials, or reported on community activities.

This treasure trove of local information and opinion is complemented by a cache of materials on Slovak Days. Newspapers were culled for anything dealing with a Slovak Day. The varied items included notices about planning meetings, pre-event publicity, contest promotions, detailed programs, committee reports, financial reports, and firsthand accounts by both organizers and participants. A similar methodology was followed for local athletic activities, especially those prior to the creation of coordinated programs by national organizations. For Slovak Days and early athletic programs, newspapers in effect constitute an archive because they are usually the only recorded sources for these activities. The same is true for local activities and most national lobbying efforts for social insurance during the Depression. Youth pages, especially the English-language sections, which were printed either as monthly supplements or as separate publications, are sources of "young" people's opinions, interests, and activities.

Due to availability, the dates examined varied, but for the period circa 1914–1942, the major organizational newspapers studied were *Dennica* (Živena), *Jednota* (First Catholic Slovak Union) *Národné noviny* (National Slovak Society), and *Slovenský hlásnik* (Slovak Evangelical Union). All these papers eventually established English-language pages; two had youth supplements: *Jaro* (First Catholic Slovak Union) and *Kruh mládeže* (National Slovak Society). Some mention should be made of the difference between the fraternal press and nonaffiliated newspapers, specifically the *Slovák v Amerike* and *Slovenská obraná*. Trying to be foreign-language equivalents of American newspapers, nonaffiliated newspapers had correspondence from readers and included some information about local communities but usually carried more national and international news. *Slovenská obraná* was generally more interested in European, especially homeland, affairs. Organizational papers, which went to all members throughout the country, carried extensive commentary from, as well as about, local communities.

Organizational almanacs and numerous other publications, which are cited in footnotes but are far too numerous and diverse to list here, were also important. Some appeared annually, others were sporadic, and some were short-lived. They yielded sometimes vastly different information. Almanacs carried wide-ranging feature stories on Slovak history and personages; American history and heroic figures; and a host of other topics, including youths and Americanization. Anniversary histories had historical data and chronicled the organizations' and many of their local branches' pasts. The chief organizational publications, whose titles could vary, consulted were *Národný kalendár* (NSS), *Kalendár Jednota* (FCSU), *Kalendár S.E.J.* (SEU), *Sborník Slovenského Katolíckeho Sokola* (SCS), and *Furdek* (Association of Slovak Catholic Students). Most issues of these publications and of the Slovak newspapers are available at IHRC, which also has materials on non-Slovak nationality days. A few scattered publications and newspaper issues are in the author's possession.

Manuscript collections were also vital. Interviews in the Ethnic Fraternal Organizations Oral History Project (University of Pittsburgh, 1975–1977), housed in the Archives of Industrial Society, were not as useful as I had hoped. More helpful manuscript collections included the Ladies Pennsylvania Slovak Catholic Union Records at the Balch Institute for Ethnic Studies in Philadelphia. They comprise primarily administrative, financial, and membership data; however, the minutes of conventions, executive meetings, and financial committee meetings refer to members' problems and appeals during the 1930s. Two collections—the National Slovak Society Records and the First Catholic Slovak Union Records, housed at the IHRC—were invaluable. Both collections contain bylaws and routine administrative, financial, and membership data. The FCSU Records have material on the organization's athletic programs. Both collections include some resolutions and memoranda, especially from the late 1930s into the 1940s. The NSS Records have files on lobbying efforts against anti-alien legislation during the 1930s. In addition to reports on indigent funds, both collections contain invaluable correspondence and petitions from members and lodge officers during the Great Depression. The Adam Podkrivacky Papers, records of a former FCSU president (also at the IHRC), have correspondence from members seeking assistance in the 1930s, membership data, and various publications.

Notes

PREFACE AND ACKNOWLEDGMENTS

1. Moses Rischin, "Just Call Me John: Ethnicity as *Mentalité*," in *American Immigrants and Their Generations: Studies and Commentaries on the Hansen Thesis after Fifty Years*, ed. Peter Kivisto and Dag Blanck (Urbana: University of Illinois Press, 1990), 78.

INTRODUCTION

1. U.S. Department of Commerce, Bureau of the Census, *Abstract of the Fourteenth Census of the United States 1920* (Washington, D.C., 1923), 74 (hereafter, *Fourteenth Census: Abstract*).

2. Derived from U.S. Department of Commerce, Bureau of the Census, *Immigrants and Their Children 1920: A Study Based on Census Statistics Relative to the Foreign Born and Native White of Foreign or Mixed Parentage*, by Niles Carpenter, Census Monographs 7 (Washington, D.C., 1927) (hereafter, Carpenter, *Immigrants and Their Children*). For a listing and explanation of "mother tongue" categories, see U.S. Department of Commerce, Bureau of the Census, *Fourteenth Census of the United States Taken in the Year 1920, Volume II, Population 1920: General Report and Analytical Tables* (Washington, D.C., 1922), 967–69 (hereafter, *Fourteenth Census: Population 1920*).

3. Derived from *Fourteenth Census: Population 1920*, 694; Carpenter, *Immigrants and Their Children*, 74, 298.

4. Carpenter, *Immigrants and Their Children*, 132; U.S. Department of Commerce, Bureau of the Census, *Fourteenth Census of the United States Taken in the Year 1920, Volume III, Population 1920: Composition and Characteristics of the Population by States* (Washington, D.C., 1922).

5. Carpenter, *Immigrants and Their Children*, 154–56.

6. Derived from ibid., 168–73.

7. Ibid., 169–70, 247–48.

8. *Fourteenth Census: Abstract*, 332; Carpenter, *Immigrants and Their Children*, 62, 63. In 1920, 2.1 percent of foreign-born whites were nine years old or younger; 1.4 percent were age ten to fourteen, inclusive (Carpenter, *Immigrants and Their Children*, 157).

9. Carpenter, *Immigrants and Their Children*, 184, 192.

10. For statistics comparing school attendance in 1910 and 1920 by region and nativity, see *Fourteenth Census: Abstract*, 412–19. For data on occupations, see Carpenter, *Immigrants and Their Children*, 279–82; J. Y. (Slovak), interviewed 4 June 1976, EFOHP.

11. Derived from *Fourteenth Census: Population 1920,* 973. For data on patterns of Slovak residential distribution, occupation, and education, see Carpenter, *Immigrants and Their Children,* 285, 411–27; on gender ratios, see ibid., 168–71, 176–77; on general occupational patterns, see ibid., 270–71, 284–86, 288–90. However, in terms of first- and second-generation work patterns and socio-economic characteristics, eastern European Jews were one group for which Slovaks were probably not representative.

12. Lizabeth Cohen, *Making a New Deal: Industrial Workers in Chicago, 1919–1939* (New York: Cambridge University Press, 1990), 8.

13. This is hardly an exhaustive list of the rapidly growing scholarship on whiteness and racialism. Representative works that discuss the twentieth century include Matthew Frye Jacobson, *Whiteness of a Different Color: European Immigrants and the Alchemy of Race* (Cambridge, Mass.: Harvard University Press, 1998); Arnold R. Hirsch, *Making the Second Ghetto: Race and Housing in Chicago, 1940–1960* (New York: Cambridge University Press, 1983); Karen Brodkin, *How Jews Became White Folks and What That Says about Race in America* (New Brunswick, N.J.: Rutgers University Press, 1998); David R. Roediger, *Towards the Abolition of Whiteness* (London: Verso, 1990); idem, *Colored White: Transcending the Racial Past* (Berkeley: University of California Press, 2002); James R. Barrett and David R. Roediger, "Inbetween Peoples: Race, Nationality and the 'New Immigrant' Working Class," *JAEH* 16 (Spring 1997): 3–44; Gary Gerstle, "Race and the Myth of the Liberal Consensus," *JAH* 82 (September 1995): 579–86. Gerstle pursues the theme that new immigrants and their offspring developed a growing sense of whiteness in *American Crucible: Race and Nation in the Twentieth Century* (Princeton, N.J.: Princeton University Press, 2001).

14. It is important to remember that, while the term "ethnicity" was not coined until the early 1940s, terms such as "ethnic," "ethnic stock," "ethnically distinct peoples," and "ethnic cohesion" were used in the 1920s. See, for example, *Fourteenth Census: Population 1920,* 967–69; Carpenter, *Immigrants and Their Children,* 20, 142–45 and passim.

15. For objections to using the term "new immigrants," see Roediger, *Colored White,* 281–82, n. 7.

16. Philip Gleason makes the same point about the ebb and flow of ethnicity in "American Identity and Americanization," *Harvard Encyclopedia of American Ethnic Groups,* ed. Stephan Thernstrom et al. (Cambridge, Mass.: Harvard University Press, 1980), 47 (hereafter, *HEAEG*).

17. On ethnic leadership, see John Higham, ed., *Ethnic Leadership in America* (Baltimore: Johns Hopkins University Press, 1978); idem, "Leadership," *HEAEG,* 642–47; Victor R. Greene, *American Immigrant Leaders, 1800–1910* (Baltimore: Johns Hopkins University Press, 1987).

18. Roy Rosenzweig, *Eight Hours for What We Will: Work and Leisure in an Industrial City, 1870–1920* (Cambridge: Cambridge University Press, 1983), 166.

19. Higham, "Leadership," 642. The definition is Higham's; the accompanying observation about national officers not being leaders is mine.

20. On Hansen's thesis, see Kivisto and Blanck, *American Immigrants.* Hansen first presented this principle in a 1937 address titled "The Problem of the Third Generation Immigrant." It is reprinted in ibid., 191–203. In a notable exception

to the general scholarship, Victor Greene challenges the principle that second-generation children wanted to forget a culture their parents wanted to remember: see Victor Greene, "Old-Time Folk Dancing and Music among the Second Generation," in ibid., 142–63; and idem, *A Passion for Polka: Old-Time Ethnic Music in America* (Berkeley: University of California Press, 1992).

21. Herbert Gans, "Symbolic Ethnicity: The Future of Ethnic Groups and Cultures in America," *Ethnic and Racial Studies* 2 (January 1979): 1–20; Richard D. Alba, *Ethnic Identity: The Transformation of White America* (New Haven, Conn.: Yale University Press, 1990); Mary C. Waters, *Ethnic Options: Choosing Identities in America* (Berkeley: University of California Press, 1990); Howard F. Stein and Robert F. Hill, *The Ethnic Imperative: Examining the New White Ethnic Movement* (University Park: Pennsylvania State University Press, 1977). On the ethnic revival "at both the intellectual and societal levels," see Rudolph J. Vecoli, "Return to the Melting Pot: Ethnicity in the United States in the Eighties," *JAEH* 5 (Fall 1985): 7–20, quote on 9.

22. Werner Sollors, *Beyond Ethnicity: Consent and Descent in American Culture* (New York: Oxford University Press, 1986); idem, "Introduction: The Invention of Ethnicity," in *The Invention of Ethnicity*, ed. Wernor Sollors (New York: Oxford University Press, 1989), ix–xx; Kathleen Neils Conzen et al., "The Invention of Ethnicity: A Perspective from the U.S.A.," *JAEH* 12 (Fall 1992): 3–41, with accompanying comments by Herbert J. Gans ("Ethnic Invention and Acculturation, A Bumpy-Line Approach," 42–52) and Lawrence H. Fuchs ("'The Invention of Ethnicity': The Amen Corner," 53–58) and a "Response" by David A. Gerber, Ewa Morawska, and George E. Pozzetta (59–63). For historiographical discussions of the literature, see Russell A. Kazal, "Revisiting Assimilation: The Rise, Fall, and Reappraisal of a Concept in American Ethnic History," *AHR* 100 (April 1995): 437–71; Gary Gerstle, "Liberty, Coercion, and the Making of Americans," *JAH* 84 (September 1997): 524–58.

23. For example, Arthur M. Schlesinger, Jr., *The Disuniting of America: Reflections on a Multicultural Society* (New York: Norton, 1992 [1991]).

24. On fragmentation, see John Higham, "Current Trends in the Study of Ethnicity in the United States," *JAEH* 2 (Fall 1982): 5–15.

25. On ethnic theory and the literature on ethnic identity, see Richard H. Thompson, *Theories of Ethnicity: A Critical Appraisal* (New York: Greenwood Press, 1989); Anya Peterson Royce, *Ethnic Identity: Strategies of Diversity* (Bloomington: Indiana University Press, 1982).

26. Essays by Philip Gleason provide especially perceptive discussions of national identity. For a compilation of his essays on this and other related topics, see Philip Gleason, *Speaking of Diversity: Essays on the Language of Ethnicity* (Baltimore: Johns Hopkins University Press, 1992). See also Lawrence Fuchs, *The American Kaleidoscope: Race, Ethnicity, and the Civic Culture* (Hanover, N.H.: University Press of New England, 1990).

27. See, for example, Gary Gerstle, *Working-Class Americanism: The Politics of Labor in a Textile City, 1914–1960* (New York: Cambridge University Press, 1989); see also his *American Crucible*. James R. Barrett, "Americanization from the Bottom Up: Immigration and the Remaking of the Working Class in the United States, 1880–1930," *JAH* 79 (December 1992): 996–1020.

28. Gleason, "American Identity," 48; Philip Gleason, "Americans All: World War II and the Shaping of American Identity," *Review of Politics* 43 (October 1981): 504–6; Gary Gerstle, "The Working Class Goes to War," *Mid-America* 75 (October 1993): 303–21. See also idem, *American Crucible*, 195–99, 220–35.

29. Gerstle, "Liberty," 552.

CHAPTER ONE

1. *Jednota*, 4 and 25 July 1917.

2. Ibid., 25 July 1917.

3. Woodrow Wilson's message sanctioning the day is reprinted in George Creel, *Complete Report of the Chairman of the Committee on Public Information* (Washington, D.C., 1920), 82.

4. Arthur S. Link, ed., *The Papers of Woodrow Wilson* (hereafter, *PWW*), 69 vols. (Princeton, N.J.: Princeton University Press, 1966–), 30:34–36, quote on 35, 35:293–310, quote on 306.

5. Theodore Roosevelt, "Americanization Day," *IAR* 1 (September 1915): 36–37. (This essay first appeared in the July 1915 issue of *Metropolitan Magazine*.) Roosevelt did caution that not all foreign-born persons were hyphenates and called on Americans to be careful in their judgment and tolerant in their actions (ibid., 37–39). See also Theodore Roosevelt, "Americanism," address delivered at Knights of Columbus meeting, New York City, 12 October 1915, as reprinted in Veterans of Foreign Wars of the United States, Americanization Department, *Americanism: Addresses by Woodrow Wilson ... Franklin K. Lane ... Theodore Roosevelt* (n.p., n.d.), 18; John Higham, *Strangers in the Land: Patterns of American Nativism, 1860–1925*, 2nd ed. (New Brunswick, N.J.: Rutgers University Press, 1992), 198–99; Frederick C. Luebke, *Bonds of Loyalty: German Americans and World War I* (DeKalb: Northern Illinois University Press, 1974), 140–42.

6. Roosevelt, "Americanization Day," 36.

7. Idem, "Americanism," 18.

8. Arthur S. Link, *Woodrow Wilson and the Progressive Era* (New York: Harper and Brothers, 1954), 247; Louis L. Gerson, *The Hyphenate in Recent American Politics and Diplomacy* (Lawrence: University of Kansas Press, 1964), 67.

9. Roosevelt, "Americanism," 24.

10. Link, *PWW*, 37:212–17, quote on 216; Roosevelt, "Americanism," 16.

11. Higham, *Strangers in the Land*, 204–5.

12. Link, *PWW*, 33:147–50, quote on 148.

13. Frances A. Kellor, "National Americanization Day—July 4th," *IAR* 1 (September 1915): 18–29, quote on 18; Edward George Hartmann, *The Movement to Americanize the Immigrant* (New York: Columbia University Press, 1948), 110–11.

14. Kellor, "National Americanization Day," 22. On the growing call to make naturalization ceremonies more "impressive," see ibid., 25; Frederic C. Howe, Commissioner of Immigration, to the Mayors of American Cities, 22 May 1915, reprinted in *IAR* 1 (June 1915): 74; Roosevelt, "Americanization Day," 33–35; Hartmann, *Movement to Americanize*, 117, n. 18.

15. Kellor, "National Americanization Day," 18–23, quote on 19–20 (Kellor clearly equated "laborers" with immigrants); "Americanization Day in 150 Com-

munities," *The Survey*, 31 July 1915, 390; Hartmann, *Movement to Americanize*, 112–22.

16. Hartmann, *Movement to Americanize*, 122–28.

17. "By-products of Americanization Day," *IAR* 1 (September 1915): 46–50; "Record of Progress" entries, *IAR*, March 1915–July 1916. Following Americanization Day 1915, the committee deleted "Day" from its name.

18. Kellor, "National Americanization Day," 26.

19. Ibid., 23.

20. Mrs. James G. Dunning, "Educational Work of the Daughters of the American Revolution," *IAR* 1 (September 1915): 51–53; Hartmann, *Movement to Americanize*, 122–63. On discrepancies between number of registrants and actual attendance at evening classes, see John F. McClymer, "The Americanization Movement and the Education of the Foreign-Born Adult, 1914–25," in *American Education and the European Immigrant: 1840–1940*, ed. Bernard J. Weiss (Urbana: University of Illinois Press, 1982), 98–99, 103–6.

21. Link, *PWW*, 37:113–16, quote on 115. As early as May 1916, Charles Pergler, an ardent Czech nationalist, confirmed the contemporary impact of Wilson's oratory. Citing the president's speech before the League to Enforce Peace, Pergler said that "no other logical conclusion can be drawn" than that the application of the speech's principles supported the creation of an independent Czech and Slovak state: see Charles Pergler, *The Bohemians (Czechs) in the Present Crisis* (Chicago: Bohemian National Alliance of America, 1916[?]), 20.

22. Kirk H. Porter and Donald Bruce Johnson, comps., *National Party Platforms, 1840–1972* (Urbana: University of Illinois Press, 1973), 195–96; Link, *PWW*, 38:537–39, quote on 539.

23. Gerson, *Hyphenate*, 68–72. For example, in 1917 Ukrainian Americans successfully lobbied for a Ukrainian relief day: see Myron B. Kuropas, *The Ukrainian Americans: Roots and Aspirations, 1884–1954* (Toronto: University of Toronto Press, 1991), 140, 142–43.

24. Gerson, *Hyphenate*, 73–83. On Poland's treatment, see idem, *Woodrow Wilson and the Rebirth of Poland, 1914–1920* (New Haven, Conn.: Yale University Press, 1953), 69–100.

25. Gerson draws the same conclusion about the unintended effects of Wilson's positions as well as the activities of the Committee on Public Information: see Gerson, *Hyphenate*, 68–70 and passim. For a contemporary illustration, see Pergler, *Bohemians*.

26. Béla Vassady, Jr., "The 'Homeland Cause' as a Stimulant to Ethnic Unity: The Hungarian-American Response to Károlyi's 1914 American Tour," *JAEH* 2 (Fall 1982): 39–64. On another group, see Alfred Erich Senn and Alfonsas Eidintas, "Lithuanian Immigrants in America and the Lithuanian National Movement Before 1914," *JAEH* 6 (Spring 1987): 6–19. On the prewar development of immigrant institutions and networks, see, for example, June Granatir Alexander, *The Immigrant Church and Community: Pittsburgh's Slovak Catholics and Lutherans, 1880–1915* (Pittsburgh: University of Pittsburgh Press, 1987).

27. Committee Political Federation of Slovaks, *An Open Letter Addressed to Count Michael Károlyi . . . April 13th 1914* (n.p., 1914[?]); Vassady, "The 'Homeland Cause,'" 54–55; Victor S. Mamatey, "The Slovaks and Carpatho-Ruthenians,"

in *The Immigrants' Influence on Wilson's Peace Policies*, ed. Joseph P. O'Grady (Lexington: University of Kentucky Press, 1967), 230–32; Gregory C. Ference, *Sixteen Months of Indecision: Slovak American Viewpoints toward Compatriots and the Homeland from 1914 to 1915 as Viewed by the Slovak Language Press in Pennsylvania* (Selinsgrove, Penn.: Susquehanna University Press, 1995), 140–46. (For a translation of the memorandum, see ibid., 192–96.) Milan Getting provides a firsthand account and a Slovak-language chronicle of Slovak and Czech nationalist activities before and during World War I in his *Americkí Slováci a vývin československej myšlienky v rokoch 1914–1918* (American Slovaks and the evolution of the Czechoslovak idea in the years 1914–1918) (n.p.: Slovenská Telocvičná Jednota Sokol v Amerike, 1933), 7–179.

28. Link, *PWW*, 30:393–94, quote on 394. One activist mocked the very idea of neutrality by noting that, "if neutrality means indifferences as between right and wrong, there is no such thing as neutrality. Concerning the greatest event of human history thinking people must have some opinions. Only people deaf, dumb and blind . . . can be devoid of opinion": see Pergler, *Bohemians*, 6.

29. See, for example, *Národný denník*, 3 and 4 March 1915; Mamatey, "Slovaks and Carpatho-Ruthenians," 233.

30. On divisions and wide-ranging activities by nationality groups, see Gerson, *Hyphenate*, 59–72, and essays in O'Grady, *Immigrants' Influence*. See also Theodore Saloutos, *The Greeks in the United States* (Cambridge, Mass.: Harvard University Press, 1964), 138–68. On Czechs, see Charles Pergler, *America in the Struggle for Czechoslovak Independence* (Philadelphia: Dorrance and Company, 1926), 21–76.

31. Kuropas, *Ukrainian Americans*, 132–39.

32. Dominic A. Pacyga, "Chicago's Pilsen Park and the Struggle for Czechoslovak Independence during World War One," in *Essays in Russian and East European History: Festchrift in Honor of Edward C. Thaden*, ed. Leo Schelbert and Nich Ceh (Boulder, Colo.: East European Monographs, 1995), 122–28; John Bodnar, *Immigration and Industrialization: Ethnicity in an American Mill Town, 1870–1940* (Pittsburgh: University of Pittsburgh Press, 1977), 118–21; Mamatey, "Slovaks and Carpatho-Ruthenians," 232–34; Prpic, "South Slavs," 176–78, 180, 182–86; Pergler, *Bohemians*, 26–27.

33. SLA to Woodrow Wilson, memorandum, 6 March 1917, Woodrow Wilson Papers, Library of Congress, Washington, D.C.

34. Victor S. Mamatey, *The United States and East Central Europe, 1914–1918* (Princeton, N.J.: Princeton University Press, 1957), 113–18, 129–35; idem, "Slovaks and Carpatho-Ruthenians," 233–35; Otakar Odlozilik, "The Czechs," in O'Grady, *Immigrants' Influence*, 211–12; Prpic, "South Slavs," 186–89; Pergler, *Bohemians*, 27–34, 41–45, 60–66; *SH*, 26 April 1917.

35. Link, *PWW*, 45:197, 534–39, quotes on 536, 537; Pergler, *Bohemians*, 68–69; Prpic, "South Slavs," 189–92; Gerson, *Hyphenate*, 76–79.

36. Mamatey, *United States and East Central Europe*, 129–32. On Selective Service requirements and policies regarding recruiting immigrants for foreign-based nationality units, see Joseph T. Hapak, "Selective Service and Polish Army Recruitment during World War I," *JAEH* 10 (Summer 1991): 38–60. On recruit-

ment for the Czechoslovak Legion, see Nancy Gentile Ford, *Americans All! Foreign-born Soldiers in World War I* (College Station: Texas A&M University Press, 2001), 31–34.

37. *SH*, 6 June 1918; Thomas Garrigue Masaryk, *The Making of a State: Memories and Observations, 1914–1918* (New York: Frederick A. Stokes Company, 1927), 217–25, 235–38, 297–99; Mamatey, *United States and East Central Europe,* 280–88. On the role of Slovak immigrants in the creation of Czechoslovakia, see Mamatey, "Slovaks and Carpatho-Ruthenians," 224–39. A less sophisticated and less balanced discussion is presented in M. Mark Stolarik, *The Role of American Slovaks in the Creation of Czecho-Slovakia, 1914–1918* (Cleveland: Slovak Institute, 1968). On the role of Czech immigrants, see Odlozilik, "Czechs," 204–13.

38. Wilson expressed his altered position in a memo to Secretary of State Robert Lansing, and, to Wilson's chagrin, Lansing released a statement announcing the change: see Mamatey, *United States and East Central Europe,* 269–73, 308–9. On the general response of other nationalities, see Gerson, *Hyphenate,* 81–82. See also Prpic, "South Slavs," 196–97.

39. Gerson, *Hyphenate,* 82; Joseph P. O'Grady, "Introduction," in idem, *Immigrants' Influence,* 27–31; Mamatey, *United States and East Central Europe,* 117–18, 131.

40. Higham, *Strangers in the Land,* 237–50; Luebke, *Bonds of Loyalty,* 210–20; David M. Kennedy, *Over Here: The First World War and American Society* (New York: Oxford University, Press, 1980), 67–69; H. C. Peterson and Gilbert C. Fite, *Opponents of War, 1917–1918* (Madison: University of Wisconsin Press, 1957).

41. Creel, *Complete Report,* 78–81; Michael D. Thompson, "Liberty Loans, Loyalty Oaths, and the Street Name Swap: Anti-German Sentiment in Ohio, Spring 1918," *Yearbook of German-American Studies* 33 (1988): 129–56.

42. Creel, *Complete Report,* 82. The quote is from a petition to Woodrow Wilson that reportedly was composed by "representatives of all the foreign-language groups" cooperating with the Committee on Public Information's Division of Work among the Foreign Born: ibid., 81.

43. Ibid., 82–83, quote on 82.

44. Link, *PWW,* 45:224, n. 1.

45. For example, *Jednota,* 11 April 1917, published an affirmation of Slovak loyalty in both English and Slovak. It was an English-language memorandum that had been sent to Secretary of War Newton Baker, asking him to assure President Wilson that "the Slovaks stand as one man behind him in his wonderful undertaking in behalf of the oppressed of the large and small nations and nationalities."

46. This change first appeared on 12 April 1917 and continued through the 21 June 1917 issue. The composite description is based on *Jednota, NN,* and *SH,* April–December 1917. For coverage in other immigrant newspapers, see, for example, Gary Hartman, "Building the Ideal Immigrant: Reconciling Lithuanianism and 100 Percent Americanism to Create a Respectable Nationalist Movement, 1870–1922," *JAEH* 18 (Fall 1998): 55–57.

47. *Jednota,* 9 August 1916; *SH,* 16 May 1918.

48. *Jednota,* 29 May 1918.

49. Gustave Kosik to Woodrow Wilson, telegram, 25 May 1917, Woodrow Wilson Papers. Kosik placed his comments within the context of a recent trip to France, England, and Russia. Although he might have inadvertently added to the animosity toward immigrant newspapers, he was concerned about papers published in Europe. Moreover, given the fact that he edited a Catholic newspaper, he probably wanted radical, left-wing publications censored. Kosik, whose name when rendered in Slovak was Košík, edited the *Katolícky sokol* (Catholic Sokol).

50. *SH*, 29 November 1917.

51. Ibid., 9 March and 29 November 1917.

52. *Jednota*, 26 June 1918; Prpic, "South Slavs," 194–95.

53. *NYT*, 5 July 1918; Creel, *Complete Report*, 83–84; Hartmann, *Movement to Americanize*, 207–8; Prpic, "South Slavs," 194–95.

54. Creel, *Complete Report*, 83.

55. *Jednota*, 24 July 1918.

56. *NYT*, 7 July 1918. According to the reporter, this "big division" also included numerous "Red Cross workers, service flags, and boy and girl scouts."

57. See Mamatey, *United States and East Central Europe*, 269–73, 308–9.

58. Kennedy, *Over Here*, 98–106.

59. Walton Rawls, *WAKE UP, AMERICA!—World War I and the American Poster* (New York: Abbeville Press, 1988), 144, 205, 210. The Food Administration went one step further in appealing to immigrants in its poster "FOOD WILL WIN THE WAR." This poster, which depicted immigrants arriving in America as a red, white, and blue rainbow curved over the Statue of Liberty, was printed in English, Hungarian, Italian, Spanish, and Yiddish versions: see ibid., 113.

60. *Jednota*, 3 April 1918.

61. Alexander Whitehead, "Our New Americans and War Activities," *The Survey*, 15 June 1918, 309–12.

62. Quotes from *Jednota*, 3 April 1918; see also, for example, *SH*, 2 May 1918.

63. *SH*, 18 October 1917. This description is also based on commentary in *Jednota* and *NN*, 1917–1918. See also Hartman, "Building the Ideal Immigrant," 57–58.

64. *SH*, 2 May 1918.

65. *Jednota*, 24 April 1918; V. S. Plátek, "Šesťdesiat liet" (Sixty [years] of summer) in NSS, *Dejiny a Pamätnica Národného Slovenského Spolku, 1890–1950* (History and memorial book of the NSS) (Pittsburgh: National Slovak Society, 1950), 105. The $64,000 amount was not small. The moneys invested by individual lodges were taken from the lodge treasuries and were thus contributions beyond those made by individual members.

66. *SH*, 3 October 1918.

67. *Jednota*, 24 July 1918.

68. Ibid., 19 June 1918.

69. *SH*, 17 May and 14 June 1917.

70. Ibid., 21 June 1917.

71. Ibid., 5 July 1917.

72. The English-language headline appeared in a report in ibid., 24 May 1917.

73. Ibid., 5 July 1917. Throughout the summer of 1917, All-Slav days were held in cities and small towns; many included parades. For a representative example of a small-town event, see ibid., 30 August 1917.

74. *Jednota*, 15 May 1918.

75. Ibid., 19 June and 2 October 1918. All of the Slovak newspapers regularly carried notices about local events to assist the homeland.

76. Ibid., 2 August 1917.

77. For a description of patriotic manifestations in a small industrial town inhabited by a large number of Slavic peoples, see Bodnar, *Immigration and Industrialization*, 121–25.

78. *SH*, 15 February and 20 December 1917. On Czech activities in Chicago, see Pacyga, "Chicago's Pilsen Park," 128–29.

79. *SH*, 5 July 1917.

80. Ibid., 31 May 1917. Brief notices sporadically appeared in *Jednota* and *SH*, April–August 1917 and April–August 1918.

81. *SH*, 17 May, 14 and 21 June 1917.

82. See, for example, ibid., 24 and 31 May 1917.

83. On the emergence of the American flag as a national, patriotic symbol, see Cecilia Elizabeth O'Leary, *To Die For: The Paradox of American Patriotism* (Princeton, N.J.: Princeton University Press, 1999), 49–58, 150–86; Robert Justin Goldstein, *Burning the Flag: The Great 1989–1990 American Flag Desecration Controversy* (Kent, Ohio: Kent State University Press, 1996), 1–5.

84. On the Ford Motor Company's oppressive policies, see Stephen Meyer III, *The Five Dollar Day: Labor, Management and Social Control in the Ford Motor Company, 1908–1921* (Albany: State University of New York Press, 1981).

85. *IAR* 2 (January 1916): 11–12, 86.

86. Esther Everett Lape, "The 'English First' Movement in Detroit," *IAR* 1 (September 1915): 46–50; Francis Kellor, "The Immigrant and Preparedness," *IAR* 2 (January 1916): 26; Higham, *Strangers in the Land*, 244.

87. *IAR* 2 (January 1916): 86.

88. "Citizenship through the Pay Envelope," *IAR* 1 (September 1915): 10; Hartmann, *Movement to Americanize*, 128–32; Higham, *Strangers in the Land*, 244–45.

89. See, for example, Helen Winkler, "Laggards at Night School: Factory Classes Essential for Americanization," *The Survey*, 26 January 1918, 462–63; "Immigrants' Program of Americanization," *The Survey*, 24 August 1918, 596–97; Hartmann, *Movement to Americanize*, 177–78, 195, 197–98, 211–12.

90. Howard Hill, "The Americanization Movement," *American Journal of Sociology* 24 (May 1919): 622–23.

91. Gerd Korman, *Industrialization, Immigrants and Americanizers: The View from Milwaukee, 1866–1921* (Madison: State Historical Society of Wisconsin, 1967), 136–86; Hartmann, *Movement to Americanize*, 129–32, 140–53.

92. Roosevelt, "Americanism," 16.

93. Higham, *Strangers in the Land*, 194–222; William J. Preston, Jr., *Aliens and Dissenters: Federal Suppression of Radicals, 1903–1933*, 2nd ed. (Urbana: University of Illinois Press, 1995); Peterson and Fite, *Opponents of War*; Kennedy, *Over Here*, 66–83.

CHAPTER TWO

1. James Ramon Felak, *"At the Price of the Republic": Hlinka's Slovak People's Party, 1929–1938* (Pittsburgh: University of Pittsburgh Press, 1994), 18–20, 20–23, 24–32; Stanislav J. Kirschbaum, *A History of Slovakia: The Struggle for Survival* (New York: St. Martin's Press, 1995), 161–65; *SH,* 20 March and 27 November 1919. Milan Getting chronicles Hungary's attempt to retain Slovakia in *Americkí Slováci,* 183–287. The purpose here is not to analyze why people in power in Czechoslovakia favored a central government. For this discussion, the key is to examine what was influencing attitudes among Slovaks in America.

2. Alexander, *Immigrant Church and Community,* 100–42.

3. The Dillingham Commission also included Slovaks as a separate nationality: see U.S. Congress, Senate, Immigration Commission, *Reports of the Immigration Commission: Dictionary of Races or Peoples,* S. 662, 61st Cong., 3rd sess., 1911, 5:132–33.

4. Alexander, *Immigrant Church and Community*; Karel D. Bicha, "Hunkies: Stereotyping the Slavic Immigrants, 1890–1920," *JAEH* 2 (Fall 1982): 16–38.

5. Ference, *Sixteen Months of Indecision,* 140–91; Mamatey, "Slovaks and Carpatho-Ruthenians," 232–39. For reports in English-language newspapers referring to "Czecho-Slovak" activities and to the "Czecho-Slovak race" and "peoples," see Getting, *Americkí Slováci,* 127–33.

6. Appeals for help and reports on relief activities appeared in Slovak newspapers, especially in *SH* and *NN.* See also NSS, *Dejiny a Pamätnica,* 380.

7. Ford, *Americans All!* 31–34.

8. For example, the Committee on Public Information's Division of Work with the Foreign Born had a "Czechoslovak Bureau": see Creel, *Complete Report,* 88–89, 98. See also George Creel, *How We Advertised America* (New York: Harper and Brothers, 1920), 175–76, 184–99 passim; *NYT,* 23 May and 5 July 1918; Jaroslav F. Smetanka, "Bohemians and Slovaks—Now Czechoslovaks," *Annals of the American Academy of Political Science* 93 (January 1921): 149–53; Thomas Čapek, *The Čechs (Bohemians) in America: A Study of Their National, Cultural, Political, Social, Economic and Religious Life* (Boston: Houghton Mifflin, 1920), 217–77. Notable exceptions to the tendency by serials to fuse these two groups were "Our Foreign-Born Citizens," *National Geographic,* vol. 31, February 1917, 95–130, and Edwin A. Grosvenor, "The Races of Europe," *National Geographic,* vol. 34 (December 1918), 441–534.

9. In 1925, it was renamed the Hlinka Slovak People's Party: see Kirschbaum, *History of Slovakia,* 172.

10. The SEU consistently presented the gradualist position: see, for example, *SH,* 19 June, 28 August, and 6 November 1919, 29 April 1920. The SEU supported the SLA, which in 1919 also supported the gradualist approach: see, for example, *SH,* 22 January 1920; Karol Sidor, "The Slovak League of America and the Slovak Nation's Struggle for Autonomy," in *Sixty Years of the Slovak League of America,* ed. Joseph Paučo (Middletown, Penn.: Jednota Press, 1967), 56–57, 62–65. The NSS also backed the league and the gradualist position: see, for example, *NN,* 24 March, 21 and 28 April, 14 July 1920. Milan Getting, who became the Czechoslovak consul in Pittsburgh, represented the centralist position: see Getting, *Americkí Slováci.*

11. *Jednota,* 5 March and 2 April 1919.

12. Konštantín Čulen, "The Cult of SS. Cyril and Methodius amongst the Slovaks in U.S.A. and Canada," trans. J. M. Kirschbaum, *Slovakia* 22 (1972): 106–8; *Jednota,* 13 July 1921, 5 July 1922.

13. *Jednota,* 30 June 1920. The writer was president of the Slovak Catholic Federation, the group most actively dedicated to establishing the Cyril and Methodius national holiday.

14. Ibid., 5 March 1919, 30 June 1920, 13 July 1921, 26 July 1922.

15. *SH,* 17 and 24 July 1919.

16. Typically, specific pages were dedicated to this type of literature. For representative samples, see *KM,* 15 January 1920, 15 May, 15 June, and 15 September 1921, 15 January and 15 February 1922; *SH,* 9 June 1921, 27 December 1923. On Jánošík, see, for example, "Národní hrdinovia" (National heroes), *KM,* 15 March 1922; Ignac Gessay, "Kto bol Jánošík? Historická stať" (Who was Jánošík? A historical essay), *Kalendár Denníka Slovák v Amerike* (Almanac of the Daily Slovak in America), 1920 (New York: Slovák v Amerike, 1920), 44–46.

17. These observations are limited to the immediate postwar era to circa 1924, when homeland issues were regularly discussed in newspapers. Over time, Protestants apparently came to support a central government.

18. For example, *Jednota,* 15 and 29 June, 20 July 1921, 28 June and 26 July 1922.

19. Ibid., 30 June 1920.

20. Ibid.

21. Ibid., 17 March 1920.

22. *SH,* 22 January 1920.

23. On persistent fears about returning to Hungarian control, see, for example, *SH,* 15 May 1918, 19 June and 6 November 1919, 29 April 1920. On the ongoing claim that the Pittsburgh Agreement could best be realized in a joint state, see ibid., 5 May 1921, 21 September, 19 and 26 October, 2 November 1922.

24. Unfortunately, most commentators who have simply turned gradualists into "Czechoslovaks" and "centralists" have not researched the editorials and position statements of relevant organizations. As late as 19 October 1922, *SH,* the official SEU organ, was editorializing in favor of implementing the Pittsburgh Agreement. The paper also printed warnings about "Czechoslovakism": see, for example, *SH,* 24 August–21 September 1922. For an example of a historical work that exhibits the arbitrary judgment described, see Stolarik, *Role of American Slovaks,* 53–54.

25. *Jednota,* 3 November 1920.

26. *NN,* 16 June and 10 November 1920. The November report asserted that the Republicans' win doomed the League of Nations.

27. *Jednota,* 23 July and 27 August 1919.

28. *NN,* 14 July and 18 August 1920.

29. Ibid., 30 June and 28 July 1920; *SH,* 26 August 1920.

30. U.S. Department of the Interior, Bureau of Education, *Proceedings: Americanization Conference Held under the Auspices of the Americanization Division, Bureau of Education Department of Interior, Washington, May 12, 13, 14, 15, 1919* (Washington, D.C., 1919), 7–20; Hartmann, *Movement to Americanize,* 228–30.

31. Hartmann, *Movement to Americanize*, 228; see also comments by Fred Butler in Bureau of Education, *Proceedings: Americanization Conference*, 36; Felix Morley, "Making Americans," *The Nation*, 31 May 1919, 878.

32. Morley, "Making Americans," 878.

33. "America's Heritage" in Bureau of Education, *Proceedings: Americanization Conference*, 293–98, quote on 298; Higham, *Strangers in the Land*, 259; Hartmann, *Movement to Americanize*, 97–98, 189–90.

34. Bureau of Education, *Report 1919*, 189–94; Fred Clayton Butler, *Community Americanization: A Handbook for Workers*, U.S. Department of the Interior, Bureau of Education, Bulletin 76 (Washington, D.C., 1919); idem, *State Americanization: The Part of the States in the Education and Assimilation of the Immigrant*, U.S. Department of the Interior, Bureau of Education, Bulletin 77 (Washington, D.C., 1919); Henry H. Goldberger, *Teaching English to the Foreign Born: A Teacher's Handbook*, U.S. Department of the Interior, Bureau of Education, Bulletin 80 (Washington, D.C., 1919); John J. Mahoney, *Training Teachers for Americanization*, U.S. Department of the Interior, Bureau of Education, Bulletin 12 (Washington, D.C., 1920).

35. Albert Mamatey, "Securing Interest of and Cooperation with Foreign-Born People Generally; from the Viewpoint of the Foreign-Born" in Bureau of Education, *Proceedings: Americanization Conference*, 221–29.

36. Ibid., quotes on 226, 227.

37. *SH*, 21 September 1922.

38. *NN*, 3 March 1920.

39. R. W. Seton-Watson [Scotus Viator], *Racial Problems in Hungary* (London: Archibald Constable & Company, 1908), 436–38.

40. M. Mark Stolarik, "The Slovak-American Press," in *The Ethnic Press in the United States: A Historical Analysis and Handbook*, ed. Sally M. Miller (New York: Greenwood Press, 1987), 353–68; Robert E. Park, *The Immigrant Press and Its Control* (New York: Harper & Brothers, 1922), 297, 300; Alexander, *Immigrant Church and Community*, 121–25; A. Y. (Slovak), interviewed 5 May 1976, EFOHP.

41. Josef J. Barton, *Peasants and Strangers: Italians, Rumanians, and Slovaks in an American City, 1890–1950* (Cambridge, Mass.: Harvard University Press, 1975), 101–4, 143–46; John Bodnar, "Schooling and the Slavic-American Family, 1900," in Weiss, *American Education*, 78–95; M. Mark Stolarik, "Immigration, Education, and the Social Mobility of Slovaks, 1870–1930," in *Immigrants and Religion in Urban America*, ed. Randall M. Miller and Thomas D. Marzik (Philadelphia: Temple University Press, 1977), 103–16.

42. Ľudmila Podjavorinská, "Žena v národe" (The woman in the nation), *KŽ*, 1924, 101–3, quotes on 103 and 102, respectively.

43. Šárka Hrbkova, "Prečo sa majú slovenské ženy učiť anglicky," *KŽ*, 1924, 113–14.

44. See, for example, *NN*, 3 March, 4 August, 20 October, and 17 November 1920. On the flexible meaning of "Americanism" and the appropriation of political language to forward diverse agendas, see Gerstle, *Working-Class Americanism*.

45. *NN*, 20 October 1920.

46. Ibid., 24 November 1920.

47. "Zápisnica" (Minutes), *SH*, 29 December 1921.

48. *NN*, 1 January, 4 August, and 20 October 1920.

49. Ibid., 4 August 1920.

50. The discussion here is a composite derived from numerous items published in the immigrant media. For representative examples, in addition to the sources cited in the following notes, see "Nepravé Prostriedky Amerikanizovania" (Wrong means of Americanization), *SH*, 22 May 1919, 19 May 1921; *NN*, 28 January, 11 February, 3 March, 4 August, and 7 July 1920; "Amerikanizácia" (Americanization), *Slovenská mládeže* (Slovak Youth), April 1919.

51. *SH*, 27 November 1919.

52. Allen H. Eaton, *Immigrant Gifts to American Life* (New York: Russell Sage Foundation, 1932), 27–31. In the summer of 1920, both *SH* (5 August) and *NN* (28 July) reprinted articles from *Collier's* that stressed the positive cultural "gifts" immigrants brought with them.

53. Higham, *Strangers in the Land*, 121–23; Eaton, *Immigrant Gifts*, 31–66, 87–91, 93; *NYT*, 30 October and 11 November 1921. At the same time, for example, the International Institute in Pittsburgh announced plans for a one-month exhibition of nationalities' folk arts and crafts: see *SH*, 15 September 1921.

54. Eaton, *Immigrant Gifts*, 91, n. 1. See also *NYT*, 30 October 1921.

55. *SH*, 1 December 1921. Based on the *NYT* report (30 October 1921), the number twenty-eight is low. The difference can be accounted for if the *SH* writer was speaking of the number of booths rather than the number of nationality groups.

56. *SH*, 15 September 1921.

57. *Jednota*, 27 June 1923.

58. Ibid., 27 June and 11 July 1923, 19 March and 9 July 1924.

59. Ibid., 16 July 1924.

60. Ibid., 9 July, 6, 13, and 27 August 1924.

61. Ibid., 9 April and 9 July 1924.

62. Ibid., 27 August 1919, 29 June 1921, 18 July 1923.

63. For example, the souvenir program for Chicago's 1930 Slovak national day devoted twenty pages to Slovak wartime activities. After noting the military service of young Slovaks, it recounted domestic support for the war effort and reproduced government and other items documenting and praising Slovak support. In addition to comparing Slovak contributions with those of other nationalities, the discussion gave "Slovaks" credit for some activities, such as bond purchases, where the totals were actually listed for "Czecho-Slovaks": see *Slovenský Deň* [Slovak Day at the] *Coliseum, Chicago, Illinois 1930: Souvenir Program of Slovak Festival Commemorating 50th Anniversary of Gen. Milan R. Stefanik* (Chicago: Mally Press, 1930). In the 1932 edition, local sokols listed those who had fought in the war and the names of women who worked for the Red Cross or had led efforts to sell liberty bonds: see *Pamätník Štvrtého Národného Slovenského Dňa* (Souvenir Program of the Fourth National Slovak Day) (Chicago: Mally Press, 1932), 63, 82–83 (hereafter, 1932 National Slovak Day, *Souvenir Program*).

64. See, for example, *Jednota*, 24 September, 1 and 15 October, 5, 12, 19, and 26 November 1919; *SH*, 25 September 1919; *Denný hlas* (Daily Voice), 3 and 5 December 1918. David Montgomery errs when he claims that the NSS did not

support the 1919 steel strike: see his "Nationalism, American Patriotism, and Class Consciousness among Immigrant Workers in the United States in the Epoch of World War I," in *"Struggle a Hard Battle": Essays on Working-Class Immigrants,* ed. Dirk Hoerder (DeKalb: Northern Illinois University Press, 1986), 331.

CHAPTER THREE

1. Preston, *Aliens and Dissenters,* 181–272; Robert K. Murray, *Red Scare: A Study of National Hysteria, 1919–1920* (St. Paul: University of Minnesota Press, 1955); Burt Noggle, *Into the Twenties: The United States from Armistice to Normalcy* (Urbana: University of Illinois Press, 1974), 84–121; Louis F. Post, *The Deportations Delirium of Nineteen-Twenty* (Chicago: Charles H. Kerr, 1923); Higham, *Strangers in the Land,* 264–99; Paul Murphy, "Normalcy, Intolerance, and the American Character," *Virginia Quarterly Review* 40 (Summer 1964): 445–59.

2. *NYT,* 24 and 25 September 1920.

3. Sean Dennis Cashman, *America in the Twenties and Thirties: The Olympian Age of Franklin Delano Roosevelt* (New York: New York University Press, 1989), 84–85; Michael E. Parrish, *Anxious Decades: America in Prosperity and Depression, 1920–1941* (New York: W. W. Norton, 1992), 3–11; Lynn Dumenil, *The Modern Temper: American Culture and Society in the 1920s* (New York: Hill and Wang, 1996), 201–49.

4. "Uncle Sam's Turnstile," *New Republic,* 17 August 1921, 314–15.

5. Harry Jerome, *Migration and Business Cycles* (New York: National Bureau of Economic Research, 1926), 106, 124–25; E. P. Hutchinson, *Legislative History of American Immigration Policy 1798–1965* (Philadelphia: University of Pennsylvania Press, 1981), 171–83. New immigrants are described here as the "major" target because, except for the Japanese, legislation had already halted Asian immigration. On "racial" elements of the legislation, see Mae M. Nga, "The Architecture of Race in Law: A Reexamination of the Immigration Act of 1924," *JAH* 86 (June 1999): 67–92.

6. *SH,* 1 July 1920.

7. *NN,* 7 July 1920. See, for example, Grover Cleveland's veto of the first literacy act passed by Congress in 1897 in James D. Richardson, comp., *A Compilation of the Messages and Papers of the Presidents,* 11 vols. (Washington, D.C.: Bureau of National Literature, 1913), 8:6189–93.

8. *NN,* 29 September 1920.

9. Ibid., 5 May 1920.

10. Kenneth L. Roberts, "The Rising Irish Tide," *Saturday Evening Post,* 14 February 1920, 3–4, 58, 61–62, 65–66, 68; idem, "Plain Remarks on Immigrants for Plain Americans," *Saturday Evening Post,* 12 February 1921, 21–22, 44, 47; idem, "The Existence of an Emergency," *Saturday Evening Post,* 30 April 1921, 3–4, 86, 89–90, 93–94. Despite the "Rising Irish Tide" title, Roberts praised the Irish as "desirable" because they belonged to the "old immigration" (quotes on 58, 4).

11. Quotes from Roberts, "Plain Remarks," 47, and idem, "Rising Irish Tide," 4.

12. The quintessential example of the genre was Madison Grant, *The Passing of the Great Race or the Racial Basis of European History*, 4th ed. rev. (New York: Scribners, 1921); see also Higham, *Strangers in the Land*, 270–77.

13. *NN*, 15 December 1920; see also ibid., 16 June 1920. With matter-of-fact reports, the Slovak press followed the legislation through Congress. See, for example, *Jednota*, 11 May, 22 June, and 21 September 1921; *SH*, 30 June 1921.

14. *Jednota*, 29 March 1922.

15. *SH*, 21 February and 12 March 1924.

16. For example, ibid., 18 and 25 October 1923.

17. Hutchinson, *Legislative History*, 187–88; *Jednota*, 6, 13, and 20 February, 12 March 1924; *SH*, 31 January, 4, 14, 21, and 28 February, 6 March 1924.

18. *Jednota*, 6 February 1924; *SH*, 31 January 1924.

19. *Jednota*, 13 February 1924; *SH*, 4 February 1924.

20. *SH*, 21 February 1924.

21. Ibid., 28 February and 6 March 1924; *Jednota*, 20 February and 12 March 1924.

22. *SH*, 21 February 1924.

23. Ibid., 6 March 1924.

24. For example, ibid., 28 February, 6 March, and 1 May 1924; *Jednota*, 12 March 1924.

25. For example, *Jednota*, 2, 9, and 30 July 1924; *SH*, 12 and 26 June, 3, 17, and 31 July 1924.

26. In 1920, the Polish newspaper *Zgoda* started publishing English items as a "self-defense to Polish emigration" and as a way "to 'Polanize'" Polish youths. The first columns are reprinted in Park, *Immigrant Press*, 211–13.

27. *Jednota*, 18 June and 2 July 1924.

28. Ibid., 3 September 1924.

29. *SH*, 3 July 1924.

30. Ibid., 8 January 1925. These were themes in a five-part series entitled "Americanization," which was also sponsored by the SLA and printed in Slovak newspapers. The final installment was particularly vehement. See ibid., 13, 20, and 27 March, 3 and 10 April 1924.

31. *NN*, 7 April 1920.

32. *SH*, 10 April 1924.

33. Wentworth Stewart, *The Making of a Nation: A Discussion of Americanism and Americanization* (Boston: Stratford, 1920), 13; emphasis added.

34. *Strangers in the Land*, 264–99.

35. Harry Rider, "Legislative Notes and Reviews," *American Political Science Review* 14 (February 1920): 110–13; Higham, *Strangers in the Land*, 260.

36. *NN*, 1 January 1920.

37. Noggle, *Into the Twenties*, 119–20; Bureau of Education, *Report 1919*, 191; Barrett, "Americanization from the Bottom Up," 1003; McClymer, "Americanization Movement," 102–5; Higham, *Strangers in the Land*, 301. For a scathing English description of the classes' content that sheds light on how ordinary immigrants probably viewed them, see *SH*, 3 April 1924.

38. For example, *SH*, 3 July 1924.

39. See Preston, *Aliens and Dissenters;* Murray, *Red Scare;* Noggle, *Into the Twenties;* Post, *Deportations Delirium;* Higham, *Strangers in the Land;* and Murphy, "Normalcy." See also Winfield Jones, *Knights of the Ku Klux Klan* (New York: n.p., 1941), 108–9, 228–30; David M. Chalmers, *Hooded Americanism: The First Century of the Ku Klux Klan* (Garden City, N.Y.: Doubleday, 1965), 31–32.

40. Higham, *Strangers in the Land,* 294–95. On Klan activities in local areas, see William D. Jenkins, *Steel Valley Klan: The Ku Klux Klan in Ohio's Mahoning Valley* (Kent, Ohio: Kent State University Press, 1990); Leonard J. Moore, *Citizen Klansmen: The Ku Klux Klan in Indiana, 1921–1928* (Chapel Hill: University of North Carolina Press, 1991); Kathleen M. Blee, *Women of the Klan: Racism and Gender in the 1920s* (Berkeley: University of California Press, 1991). See also Shawn Lay, *Hooded Knights on the Niagara: The Ku Klux Klan in Buffalo, New York* (New York: New York University Press, 1995); and Kenneth T. Jackson, *The Ku Klux Klan in the City, 1915–1930* (New York: Oxford University Press, 1967).

41. *SH,* 13 October 1921.

42. *Svedok,* 1 January 1923.

43. On anti-Klan activities, see David J. Goldberg, "Unmasking the Ku Klux Klan: The Northern Movement against the KKK, 1920–1925," *JAEH* 15 (Summer 1996): 48.

44. *Steubenville Herald-Star,* 16, 17, 18, 20, and 22 August 1923; *Steubenville (Weekly) Herald,* 23 August 1923; *NYT,* 17 and 31 August 1923.

45. *NYT,* 17 August 1923; Goldberg, "Unmasking," 34, 36; Chalmers, *Hooded Americanism,* 39–99, 119–97, 215–53. See also, Charles C. Alexander, *The Ku Klux Klan in the Southwest* (Lexington; University of Kentucky Press, 1965); Shawn Lay, ed., *The Invisible Empire in the West: Toward a New Historical Appraisal of the Ku Klux Klan of the 1920s* (Urbana: University of Illinois Press, 1992).

46. Higham, *Strangers in the Land,* 294.

47. *Steubenville Herald-Star,* 16 August 1923; *NYT,* 26 August 1923.

48. For confirmation of lingering memories, see, for example, *SH,* 3 April 1924. See also Montgomery, "Nationalism," 335.

49. Alexander, *Immigrant Church and Community,* 26. On an awareness by immigrants of this contemporary desire for "public rallies and flag raisings," see *SH,* 13 March 1924.

50. *Jednota,* 9 June 1920.

51. *KM,* 15 June 1920.

52. "Loyalty pictures" is my designation for this photo genre.

53. On the number and content of foreign-language newspapers, see Park, *Immigrant Press,* 113–247, 297.

54. This is a composite description derived from secular and religious publications. For representative examples, see *Jednota,* 9 June 1920, 2 July 1924. SEU, *Kalendár, 1924,* contained thirty-three pictures of local lodges, and nearly all included a flag conspicuously displayed. Sokol publications regularly reproduced pictures of their local teams that included people holding flags or prominently featuring them.

55. *KM,* 15 May 1922.

56. *SH,* 26 January 1922; see also ibid., 26 June 1924.

57. Hutchinson, *Legislative History,* 172, n. 43.

58. American Russian [Carpatho-Rusin] Sokol Union, *Kalendar' Amerikanskaho Russkaho Sokola Sojedinenija, 1922* (Homestead, Penn.: n.p., 1922), 72.

59. This constant theme in organizations' publications was also evident in programs distributed at Slovak Days. See, for example, *Pamätník Štvrtého* and *Pamätník Piateho Slovenského Národného Dňa* (Souvenir Program of the Fifth Slovak National Day) (Chicago: Mally Press, 1933), 75–85 (hereafter, 1933 Slovak National Day, *Souvenir Program*).

60. The pre-1929 figures were in a U.S. House of Representatives report reprinted in the SLA's series "Restricted Immigration" in *SH*, 21 February 1924. For the 1929 revised totals, see Maurice R. Davie, *World Immigration: With Special Reference to the United States* (New York: Macmillan, 1936), 378.

61. Konštantín Čulen, *Dejiny Slovákov v Amerike* (History of Slovaks in America), 2 vols. (Bratislava: Slovenská Liga na Slovensku, 1942), 1:47–48.

62. *Jednota*, 16 July 1924.

63. See, for example, Frederick Lewis Allen, *Only Yesterday: An Informal History of the 1920's* (New York: Harper and Brothers, 1931); Cashman, *America in the Twenties and Thirties*; Cohen, *Making a New Deal*, 53–211; William E. Leuchtenburg, *The Perils of Prosperity, 1914–1932* (Chicago: University of Chicago Press, 1958); Parrish, *Anxious Decades*; Dumenil, *Modern Temper*; Frank Stricker, "Affluence for Whom?—Another Look at Prosperity and the Working Classes in the 1920's," *Labor History* 24 (Winter 1983): 5–33.

CHAPTER FOUR

1. See, for example, *Furdek*, March 1931, 18–19; *NN*, 30 May, 27 June, and 8 August 1928, 21 May 1930, 7 November 1934; *SH*, 8 January 1925, 2 September and 28 October 1926, 31 January 1931, 29 March 1934.

2. Čulen, "Cult of SS. Cyril and Methodius," 98–99, 107–8; Stephan J. Palickar, "The 'Slovak Day' in America: Its Character and Purpose," address delivered at Slovak Day, Bayonne, New Jersey, 4 July 1927, partially reprinted in *Jednota*, 6 July 1927.

3. See, for example, *Jednota*, 6 July 1927; *NN*, 11 July 1928, 6 April 1932.

4. *Jednota*, 29 June 1927.

5. For methodology, see the Bibliographical Note. The immense number of items regarding Slovak Days precludes citing every relevant item; moreover, the remarkable similarity of the published items would increase the individual endnotes to unwieldy lengths without substantially enhancing the documentation. Therefore, except in a few instances where the text requires representative citations or where the text is derived from limited instead of aggregate notes or sources, specific citations are not provided. Specific sources are, of course, provided for direct quotes. While nonaffiliated newspapers were not major sources for Slovak Day items, they occasionally included some materials; see, for example, *SvA*, 5, 10, 13, 16, 20, 24, and 27 June, 9, 11, and 15 July 1931, and summer issues for 1932 and 1933.

6. *NN*, 6 April 1932. Scholars support contemporary perceptions of St. Patrick's Day: see, for example, Timothy J. Meagher, "'Why Should We Care for a Little Trouble or a Walk through the Mud': St. Patrick's and Columbus Day

Parades in Worcester, Massachusetts, 1845–1915," *New England Quarterly* 58 (March 1985): 5–26.

7. Čulen, "Cult of SS. Cyril and Methodius," 98–134.

8. *Jednota*, 21 May 1930, 12 July and 9 August 1933, 22 August 1934, 21 and 28 August 1935, 5 July 1937; *NN*, 15 August 1934; *SH*, 12 May 1932.

9. *NN*, 17 April, 3 and 24 July, 4 September 1935; *Jednota*, 3 June 1931, 21 and 28 June 1933, 10 April and 3 July 1935, 8 July 1936.

10. *NN*, 27 August 1930.

11. Based on admission-ticket sales, attendance figures were probably relatively accurate: see, for example, ibid., 16 July 1930, 15 July and 16 September 1931; *Jednota*, 15 July 1931, 29 June, and 27 September 1933; *SvA*, 10 July 1931.

12. *NN*, 13 September 1933.

13. *SH*, 25 June 1925; *Jednota*, 22 April and 30 May 1925.

14. *Jednota*, 10 March 1926.

15. Ibid., 30 June 1926.

16. Ibid., 14 and 21 July 1926, quote from 21 July.

17. The explanation about the 1926 Slovak Day was included in publicity for South Orange's 1929 day (ibid., 17 April 1929). On the visits, see ibid., 23 June and 14 July 1926; Sidor, "Slovak League of America," 66–67.

18. *SH*, 9 August 1928; *Jednota*, 15 August 1928, 20 March and 19 June 1929; *NN*, 8 August 1928, 19 June, 3 and 17 July, and 21 August 1929.

19. *Jednota*, 24 April and 17 July 1929; *NN*, 1 May and 3 July 1929.

20. *Jednota*, 18 June 1930.

21. Ibid., 11 June 1930; *NN*, 30 August 1933.

22. *NN*, 5 August 1931, 24 May and 30 August 1933, 7 August 1935; *Jednota*, 22 August 1934, 24 July 1935, 19 August 1936, 14 April 1938; *SH*, 18 July 1935.

23. *Jednota*, 3 June and 22 July 1931.

24. *NN*, 21 October 1931, 6 April 1932, 23 August and 6 September 1933; *Jednota*, 6 September 1933.

25. The plea was reiterated year after year. For representative examples, see *NN*, 19 June 1929, 2 September 1931, 7 June 1933.

26. *SH*, 16 July and 24 September 1936.

27. Ibid., 18 March, 22 April, 6 and 20 May, 10 June, 8 July, and 12 August 1937, 19 May 1938.

28. *Jednota*, 3 September 1930, 11 July 1934.

29. Ibid., 8 July 1936.

30. *NN*, 26 May 1937; *SH*, 24 June 1937; *Jednota*, 26 May 1937, 27 April 1938.

31. *NN*, 8 March 1933.

32. *Jednota*, 3 June and 22 July 1931. Publicists for a Slovak Day in eastern Pennsylvania indicated they knew what Slovaks elsewhere were doing because "articles in Slovak periodicals show that Slovak Day is celebrated throughout the United States" (ibid., 28 May 1930). In 1938, organizers of the first Slovak Day in Joliet, Illinois, lamented that all the newspapers carried stories about Slovak Days elsewhere; it was time for them to follow suit (ibid., 25 May 1938).

33. Ibid., 19 July 1933.

34. Ibid.

35. Ibid., 25 July 1934.

36. *NN*, 24 June 1931. This same terminology was used repeatedly throughout the 1930s.

37. Ibid., 7 August 1935.

38. Ibid., 1 May 1929.

39. *Jednota*, 9 August 1933; *SH*, 10 August 1933; *NN*, 9 August 1933.

40. Michael V. Simko, "Slovak Day Benefits," *Furdek* 15 (1936), 10. The writer was an American-born Slovak who cited specific benefits the second generation, especially business owners and professionals, could reap from Slovak Days.

41. *SH*, 7 August 1930.

42. *NN*, 15 August 1928; *SH*, 30 August 1928.

43. *NN*, 17 June 1931, 28 June 1933, 30 May 1934; *Jednota*, 10 July 1935, 8 July 1936, 30 June 1937, 29 June and 3 August 1938; *SvA*, 25 June and 7 July 1931.

44. The sign read, "SLOVAK DAY WILL BE HELD HERE, JULY 27TH 1930": *NN*, 6 August 1930.

45. *Jednota*, 9 August 1933.

46. Ibid., 8 July 1925, 15 August 1934, 1 July 1936. The state labor inspector spoke at Detroit's 1928 day (*SH*, 30 August 1928), and the superintendent of mines addressed the 1932 Greene County, Pennsylvania, Slovak Day (*NN*, 24 August 1932).

47. For example, *Jednota*, 17 July 1929, 16 July 1930, 15 and 29 July 1931, 10 and 17 July 1935; *NN*, 10 July and 25 September 1929, 10 June and 29 July 1931, 4 September 1935; *SH*, 14 October 1937.

48. *NN*, 17 June 1931; *Jednota*, 24 June 1931; *SvA*, 25 June and 7 July 1931.

49. *Jednota*, 26 July 1933. In part, the text said that "men and women of Slovak descent . . . desire to pay our respects to the President of the U.S. assuring him of our highest admiration and respect and of our readiness to perform all of the duties we devolve upon us as citizens, and further to assure him of our sincere belief and allegiance to the Constitution of the U.S., and the laws thereof."

50. Ibid., 10 July 1935.

51. Ibid., 11 July 1928. In 1933, Slovaks in Trenton, New Jersey, used remarkably similar language when they called on Slovaks to attend the 1933 day "as American citizens to celebrate the independence of this new country and as Christians to celebrate our apostles Saints Cyril and Methodius": ibid., 21 June 1933. Throughout the 1930s, Slovaks in numerous other communities employed the same rhetoric.

52. In 1932, references to Washington appeared in the overwhelming majority of published items on Slovak Days. The quote is from *NN*, 29 June 1932. On Perth Amboy, see *Jednota*, 29 June 1932. The plethora of feature articles on Washington that appeared in Slovak publications in 1932 stressed the same themes for Slovak Day. For the claim that a reverence for Washington by eastern and southern Europeans somehow reflected a desire for "'Nordic' ancestors," see Gerstle, *American Crucible*, 167–68.

53. *Jednota*, 13 July 1927, 6 August 1936; *NN*, 22 June 1932; *SH*, 6 August 1936.

54. *Jednota*, 17 July 1929. On Chicago, see *NN*, 25 May 1932. In South Orange, New Jersey, a former governor presented an American flag to a Perth Amboy

parish and its lodges because they had the largest number of participants at Slovak Day: ibid., 10 July 1929.

55. *NN*, 30 August 1933; *Jednota*, 28 September 1938.

56. *Jednota*, 15 June 1938.

57. On the ongoing need for ethnic groups to demonstrate their loyalty and pay homage to America in public exhibitions, see John Bodnar, *Remaking America: Public Memory, Commemoration, and Patriotism in the Twentieth Century* (Princeton, N.J.: Princeton University Press, 1992), 95–103.

58. No systematic study of "nationality" days has been undertaken, and specific studies only allude to these events. Yet both contemporary sources and programs from latter-day events show that they were common. For example, by the early 1920s Poles in Chicago were holding Polish Days, and in 1931 Pittsburgh Poles scheduled their first day: see Central Council of Polish Organizations, *45th Annual Polish American Day* (n.p., 1975). On Croatian Days, see Peter Rachleff, "Class, Ethnicity, and the New Deal: The Croatian Fraternal Union in the 1930s," in *The Ethnic Enigma: The Salience of Ethnicity for European-Origin Groups*, ed. Peter Kivisto (Philadelphia: Balch Institute Press, 1989), 102. Items in Slovak religious and secular newspapers habitually referred to the "national days" arranged by "other nationalities": see, for example, *NN*, 8 July 1931.

CHAPTER FIVE

1. *Jednota*, 18 July 1934.

2. *NN*, 14 July 1937.

3. *Jednota*, 15 July 1931. Similar appeals regularly appeared: see, for example, ibid., 15 August 1928; *SH*, 27 July 1933, 28 July 1938; *NN*, 17 July 1929.

4. *SH*, 28 July 1938.

5. Ibid., 1 July 1937.

6. Ibid., 23 August 1934; *Jednota*, 22 August 1934.

7. *Jednota*, 25 June 1930; see also ibid., 22 June 1927, 3 September 1930. Slovaks in Luzerne and Lackawanna counties were not the first to introduce more innovative programs. In 1925, Youngstown Slovaks had a baseball game and "games and races for children, young and old, men and women," but published descriptions of the activities are ambiguous: see ibid., 17 June 1925.

8. Ibid., 18 May 1927.

9. Ibid., 4 July 1928. Tellingly, the announcement about athletic activities was in English in capital letters. The description of the rest of the program was in Slovak, and that version merely referred to recreational activities in general terms.

10. Ibid., 22 June 1927, 29 June 1929.

11. This is a composite description based on countless programs and firsthand accounts published in Slovak newspapers. For an explanation of the methodology used for crafting descriptions of local Slovak Days, see chap. 4, n. 5.

12. *SH*, 8 September 1927.

13. *Jednota*, 6 July 1932, 4 July 1934; *SH*, 3 September 1936; *NN*, 24 July and 18 August 1920; Jules Tygiel, *Past Time: Baseball as History* (New York: Oxford University Press, 2000), 64–86; Parrish, *Anxious Decades*, 168–69.

14. *Jednota,* 26 June 1929. The Middletown orphanage was the FCSU's. *NN,* 4 July 1928, had, without great fanfare, mentioned Wagner's participation in the 1928 event. On Wagner, see Dennis DeValeria and Jeanne Burke DeValeria, *Honus Wagner: A Biography* (Pittsburgh: University of Pittsburgh Press, 1998). Information on the other players mentioned here and later was obtained from http://sportsillustrated.cnn.com/mlb/all_time_stats/rosters.

15. *Jednota,* 6 July 1932; see also preceding note.

16. *NN,* 24 July 1935; *Jednota,* 15 June 1938.

17. *SH,* 15 April 1937, 27 July, 4 and 11 August 1938.

18. Ibid., 17 June 1929, 2 July 1931; *Jednota,* 6 June 1928, 24 June 1936; *SH,* 15 April 1937. These youths were members of the Catholic Sokol and Youth Division of the FCSU. See, "Účet spojene zo Slovenským Dňom v Kennywood," FCSU Records, box 120, folder 1392. On fraternal teams, see chap. 6.

19. *Jednota,* 18 June 1930.

20. For example, *NN,* 2 July 1930.

21. *Jednota,* 3 August 1927; *SH,* 8 September 1927; *NN,* 18 July 1928.

22. *Jednota,* 25 May 1932.

23. *Stanovy Mládeneckého a Sokolského Oddelenia I. Kat. Slov. Jednoty*[.] *By-Laws of the Junior Branch and Sokol Branch of the First Catholic Slovak Union* (Middletown, Penn.: First Catholic Slovak Union, 1931). The title page is in both Slovak and English.

24. *NN,* 8 and 15 July 1936.

25. *Jednota,* 22 June 1927, 25 June 1930. In 1929, the program advertised a "beauty contest for girls between the ages of 14 and 20": ibid., 26 June 1929.

26. Ibid., 15 July 1931.

27. Ibid., 17 June 1931, 29 August 1934, 24 June 1936; *NN,* 26 July 1933, 28 August 1935, 7 July 1937; *SvA,* 16 June 1931; *SH,* 20 July 1933, 14 November 1935. On photos, see, for example, 1933 Slovak National Day, *Souvenir Program;* *Pamätník Tretieho Kat. Slov. Dňa v Chicagu* (Souvenir Program of the Third Catholic Slovak Day in Chicago) (Chicago: Osadné Hlasy, 1933) (hereafter, 1933 Catholic Slovak Day, *Souvenir Program*).

28. *Jednota,* 17 June 1931.

29. *SH,* 5 July 1934; *Jednota,* 24 July 1935. On Slovak regionalism, see Alexander, *Immigrant Church and Community,* 6, 21, 93, 101–16.

30. *NN,* 17 June 1936.

31. *SH,* 1 June 1933.

32. Ibid., 5 July 1934.

33. *NN,* 22 June 1938.

34. Compact in author's possession; *Jednota,* 27 May 1936.

35. Ibid., 25 July 1934.

36. Ibid., 18 May 1938.

37. *NN,* 23 May 1928, 14 May 1930; 1933 Slovak National Day, *Souvenir Program;* 1933 Catholic Slovak Day, *Souvenir Program.*

38. *NN,* 6 June 1934; *Jednota,* 29 June 1938.

39. In 1936, Milwaukee's queen was the woman with "the most beautiful costume." The next year, Philadelphia also used a costume-based criterion, but

organizing committees in these cities were going against the trend: *NN*, 17 and 24 June 1936, 30 June and 7 July 1937.

40. *SH*, 1 August 1929; *NN*, 5 August 1931.

41. *Jednota*, 27 June 1932; *NN*, 28 June 1933. *Kroje* is the plural form.

42. *Jednota*, 16 June 1937; see also *NN*, 6 July 1938.

43. *Jednota*, 14 August 1935.

44. Ibid., 10 April 1935.

45. For the 1931 Slovak Day in Pennsylvania's Greene County, ads announced that prizes would be awarded to "every young man and young girl who sells the most tickets in their town": ibid., 26 August 1931. Since most Slovak Day ads mentioned popularity contests and almost invariably described the contestants as female, it seems clear that popularity contests for males occurred but rarely.

46. *Jaro*, 29 June 1938. Using a wide range of Slovak terms with various English equivalents, typically ads simply noted there would be an exhibition of Slovak "artistic objects," "handicrafts," "art," embroidery, and costumes.

47. *Jednota*, 17 June and 22 April 1931; *SH*, 2 July 1931.

48. *Jednota*, 28 July 1937.

49. Ibid., 25 July 1928.

50. Ibid., 5 September 1928, 6 August 1930.

51. For example, ibid., 2 July 1930, 17 June and 2 July 1931, 15 June 1938; *SH*, 1 August 1935; *NN*, 14 July 1937.

52. *Jednota*, 2 and 16 July 1930; *NN*, 16 July 1930.

53. *NN*, 22 September 1937.

54. *Jednota*, 12 July 1933.

55. Ibid., 14 June 1936, 15 June 1938.

56. Ibid., 4 July 1928, 18 July 1934, 3 July 1935.

57. Ibid., 27 June 1928; *NN*, 7 July 1937.

58. *NN*, 24 July 1935, 22 August 1938.

59. On commemorative events in the twentieth century, see Bodnar, *Remaking America*. For analysis of a commemorative event that emphasizes middle-class influence, see April Schultz, *Ethnicity on Parade: Inventing the Norwegian American through Celebration* (Amherst: University of Massachusetts Press, 1994).

60. *NN*, 30 August 1933. Chicago's planning meetings occurred at the Slovak Business Men's Club, but that does not mean all participants were businessmen. The 1933 program did not identify committee members for the Slovak National Day (1933 Slovak National Day, *Souvenir Program*), but the 1933 program for the "Catholic" day included biographies revealing that, except for the clergy, the majority of committee members were professional or business people (1933 Catholic Slovak Day, *Souvenir Program*).

61. Simko, "Slovak Day Benefits," 10–11.

62. Given the composition of the American Slovak population, by "intelligentsia" he undoubtedly meant "educated" people, and this probably included business owners and professionals.

63. *NN*, 23 August 1933.

64. As the historian Victor Greene has shown, second-generation offspring did develop an appreciation or a liking for traditional dance and folk music: see his "Old-Time Folk Dancing and Music," 142–63, and *A Passion for Polka*.

CHAPTER SIX

1. *KM*, 25 December 1931.
2. Ibid., 25 November 1931.
3. *Jednota*, 15 September 1926; *SH*, 18 February 1926. These types of expressions regularly appeared in publications: see, for example, *Slovenský národ* (The Slovak nation), 1 (October 1925), 13, 33.
4. Michal Laučik to Bratia Úradníci Výkonného Úradu N.S.S. (Brother officers of the executive committee of the NSS), 4 December 1926, NSS Records, box 4, folder K/L; Ján Orságh and Michal Laučik, comps., *Spevník Kruhu Mládeže Národného Slovenského Spolku v Spojených Štátoch Amerických* (Songbook of the Young Folks' Circle of the NSS in the United States of America) (Pittsburgh: n.p., 1928).
5. *SH*, 28 January and 6 June 1926.
6. *NN*, 18 April 1928; *SH*, 28 January and 4 February 1926.
7. NSS Records, box 4, folders B, D, H/I/J, K/L, M, N/O, P/Q, R, S, contain numerous letters from local elders requesting these materials in the mid- to late 1920s. See also *NN*, 18 April 1928; *Jednota*, 27 April 1927.
8. *KM*, 15 February 1926, 25 March 1930.
9. *NN*, 6 September 1933.
10. *Jaro*, 13 April 1927. At its 1929 convention, the Croatian Fraternal Union used the same procedure and voted on whether to include an English-language section in its official organ: see Rachleff, "Class, Ethnicity, and the New Deal," 98.
11. *Slovenský sokol*, 31 January 1931.
12. By introducing English, Slovaks were adhering to a pattern common among nationality groups: see Joshua A. Fishman et al., "The Non-English and the Ethnic Group Press, 1910–1960," in *Language Loyalty in the United States: The Maintenance and Perpetuation of Non-English Mother Tongues by American Ethnic and Religious Groups*, ed. Joshua A. Fishman et al. (The Hague: Mouton and Company, 1966), 51–74.
13. *Jaro*, 21 March 1928; "Our Dear Slovak Language," *Furdek*, August 1928. Despite its English title, this was a Slovak-language essay appealing for language maintenance.
14. *NN*, 14 January 1931.
15. Ibid., 25 November 1931. On the "conflict between a leadership of accommodation and a leadership of protest," see John Higham, "Introduction: The Forms of Ethnic Leadership," in idem, *Ethnic Leadership*, 3–7, quote on 3.
16. *Jaro*, 13 April 1927; *Dennica*, 15 January 1929; *NN*, 30 October 1934 (this newspaper had been printing an English column since 1928).
17. *KM*, 25 December 1931.
18. Ibid., 25 July 1931.
19. *Jaro*, 18 January 1928.

20. Ibid., 20 March 1929.

21. *Slovenský sokol*, 31 January 1931.

22. Joshua A. Fishman and Vladimir C. Nahirny, "Organizational and Leadership Interest in Language Maintenance," in Fishman et al., *Language Loyalty*, 179–84.

23. Introducing its English-language page in 1928, *SH* (8 March 1928) acknowledged that, while many could speak Slovak, "you have been deprived of the opportunity to learn to read and write in Slovak." See also ibid., 29 March 1928, 7 January 1935; *Jaro*, 30 January 1935. For latter-day evidence about language usage, see S. C. (Slovak), interviewed 13 February 1977; J. H. (Slovak), interviewed 14 June 1976; A. L. (Slovak), interviewed 12 May 1976; S. V. (Slovak), interviewed 28 May 1976, all in EFOHP.

24. *Jaro*, 18 January 1928.

25. *KM*, 25 February 1931.

26. Derived from *Jednota*, 15 March 1933. On early-twentieth-century Slovak schools without Slovak teachers, see, Alexander, *Immigrant Church and Community*, 121–25.

27. *Jednota*, 1 February 1928.

28. *Jaro*, 21 March 1928.

29. *NN*, 7 February 1934.

30. *Jaro*, 23 May 1928.

31. *Furdek*, December 1932. In October 1930, *Furdek* reversed its policy against English.

32. *KM*, 25 November and 25 December 1932, 25 January–25 December 1933.

33. Ibid., 25 March 1930; see also ibid., 25 October 1930; Memorandum to President Roosevelt, 23 May 1934, in Minutes of Annual Convention, LPSCU Records, reel 3.

34. Fishman and Nahirny ("Organizational and Leadership Interest," 184) allege that "knowledge of the ethnic mother tongue is positively related to organizational involvement." Earlier in their discussion they note the qualification that there were instances of "unaffiliated children" who had mastered the ethnic tongue and of "affiliated children" who had not; however, these do not, they assert, constitute the common "relationship between the variables": ibid., 179.

35. *NN*, 23 April 1930.

36. After about 1933, these terms appeared regularly in a wide range of Slovak publications.

37. A. M. Palkovič, "Greetings from the President," in SCS, *Sborník* (Almanac) *1933*, 151–55, quotes on 151, 154 (emphasis added), 155.

38. *SH*, 9 April 1936.

39. *Jednota*, 17 March 1926; *NN*, 27 June 1928.

40. *NN*, 11 September 1929.

41. *SH*, 28 August 1924; *Jednota*, 7 September 1927; *Jaro*, 18 January 1928; NSS Records, box 4, folders D, E/F.

42. It is difficult to determine the exact number of youth memberships. A few organizations did not have separate youth divisions, and others either reported aggregate membership numbers or did not regularly report youth membership figures. The estimate here is based on membership in the FCSU,

SEU, NSS, and LPSCU and scattered references to membership figures for the SELU and Živena.

43. *NN,* 20 March 1929.

44. Correspondence: Supreme Secretary [Michal] Simko, FCSU Records, box 113, folder 1303; NSS Records, box 4, folders B, D, E/F, H/I/J, K/L, M. People seeking information about establishing an adult lodge were told that they should also simultaneously establish an affiliated youth branch: see, for example, Michal Simko to J. P., 12 March 1924, FCSU Records, box 113, folder 1303.

45. For example, *Jednota,* 11 January 1928; *NN,* 13 June 1928, 20 March 1929, 24 September 1930.

46. *NN,* 19 June 1929. On turn-of-the-century to prewar rhetoric to attract new members, see Alexander, *Immigrant Church and Community,* 18–24.

47. For example, *NN,* 1 August 1928, 9 January and 17 July 1929, 26 February 1930; *SH,* 8 October 1925; *Jednota,* 13 July 1927.

48. T. P. to M. Laučik, 21 May 1925, NSS Records, box 4, folder P/Q.

49. Š. E. to Michal Laučik, 9 August 1927, NSS Records, box 4, folder E/F.

50. For example, *Jednota,* 7 September 1927.

51. *NN,* 27 June 1928.

52. Ibid., 24 July 1929.

53. See *SH,* 1919–1931 (membership statistics were normally published in a spring issue of the paper); "Dejiny I.K.S.J. v náčrte" (A history of the FCSU in brief), *KJ,* 1940, 55; NSS, *Dejiny a Pamätnica,* 214.

54. *Jednota,* 26 March 1919.

55. Ibid., 26 July 1922. Lizabeth Cohen notes that, in the 1920s, Chicago's ethnic groups were also sponsoring their own athletics to counter those being organized by the YMCA and other groups. Based on Cohen's sources, it appears that Chicago's ethnic groups were promoting athletics traditionally linked to their culture: see Cohen, *Making a New Deal,* 55; see also John Daniels, *America via the Neighborhood* (New York: Harper and Brothers, 1920), 126–33.

56. Slovak sokols in Duquesne and McKees Rocks, Pennsylvania, had teams by 1922. These teams announced they were playing "Slovak" and non-Slovak teams. In 1922, going to play the best team in South Bethlehem, Pennsylvania, during the sokol convention, Duquesne challenged baseball teams in the Johnstown area to play. Since the announcement appeared in *Jednota,* the team was clearly directing its challenge to "Slovak" teams in the area: see *Jednota,* 30 August 1922, for the quote; see also ibid., 26 July and 16 August 1922; *Sborník Rímsko a Grécko Katolíckej Telocvičnej Slovenskej Jednoty,* 1922 (Almanac of the Roman and Greek Catholic Gymnastic Union), 122.

57. *Jednota,* 16 April 1924.

58. Ibid., 15 July 1931. The founding date is based on a reference to the team's having been organized six years earlier.

59. *Jaro,* 18 April 1928; *Jednota,* 30 May 1928.

60. *Jednota,* 13 April 1927.

61. *NN,* 9 October 1929.

62. *Jednota,* 22 October 1930.

63. Ibid., 21 September 1927.

64. *NN,* 15 October 1930.

65. Ibid., 9 October 1929.
66. *Jaro,* 18 April 1928.
67. Ibid., 18 January 1928.
68. *SH,* 11 April 1929.
69. *Jaro,* 22 May 1929.
70. *NN,* 29 August 1928; *Jednota,* 23 April 1930, 8 July 1931.
71. *Jednota,* 12 March 1930.
72. *SH,* 14 March, 11 April, and 9 May 1929.
73. Ibid., 9 May 1929.
74. "Constitution of Western Pennsylvania Jednota Baseball League (adopted 5 June 1931)," Slovak Collection, IHRC. The league included teams from industrial towns (McKees Rocks, Duquesne, Clairton, Donora, Homestead, and Ford City) in the Pittsburgh area but none from the Steel City.
75. Edward Minarcak, "The Steady Expansion of Baseball Activities in the Jednota," *KJ,* 1933, 83–87.
76. A Raritan, New Jersey, team made the total number of teams belonging to the eastern Pennsylvania league twenty-three: see ibid., 83–85, 87–88; correspondence from tajmoník Okresu Štefan Furdek to Ročnej Schôdze, IKSJ, 16 January 1932, FCSU Records, box 120, folder 1392.
77. Zápisnica II Ročnej Schôdze, Hl. Odboru NSS po XV konvencu (Minutes of the second annual meeting of the Supreme Branch of the NSS following the 15th convention), published in *NN,* 8 August 1928. See ibid., 24 October 1928, 29 September 1931. Peter Rachleff discusses the promotion of athletics by Croatian fraternal organizations but suggests the impetus there came from the national leadership. He also indicates that promoting athletics and other social activities encountered opposition from the first generation: see his "Class, Ethnicity, and the New Deal," 98–101.
78. Published in *SH,* 3 October 1929.
79. Minarcak, "Steady Expansion," 83–85; *NN,* 5 and 12 April 1933; *KM,* 25 June 1933; FCSU Records, box 120, folder 1393; Podkrivacky Papers, box 18.
80. "[FCSU] Report: Teams Active in Baseball and Basketball and Softball, 1935," FCSU Papers, box 127, folder 1519 (hereafter, "FCSU Report, 1935"); Edward Minarcak, "Jednota Athletic Review of 1937," *KJ,* 1938, 193, 195, 198, 201. "Independent" FCSU lodge teams were affiliated with local Catholic, city, regional, or church leagues. They played Slovak and non-Slovak teams in their divisions. By 1936, the NSS also had a regular athletics director and was sponsoring a national tournament: see *NN,* 13 May 1936.
81. "FCSU Report, 1935."
82. *SH,* 15 May 1930, 22 January and 5 February 1931. The districts were Pittsburgh, Cleveland, and Michigan. Pittsburgh and Cleveland each had six teams; the newspaper did not report the number of teams in Michigan: see article submitted by the "Commissioner and National President SEU Young People's Association," ibid., 20 October 1932.
83. *KM,* 25 November 1933.
84. "FCSU Report, 1935." FCSU activities also included golf and a few "lesser sports maneuvers." However, as a review of 1938 indicated in a subheading, "Baseball Remains King in Jednota Sports": see Minarcak, "Jednota

Athletic Review," 193–205; Edward Minarcak, "Presents a Review of the 1938 Jednota Athletic Program," *KJ*, 1939, 223–31, quotes on 223; idem, "Review of 1939," *KJ*, 1940, 87–95. The SEU had twenty basketball, baseball, and mushball teams affiliated with its districts; it also had thirteen bowling teams: see *SH*, 16 November 1939.

85. *SH*, 3 June 1937.

86. Ibid., 19 October 1939. Other organizations also promoted bowling: see "[FCSU] Report: Teams Active in Baseball, Basketball, Softball, Bowling, 1939," FCSU Records, box 127, folder 1520; Minarcak, "Presents a Review," 230.

87. *NN*, 4 March 1936.

88. *Jednota*, 10 May 1933.

89. *SH*, 14 March 1929.

90. *NN*, 26 July 1933.

91. *Jednota*, 21 March 1934.

92. *KM*, 25 July 1933; *SH*, 7 March 1929, 15 January 1931, June–September 1932; *NN*, 12 October 1938; "FCSU Report, 1935"; Jack McCallum and Chuck Bednarik, *Bednarik: Last of the Sixty-Minute Men* (Englewood Cliffs, N.J.: Prentice-Hall, 1977), 41. Bednarik was a second-generation Slovak who identified himself as a Slovak. He opted to play with a mixed team because it included "buddies" with whom he went to school or who lived near him. According to Bednarik, he was queried about why he did not play on a Slovak sokol team. Clearly, the second-generation youths who played on the area Slovak sokol teams identified themselves as Slovak and emphasized playing for a "Slovak" team.

93. Since parishes, schools, sokols, and local branches of national organizations had teams, there is no way to determine how many Slovak sports teams existed. Nevertheless, the number was much higher than the official statistics of the national organizations. Information on local athletic teams is confined to parish and school jubilee histories, and often these publications have only short, celebratory descriptions. Even scholarly studies of Slovak communities reflect the celebratory style of jubilee books, mention local teams only in passing, and fail to provide solid information: see, for example, M. Mark Stolarik, *Growing Up on the South Side: Three Generations of Slovaks in Bethlehem, Pennsylvania, 1880–1976* (Lewisburg, Penn.: Bucknell University Press, 1985), 84–87; Joseph Semancik, "Slovaks," in *Peopling Indiana: The Ethnic Experience*, ed. Robert M. Taylor, Jr., and Connie A. McBirney (Indianapolis: Indiana Historical Society, 1996), 526.

94. *SH*, 7 February 1929, 2 January and 8 October 1936.

95. "The Constitution, By-Laws and the Essential Rules of the Slovak Evangelical Union Young People's Association of the United States of America," *SH*, 9 November 1933. This association was established to promote and oversee SEU athletic activities. The FCSU's 1931 convention established a fund to support youth athletics; see "Zpráva výboru sokolstva, atleticky a mládeže KJ" (Report of the committee on sokol members, athletes and youth Jednota), *Jednota*, 30 December 1931; see also ibid., 3 February 1932. The NSS sponsored teams and leagues but did not establish a national financial-support system until 1938: see *NN*, 24 October 1928, 23 September 1931, 4 January 1933; NSS, *Dejiny a Pamätnica*, 149.

96. FCSU Papers, box 120, folders 1392, 1393; ibid., box 127, folders 1518, 1520; Podkrivacky Papers, box 18; *Jednota,* 5 July 1933.

97. Minarcak, "Jednota Athletic Review," 193. For pictures of sporting events that depict the large number of spectators, see idem, "Sketching the 1936 Jednota Sport Enterprise," *KJ,* 1937, 193–98.

98. *Jednota,* 12 December 1934.

99. See, for example, pictures of girls' teams in SCS, *Sborník 1933,* 150–62 passim.

100. J. M. to Brat [brother] Prusak, 19 September 1931, Podkrivacky Papers, box 18.

101. Kenneth Baka, "The First Catholic Slovak Ladies Association: A History," in *Slovaks in America: A Bicentennial Study,* comps. Joseph C. Krajsa et al. (Middletown, Penn.: Jednota Slovak American Publishing House, 1978), 174.

102. *Furdek,* June 1930. Throughout the 1930s, sokol publications carried stories featuring female or male and female teams. Females participated in local and national competitions.

103. *Jednota,* 27 June 1934.

104. *SH,* 30 October and 7 November 1929, 2 January 1936, 31 March 1938, 4 May 1939, 27 March 1941.

105. For example, *NN,* 3 June 1936; *KM,* 15 April 1927. The first female section that appeared in this NSS youth publication consisted of recipes. By 1929, the girls' page was sporadic, but the content still typically featured items focusing on the domestic arts.

106. *NN,* 25 March 1931.

107. *SH,* 5 April and 10 May 1928.

108. *NN,* 31 August 1938. There were other jewelry and domestic-style prizes for those who placed lower. These prizes included a wristwatch, a gold ring with the NSS emblem, a coffee percolator, a chime clock, and a set of silverware. The LPSCU offered cash prizes to its members: see LPSCU Records, 1934 ad, book 3, reel 1.

109. *SH,* 7 May 1936.

110. *NN,* 2 August 1933.

Chapter Seven

1. Thomas Bell, *Out of This Furnace* (New York: Little, Brown, 1941), 269.

2. Thomas R. Supe, "Let Us Honor and Respect the Traditions of Our Ancestors," *NN,* 18 March 1931.

3. Both John J. Bukowczyk (*And My Children Did not Know Me: A History of Polish-Americans* [Bloomington: Indiana University Press, 1987], 79) and Caroline Golab ("Stellaaaaaa. . . . . . ! ! ! ! ! ! ! !: The Slavic Stereotype in American Film," in *The Kaleidoscopic Lens: How Hollywood Views Ethnic Groups,* ed. Randall M. Miller [Englewood, N.J.: Jerome S. Ozer, Publisher, 1980], 139, 141) erroneously describe the Joe Radek character as Polish. In 1966, when Michael A. Musmanno finally published *Black Fury* (New York: Fountainhead Publishers), the lead character, Jan Volkanik, was born in Poland. The 1935 movie, however, was based on a narrative Warner Brothers acquired from Musmanno in 1934 (*Black*

Fury, 373). The character Muni portrayed in the film was Slovak, and the film audience did hear Muni speak Slovak.

4. *Jednota,* 12 December 1934. The reviewer gave the title of this upcoming "Purely Slovak" movie as "Black Hell."

5. Ibid., 17 April 1935; *SH,* 18 April 1935; *NN,* 10 and 17 April 1935.

6. *NYT,* 11 April 1935.

7. *NN,* 3 and 24 July 1935; *Jednota,* 3 and 17 July 1935.

8. Quote from *Jednota,* 1 October 1919; see also ibid., 24 September 1919; *SH,* 25 September 1919; June Granatir Alexander, "Ethnic Fraternalism and Working-Class Activism: The Expanding Role of Slovak Fraternal Organizations in the United States during the Interwar Years," in *Etnični fraternalizem v priseljenskih deželah* (Ethnic fraternalism in immigrant countries), ed. Matjaž Klemenčič (Maribor, Slovenia: University of Maribor, 1996). In a subsequently published article, M. Mark Stolarik echoes the conclusion that organizations supported the strike: see his "Slovak Americans in the Great Steel Strike," *Pennsylvania History* 64 (Summer 1997): 407–18.

9. Given the stipulations for using these sources, the names of individual writers and recipients of letters found in manuscript collections will not be given unless the individuals involved were national officers. Each letter will be identified by date and by the community from which it was sent. Conclusions about Slovak participation in strikes and fraternal support for them are based on J. S. to John Sabol, 13 December 1927, FCSU Records, box 120 folder 1396; and reports, editorials, and other items that regularly appeared in *Jednota,* 1921–1929; *NN,* 1921–1929; and *SH,* 1921–1929. In 1920, the leadership of the SEU maintained that strikes hurt many people and that there must be a better way to improve the situation for "the working class." By 1922, the SEU offered full support for strikes, especially in the mining industry: see *SH,* 16 September 1920, May–August 1922, 7 March 1925; Alexander, "Ethnic Fraternalism," 163–65.

10. *Jednota,* 18 April 1928. Names of donors typically appeared weekly in *Jednota.*

11. For example, *NN,* 14 March 1928; see also, for example, *SH,* 5 April 1928.

12. *Jednota,* 24 October 1928. The committee was mandated to help all members who were "unemployed" because of the strike or for other reasons.

13. Ibid., 24 October 1928, 13 and 27 February 1929.

14. Ibid., 24 October 1928.

15. Ibid., 20 March 1929. Another writer declared that 95 percent of all Slovaks were workers: ibid., 4 December 1929.

16. *NN,* 22 January 1930.

17. *Jednota,* 6 April 1927; *NN,* 8 August 1928.

18. *Historical Statistics of the United States: Colonial Times to 1957* (Washington, D.C., 1961), 73.

19. *SH,* 1934–1935 (membership statistics were normally published in the paper's spring issue); "Dejiny I.K.S.J. v náčrte," 55; NSS, *Dejiny a Pamätnica,* 214. Smaller organizations obviously declined as well: see, Supreme Officers Meeting, minutes, 21 January 1935, LPSCU Records, reel 2.

20. Slovak organizations did establish plans to keep members from being expelled, but people had to draw on a policy's reserve value. Organizations also

modified rules to let delinquents rejoin within specified time periods if they fully paid past dues. However, "The rules are the rules," FCSU President Adam Podkrivacky told one member of more than thirty years whose delinquency made him ineligible for sick benefits, "and there are no exceptions": see his letter sent to Iselin, Pennsylvania, 9 January 1932, Podkrivacky Papers, box 18.

21. FCSU Records, box 125, folder 1469. The request was denied.

22. Ibid.

23. Homestead, Pennsylvania, 5 January 1933, FCSU Records, folder 1468.

24. Apparently, the family had depleted the death benefits it had received when the husband died: see FSCU Records, folder 1481.

25. Ibid., folder 1482.

26. NSS Records, box 4, folder S; Podkrivacky Papers, box 18. As president of the FCSU, Podkrivacky received numerous letters asking him to intervene on someone's behalf. The vast majority of this correspondence is for 1932.

27. Mammoth, Pennsylvania, 16 January 1933, FCSU Records, box 125, folder 1469. The perennial problem of delinquent dues and the constant appeals for assistance local officers addressed throughout the 1930s were recorded in the minute book of a NSS Assembly in Alverton, Pennsylvania. See Record Book [Minutes], NSS odbor 107, 1 November 1925–11 October 1951, NSS Records, box 172; see also Finance Committee Meeting, minutes, 16 July 1935, LPSCU Records, reel 2.

28. NN, 13 January 1933, 11 April 1934. For representative examples of the sundry correspondence, see letters from Houtzdale, Pennsylvania, 8 October 1932, Čislo 95, 15 January 1932, and Connellsville, Pennsylvania, 24 August 1932, to Adam Podkrivacky, and Adam Podkrivacky to Ján Sabol, 2 October 1931, in Podkrivacky Papers, box 18; letter to Supreme Officers in Newton Falls, Ohio, 18 December 1932, FCSU Records, box 124, folder 1467; Uniontown, Pennsylvania, 19 February 1932, NSS Records, box 4, folder D; Sprava Hlavného Podpredsedu I.K.S.J (1933) (Report of the supreme vice-president of the FCSU), FCSU Records, box 125, folder 1473.

29. Detroit, 17 December 1932, FCSU Records, box 124, folder 1467.

30. The lament "through no fault of my own" was common in letters from ordinary people to both Franklin and Eleanor Roosevelt: see Robert S. McElvaine, ed., Down and Out in the Great Depression: Letters from the "Forgotten Man" (Chapel Hill: University of North Carolina Press, 1983).

31. Dennica, 15 November 1932.

32. FCSU Records, box 124, folder 1467.

33. Detroit, 17 December 1932, ibid. Numerous similar letters are contained in folders filed in FCSU Records, boxes 124 and 125.

34. Natrona, Pennsylvania, 9 January 1933, FCSU Records, box 125, folder 1468.

35. NN, 21 January 1931. For another representative example of regular appeals in the Slovak press, see ibid., 5 November 1930.

36. FCSU Records, box 125, folder 1468.

37. Nemacolin, Pennsylvania, 30 December 1932, FCSU Records, box 124, folder 1467.

38. Mammoth, Pennsylvania, 16 January 1933, FCSU Records, box 125, folder 1469.

39. Canton, Ohio, 25 January 1935, FCSU Records, box 126, folder 1482.

40. Rankin, Pennsylvania, 1934(?), FCSU Records, box 126, folder 1489. The single-word name for the FCSU was "Jednota," which was "union" in Slovak. A member of the FCSU thus was often referred to as a "Jednotar."

41. FCSU Records, box 126, folder 1481.

42. Uniontown, Pennsylvania, 9 January 1933, FCSU Records, box 125, folder 1468.

43. J. F. to Adam Podkrivacky, 17 September 1932, Podkrivacky Papers. J. F. was conveying the position of one elderly lodge member who was demanding some assistance.

44. FCSU Records, box 125, folder 1468.

45. Č[islo] 7 of Houtzdale, Pennsylvania, to Adam Podkrivacky, 8 October 1932, Podkrivacky Papers.

46. Nemacolin, Pennsylvania, 30 December 1932, FCSU Records, box 124, folder 1467. Similar sentiments were expressed in Starford, Pennsylvania, 24 October 1932, Podkrivacky Papers.

47. For similar letters from ordinary Americans expressing the same sentiments evident in the Slovak letters, see McElvaine, *Down and Out*. For firsthand reports on the everyday experiences of ordinary Americans, see Richard Lowitt and Maurine Beasley, eds., *One Third of a Nation: Lorena Hickock Reports on the Great Depression* (Urbana: University of Illinois Press, 1981). See also John F. Bauman and Thomas H. Coode, *In the Eye of the Great Depression: New Deal Reporters and the Agony of the American People* (DeKalb: Northern Illinois University Press, 1988).

48. 1932 National Slovak Day, *Souvenir Program*; 1933 Slovak National Day, *Souvenir Program*; 1933 Catholic Slovak Day, *Souvenir Program*; *Jednota*, 9 May 1934, 4 September 1935, 14 July 1937; *NN*, 15 and 22 August 1934. It would thus be rash to expand Lizabeth Cohen's description of the fund-raising objectives of Chicago's 1934 Slovak Catholic day as representative of Slovak Catholic days during the Depression: see her *Making a New Deal*, 221. Some Slovak parishes in America engaged in philanthropic activities such as running soup kitchens and providing food, but their activities, which must have been limited, were not well documented.

49. *SH*, 14 April 1932.

50. *NN*, 18 November and 16 December 1931, 23 and 30 November 1932, 28 August 1935, 9 December 1936. A "Milodar" (donation) list, as well as handwritten and typed rosters prepared by the Výbor Žiadosty a Prosieb (Committee on Petitions and Requests), are in FCSU Records, box 125, folder 1470. Beginning with the 28 June 1933 issue of *NN* and continuing until 9 August 1933, the lists of recipients of NSS funds were published weekly. See also SEU, "Zpráva výboru žiadostí a sťažností" (Report of the petition and grievance committee), *SH*, 18 February 1932.

51. William E. Leuchtenburg, *Franklin D. Roosevelt and the New Deal* (New York: Harper and Row, 1963), 122–24; David M. Kennedy, *Freedom from Fear: The*

American People in Depression and War, 1929–1945 (New York: Oxford University Press, 1999), 176–77.

52. Arthur M. Schlesinger, Jr., *The Coming of the New Deal* (Boston: Houghton Mifflin, 1958), 303; U.S. Congress, House, 73rd Cong., 1st Sess., H.R. 7598, *Congressional Record*, 78:1895.

53. Leuchtenburg, *Roosevelt*, 103–6; Kennedy, *Freedom from Fear*, 224–25; Alan Brinkley, *Voices of Protest: Huey Long, Father Coughlin, and the Great Depression* (New York: Knopf, 1982), 222–26.

54. Brinkley, *Voices of Protest*; David H. Bennett, *Demagogues in the Depression: American Radicals and the Union Party, 1932–1936* (New Brunswick, N.J.: Rutgers University Press, 1969). For a contemporary elderly American's view, see McElvaine, *Down and Out*, 103–4.

55. An unsigned standard letter of reply, NSS Records, box 7. The LPSCU developed similar plans, especially for older members; see Finance Committee Meeting, minutes, 31 January and 26 October 1933, LPSCU Records, reel 4; Minutes 20th Convention, 21–26 May 1934, LPSCU Records, reel 3; Supreme Officers Annual Meeting, minutes, 21 January 1935, LPSCU Records, reel 2.

56. Third Special Convention (1934), Resolution, NSS Records, Box 7.

57. *NN*, 23 May 1934.

58. Ibid., 6 June 1934. The LPSCU was simultaneously dealing with the same ongoing membership issues but did not discuss social-insurance legislation: see Finance Committee Meeting, minutes, 20 February 1935, LPSCU Records, reel 4.

59. Samuel I. Rosenman, comp., *The Public Papers and Addresses of Franklin D. Roosevelt*, 13 vols. (New York: Random House, Macmillan [vols. 6–9], Harper and Brothers [vols. 10–13], 1938–1950), 3:291–92, 3:321–22, quotes on 291. On Roosevelt's established position on social insurance, see Frances Perkins, *The Roosevelt I Knew* (New York: Viking, 1946), 278–79.

59. Rosenman, *Public Papers*, 3:321–22.

60. *NN*, 25 July 1934.

61. *Congressional Record*, 78:1895, 79:4970. There is no credible evidence that Lundeen was a member of the Communist Party: cf. Schlesinger, *Coming of the New Deal*, 296, and Harvey Klehr, *The Heyday of American Communism: The Depression Decade* (New York: Basic Books, 1984), 289.

62. Klehr, *Heyday*, 49–52, 283–89.

63. The most conveniently available printing of the Lundeen bill is in *Congressional Record*, 79:4970–71.

64. *NN*, 31 October 1934.

65. Ibid., 25 July, 19 September, and 17 October 1934; *SH*, 6 September 1934; *Jednota*, 17 October and 14 November 1934.

66. *Jednota*, 14 November 1934.

67. *NN*, 19 September and 17 October 1934.

68. Some left-wing Slovak groups did not support the Lundeen bill. In 1935, Slovak socialists in Chicago printed a history of Slovaks in America and, offering radical solutions to the workers' plight, found the Lundeen bill wanting. See *Slováci v Amerike* (Slovaks in America) (Chicago: Slovak Progressive Printing Association, 1935).

69. *NN,* 10 October 1934; *Jednota,* 17 October 1934.

70. While the FCSLU vice-president announced that the FCSLU endorsed the bill, no published statements verify that. Živena publicized its endorsement of the Lundeen bill in *NN,* 20 March 1935.

71. Ibid., 10 October 1934.

72. See, for example, ibid., 17 October 1934; *Jednota,* 14 November 1934; *SH,* 13 December 1934.

73. *NN,* 12 December 1934; *SH,* 13 December 1934; *Jednota,* 12 December 1934, 9 January 1935. The 9 January 1935 issue of *Jednota* printed a report on the 20 December 1934 meeting called to select delegates.

74. *NN,* 2 January 1935. By 1934, the NSS had chartered 799 local assemblies, so this represented at least 50 percent of its lodges.

75. *SH,* 10 January and 7 February 1935; *NN,* 23 January and 6 February 1935.

76. *NN,* 6 February, 20 March, and 10 April 1935; *SH,* 14 February 1935. Arthur J. Altmeyer, *The Formative Years of Social Security* (Madison: University of Wisconsin Press, 1966), 28–29; Perkins, *The Roosevelt I Knew;* 296–97; *Congressional Record,* 79:4971.

77. *NN,* 6 February, 20 March, and 10 April 1935; *SH,* 14 February 1935.

78. *NN,* 20 March 1935.

79. Ibid., 3, 10, and 24 April, 15 May 1935; *SH,* 25 April 1935.

80. *Jednota,* 13 March 1935; *NN,* 3 April 1935. As a result of the NSS's vigorous activities supporting the Lundeen bill, the chairman of a congressional subcommittee invited the society to send representatives to testify at congressional hearings: see Matthew A. Dunn, chairman, Sub-Committee of the House Labor Committee, to NSS, January 1935, as reprinted in *NN,* 1 May 1935.

81. Ibid.

82. Altmeyer, *Formative Years,* 3–4, 29, 37–42.

83. For example, *NN,* 21 August 1935, 12 and 26 August, 12 September, 14 and 21 October 1936.

84. Once the Social Security bill was enacted, this was the typical response by working-class Americans: see Cohen, *Making a New Deal,* 272.

85. "To Victory in the Fight for Bread and Justice," *Jednota,* 13 March 1935.

86. Letter to Senator Robert Wagner, 9 February 1935, and accompanying "Resolution of the Supreme Officers of the First Catholic Slovak Union," FCSU Records, box 126, folder 1484. Copies of the resolution were also sent to Senator Pat Harrison, chairman of the Senate Finance Committee, and to the House Ways and Means Committee. In both documents, the officers carefully noted that this endorsement was being made by the FCSU's "Supreme Officers."

87. *Jednota,* 19 September 1934. Cf. *NN,* 10 October 1934; *Jednota,* 17 October 1934. Tellingly, the *Jednota* version of a report on one public affair deleted a synopsis of comments by the Slovak IWO speaker as well as the meeting's resolution calling for all Slovak lodges in the region to form a federation. Materials submitted to official organs were most likely scrutinized by editors and possibly rejected or altered.

88. Michal Laučik, "Problémy, jakým dnes čelia bratské podporné organizácie" (The kind of problems support societies are contending with today), *NK,* 1935, 34–41; *NN,* 20 March 1935.

89. *NN*, 1 August 1934.

90. Ibid., 14 August 1935.

91. *Dennica*, 20 March 1935.

92. Klehr, *Heyday*, 162–65; Harvey Klehr and John Earl Haynes, *The American Communist Movement: Storming Heaven Itself* (New York: Twayne Publishers, 1992), 74–75.

93. Klehr, *Heyday*, 87, 166, 232, 284, 384–85. For a description and brief history of the IWO, see Roger Keeran, "National Groups and the Popular Front: The Case of the International Workers Order," *JAEH* 14 (Spring 1995): 23–51; *NN*, 10 October 1934, 3 April 1935.

94. Perkins, *The Roosevelt I Knew*, 215–21.

95. *Jednota*, 9 August 1933. One sentence of this English-language resolution stated, "bestowing signal recognition and honor on all people of Slovak birth"; the second reference stated, "heartfelt gratitude for the signal recognition and honor bestowed upon all Slovaks." Although the published resolution used "signal" twice, the authors probably meant "single" or "singular."

CHAPTER EIGHT

1. *SH*, 9 and 30 April, 7 May, 16 and 23 July 1942; *NN*, 24 June 1942.

2. *NN*, 14 May 1941; *SH*, 14 May 1942. Although the Slovak press earlier mentioned "I Am an American" days, it was in 1943 that President Roosevelt proclaimed a national day: see Lawrence R. Samuel, *Pledging Allegiance: American Identity and the Bond Drive of World War II* (Washington, D.C.: Smithsonian Institution, 1997), 114.

3. Derived from U.S. Department of Commerce, Bureau of the Census, *Sixteenth Census of the United States: 1940 Population Nativity and Parentage of the White Population Mother Tongue* (Washington, D.C., 1943), 7, 35, 37–38. Census statistics were based on a 5 percent sample. The total number of Slovak Americans was recorded as 484,360. Based on data by "mother tongue," the numbers were: foreign born, 171,589; native born, 321,780; native born of native parentage, 29,560. The second generation total is most likely an undercount because in 1940 the census changed the definition of "mother tongue." Instead of using procedures from earlier censuses and defining mother tongue as the language spoken by the parents, it was defined as "the principal language spoken in the home of the person in his earliest childhood." This change probably also largely explains the 17 percent decline between the 1920 and 1940 tallies of second-generation Slovaks: ibid., 51.

4. Following a speech by Hitler in February 1938 where he declared Germany's commitment to defending Germans in Austria and Czechoslovakia, *NN* (23 February 1938) instituted a "zo Slovenska" (from Slovakia) column. In September 1938, representatives of the NSS, Slovak Gymnastic Union Sokol of America, SEU, and Živena sent a telegram to the secretary of state. "As Americans of Slovak birth or ancestry," they told Secretary Hull that "Czechoslovakia must not be sacrificed on the altar of European Militaristic expediency": see appeal to Cordell Hull, 23 September 1938, NSS Records, box 168, folder "Americanism."

5. See, for example, *NN*, 19 October 1938; see also *SH*, 5 and 12 October 1938. For a Catholic view, see, for example, *Jednota*, 5 October 1938, and especially the youth section, *Jaro*, 5 October 1938.

6. On the Sudetenland problem, the Munich Agreement, and Slovak autonomy, see Felak, *"At the Price of the Republic,"* 205–8; Keith Eubank, "Munich," in *A History of the Czechoslovak Republic, 1918–1948*, ed. Victor S. Mamatey and Radomír Luža (Princeton, N.J.: Princeton University Press, 1973), 239–52; Jörg K. Hoensch, "The Slovak Republic, 1939–1945," in ibid., 271–74; William V. Wallace, *Czechoslovakia* (Boulder, Colo.: Westview Press, 1976), 190–218; Dorothea H. El Mallakh, *The Slovak Autonomy Movement, 1935–1939: A Study in Unrelenting Nationalism* (Boulder, Colo.: East European Monographs, 1979), 86–129.

7. Kirschbaum, *History of Slovakia*, 181–83, 186, 190–91.

8. NSS Records, box 168, folder "Slovak League of America"; *Jednota*, 1920–1937; *NN*, 1920–1937; *SH*, 1920–1937; *Dennica*, 1924–1931, 1932–1933, 1935–1937; *Resolution [to President Herbert Hoover] Accepted at Slovak Day July 20, 1930 Coliseum—Chicago* (Chicago: Mally Press, 1930).

9. See, for example, *SH*, 3 and 17 November 1938, January–June 1939. In 1933, Milan Getting had published extracts from papers allegedly documenting the close ties between Catholic priests and Hungary: see Getting, *Americkí Slováci*, 288–94.

10. *Jednota*, 12 and 26 October 1938; *Jaro*, 12 and 19 October, 30 November 1938; Carol Skalnik Leff, *National Conflict in Czechoslovakia: The Making and Remaking of a State, 1918–1987* (Princeton, N.J.: Princeton University Press, 1988), 153.

11. See, for example, *NN*, 12 October, 23 and 30 November, 14 and 21 December 1938, 4 January and 15 February 1939; *Dennica*, 5 and 20 October 1938, November 1938–January 1939 passim.

12. *Jednota*, 7 June and 23 August 1939.

13. See, for example, ibid., 22 March and 19 April 1939; *Jaro*, 29 March, 17 and 12 April, 31 May 1939. *Jednota* carried Tiso's message in its 7 June 1939 issue; the constitution appeared in the 23 August 1939 issue.

14. *NN*, 15 March 1939; *SH*, 23 March 1939. The claim that Tiso was selling out to Hungary was unfair: see Kirschbaum, *History of Slovakia*, 190–91.

15. On the emotional power of homeland issues across generations, see Matthew Frye Jacobson, *Special Sorrows: The Diasporic Imagination of Irish, Polish, and Jewish Immigrants in the United States* (Cambridge, Mass.: Harvard University Press, 1995), esp. 217–43.

16. See, for example, *Jaro*, 22 and 29 March, 14 June 1939.

17. *SH*, 8 February 1940. As early as December 1938, Lutherans were claiming that Jews were being persecuted in Czechoslovakia: ibid., 8 December 1938, 26 January 1939. See also *NN*, 4 January 1939.

18. See esp. *SH*, 8 December 1938, 26 January, 27 July, 31 August, and 28 September 1939.

19. *Jaro*, 17 and 31 May 1939; *NN*, 4 January 1939; see also "Slovak League Congress," *NN*, 19 October 1938.

20. See, for example, *Jednota*, 7 June 1939; *Jaro*, 17 and 31 May 1939. One English-language commentator (*Jaro*, 23 August 1939) referred to Slovaks who

criticized the independent state as "pseudo Slovaks" and implicitly differentiated between them and "true Slovaks."

21. *Jednota,* 17 May 1939.

22. The statement "THIS NEWSPAPER IS FOR THE RESTORATION OF THE FREE AND INDEPENDENT CZECHOSLOVAK REPUBLIC" appeared in every issue from 28 November 1940 through 24 July 1941.

23. For example, *Jednota,* 22 March and 19 April 1939; *Jaro,* 22 March, 31 May 1939; J. M. Gay, "Historické chvíle na Slovensku" (Historical moments in Slovakia), *KJ,* 1940, 97–104; *NN,* 15 and 22 March 1939; *SH,* 23 March 1939.

24. "Slovakia Betrayed," *NN,* 22 March 1939.

25. In the spring and summer of 1939, *NN* and *SH* regularly carried notices about local meetings regarding European affairs. Some were announced as "protest" rallies; others were called to affirm support for a position; some aimed to develop plans to help people in Slovakia; finally, some were merely informational. They also advertised "Czecho-Slovak Days" (spelled both with and without the hyphen), which were arranged in local communities and dedicated to the restoration of Czechoslovakia.

26. *NN,* 29 June 1938; *SH,* 30 June 1938.

27. *Jednota,* 20 and 27 July, 10 August 1938; *Jaro,* 20 July 1938.

28. *Jednota,* 26 July 1939.

29. Ibid., 19 July 1939.

30. Ibid., 5 July, 9 and 23 August 1939.

31. Ibid., 12 and 19 July 1939.

32. Ibid., 7 June 1939.

33. *NN,* 12 and 19 July 1939; *SH,* 27 July 1939; *Jednota,* 7 June 1939.

34. *NN,* 9 August 1939.

35. *SH,* 4 May, 10 August 1939.

36. *NN,* 26 July, 9 August 1939.

37. *SH,* 23 June 1938.

38. *NN,* 26 July 1939.

39. *Jednota,* 2 August 1939.

40. *NN,* 23 August 1939.

41. *Jednota,* 28 September 1938.

42. Ibid., 7 June 1939.

43. Ibid., 14 June 1939.

44. Ibid., 1 May, 24 July, and 14 August 1940.

45. *NN,* 10 July 1940.

46. NSS, *Constitutions and By-laws of the Young Folks' Circle* (Pittsburgh: National Slovak Society, 1941), 3.

47. Address by John A. Willo at the eighteenth annual convention of the NSS in 1941, reprinted as "Our Society . . . Yesterday, Today and Tomorrow," *NK,* 1943, 102–6. He gave practically the same address at an SLA convention: see address to the Twenty-third Congress of the Slovak League, NSS Records, box 168, folder "Slovak League of America." It is likely that Willo also presented this speech or portions of it on other occasions.

48. *NN,* 17 and 31 December 1941, 14 January 1942. Stanley Kirschbaum (*History of Slovakia,* 204) argues that the Slovak state did not formally declare

war on either the United States or Great Britain. He maintains that the claim that Slovakia had made such a declaration was based on a German press report stating that Vojtech Tuka, Slovakia's prime minister, had declared war. However, on 17 December 1941, *NN* did announce that a radio station had reported news of the declaration. Later, *NN* (14 January 1942) reported on a statement by a former Czechoslovak minister to the Czechoslovak Press Bureau (both in exile) denouncing the "declaration by Tiso and Tuka." Regardless of whether Slovakia formally declared war, the Slovak press in America reported that it had, and during the war Slovakia was allied with Germany. Slovaks in America acted on the belief that Slovakia was a nation at war with the Allied Powers.

49. *NN*, 21 January 1942. The motto was "Ja som pyšný, že som Slovák," which translates "I am proud that I am Slovak." Criticism of the league continued: *Slovenská obrana* (*Slovak defense*), 18 May 1943.

50. *NN*, 15 July 1942.

51. Ibid., 17 December 1941. On 12 December 1941, Franklin Roosevelt sent Secretary of State Hull a short memo noting, "I see by tonight's bulletins that the Government of Slovakia has declared the existence of a state of war with the United States." Saying he expected Germany's "other puppet Governments" to do the same, Roosevelt added, "It is my present thought that the United States should pay no attention to any of these declarations of war against us by puppet Governments." Roosevelt wanted Hull to let congressional leaders know his views: See Cordell Hull, *The Memoirs of Cordell Hull*, 2 vols. (New York: Macmillan, 1948), 2:1175–76.

52. *NN*, 21 January 1942.

53. *SH*, 1 October 1942; *NN*, 6 December 1942; World War Resolution, NSS Records, box 168; Senator James J. Davis of Pennsylvania submitting resolutions by Slovak Americans, *Congressional Record*, 88:8851–53.

54. *NN*, 27 August 1941.

55. Resolution of 13 June 1940 passed at the quarterly meeting of the Executive Committee of NSS, NSS Records, box 169, folder "Service Flag Unveiling."

56. *Jaro*, 29 May 1940.

57. Hutchinson, *Legislative History*, 214–58; Robert A. Divine, *American Immigration Policy, 1924–1952* (New Haven, Conn.: Yale University Press, 1957), 92, 104–9. On state registration laws and the impact of the Alien Registration Act of 1940, see Geoffrey Perrett, *Days of Sadness, Years of Triumph: The American People 1939–1945* (New York: Coward, McCann and Geoghegan, 1973), 89–90; NSS Records, box 168, folder "Anti-Alien Legislation in Congress"; *NN*, 9 June 1937, 26 April 1939.

58. John W. Jeffries, *Wartime America: The World War II Home Front* (Chicago: Ivan R. Dee, 1996), 125–26; Perrett, *Days of Sadness*, 98–99; Reed Ueda, "The Changing Path of Citizenship: Ethnicity and Naturalization during World War II," in *The War in American Culture: Society and Consciousness during World War II*, ed. Lewis A. Erenberg and Susan E. Hirsch (Chicago: University of Chicago Press, 1996), 202–3. For a discussion that dismisses any "fear factor" by interpreting increased naturalizations as evidence of the "ethnic workers' desire for integration into American society," see Gerstle, "Working Class," 314. On naturalization during World War II, see Reed Ueda, *Postwar Immigrant America: A Social*

History (Boston: St. Martin's Press, 1994), 124–25, and idem, "Naturalization and Citizenship," *HEAEG*, 747.

59. On ethnic bond drives, see Samuel, *Pledging Allegiance*, 99–123.

60. In August 1942, the SEU passed a resolution encouraging members to give 10 percent of their monthly earnings to war bonds; it promised assemblies and individuals that names of those purchasing bonds would be published in an "Honor Roll": see *SH*, 6 August and 24 September 1942; see also Mikuláš Šprinc, "Slovak League of America and Independent Slovakia," in Paučo, *Sixty Years*, 92–95; V. E. Andic, "American Slovaks at War," *NK*, 1946, 163–67.

61. Andic, "American Slovaks," 155, 159; *Congressional Record*, 89:A5570–71, 90:149–50.

62. Andic, "American Slovaks," 166–67.

63. *SH*, 12 November 1942; *The American Slav* (hereafter, *TAS*), December 1942; Andic, "American Slovaks," 163–67; Samuel, *Pledging Allegiance*, 114–19; Program Committee for Western Pennsylvania Slovak Day, *50th Anniversary American Slovak Day* (Swissvale, Penn.: Krohmaly's Printing, 1973) (hereafter, Western Pennsylvania, *50th Anniversary*).

64. *SH*, 12 November 1942. See also, *The Minute Man* (hereafter, *TMM*), 1 March 1943, 41–42; ibid., 15 May 1943, 23. For descriptions of activities in other communities, see, for example, ibid., 3–4, 23–24; ibid., 1 March 1943, 31; ibid., 1 May 1943, 37–39.

65. Andic, "American Slovaks," 164–65. For efforts during a Slovak Day, see *Slovenská obrana*, 28 July 1944.

66. Andic, "American Slovaks," 163; *TAS*, April 1944. A contributor to the official history of the SLA places the total amount of bond purchases credited to Slovak Americans by October 1944 at approximately $53 million. This total was derived from official reports by the league in 1944: see Šprinc, "Slovak League," 93.

67. Andic, "American Slovaks," 164.

68. The same is true for other nationality groups. See, for example, *TMM*, 1 April 1943, 19; ibid., 1 June 1943, 44–45.

69. Andic, "American Slovaks," 165.

70. *TMM*, 1 March 1943, 7–8; ibid., 1 May 1943, 38–39; ibid., 15 May 1943, 3–4, 45. For commentary noting competition among "foreign origin groups," see, for example, ibid., 1 March 1943, 42.

71. *SH*, 17 September 1942.

72. *TAS*, December 1942.

73. *TMM*, 15 May 1943, cover, 23. *KJ* (1944, 131) reproduced this picture; reproduction also appeared in the unpaginated Western Pennsylvania, *50th Anniversary*, published in 1973.

74. *KJ*, 1944, 124.

75. Andic, "American Slovaks," 166.

76. Ibid.; *TAS*, April 1944; *Jane's Fighting Ships 1946–47* (*corrected to April 1947*) (New York: Macmillan, 1947), 370 ("note" to section on Rudderow Class), 390; *TMM*, 15 May 1943, cover.

77. For example, Andic, "American Slovaks," 166; *KJ*, 1944, 124, 131; *TAS*, December 1942.

78. In his discussion of ethnic bond drives, Lawrence Samuel (*Pledging Allegiance*, 94–119, esp. 118–19) draws the same conclusion about the government's use of ethnicity to promote support for the war effort.

79. *TMM*, 1 March 1943, 31.

80. See, for example, ibid., 1 May 1943, front cover; ibid., 15 May 1943, 23; ibid., 1 June 1943, 44–45. See also ibid., 1 March 1943, 31; Samuel, *Pledging Allegiance*, 114–23; Western Pennsylvania, *50th Anniversary.*

81. Baka, "First Catholic Slovak Ladies Association," 174; Western Pennsylvania, *50th Anniversary.* Samuel does not specifically mention Kuzma, but accompanying pictures (*Pledging Allegiance*, 122) show her as one of five women prominently involved in the Victory Nationality Booth in Homestead.

82. Samuel (*Pledging Allegiance*, 118) draws the similar conclusion that "national and ethnic identity can not only coexist but also be synergistic in expression."

83. Howard F. Stein and Robert F. Hill assert that "fierce American patriotism was the prevailing ideology as ethnic group competed with ethnic group ... to buy more war bonds." Thus, although they dismiss ethnic activities as only competition, they note that individual ethnic groups coalesced to promote the war effort. Rather than disproving the reality of ethnicity as a force, they seem to be confirming its existence: see Stein and Hill, *Ethnic Imperative*, 83.

84. In all likelihood, people who bought bonds as part of an ethnic drive also purchased bonds through employers, through their unions, or in other nonethnic drives. For example, Gerstle describes bond purchases through unions: see his "Working Class," 307–11. See also Richard Polenberg, *War and Society: The United States 1941–1945* (New York: J. B. Lippincott Co., 1972), 30.

85. For example, Cohen, *Making a New Deal*, 249.

86. *NN*, 6 November 1940; "Report of the [FCSU] Sports Director," *Jednota*, 9 October 1940; Edward Minarcik, "1940—Jednota Sports Review," *KJ*, 1941, 185–94.

87. *SH*, 20 November 1941.

88. Ibid., 19 February 1942.

89. *TAS*, June 1942; Jeffries, *Wartime America*, 30.

90. See, for example, *KJ*, 1943, 1944, 1945; SCS, *Sborník Slovenského Katolíckeho Sokola* (Almanac of the SCS), 1943; ibid., 1944; ibid., 1945; *SH*, 11 December 1941, 19 March 1942; *Slovenská obrana*, 18 May 1943, 28 July and 29 August 1944.

91. *NN*, 12 August 1942.

92. *SH*, 23 April 1942.

93. Ibid., 14 May 1942.

94. Ibid., 19 November, 3 and 17 December 1942.

95. McCallum and Bednarik, *Bednarik*, 40–42.

96. Gerstle, "Working Class," 313. Focusing on "ethnic workers," this is Gerstle's description of the impact that the war had on new immigrant generations.

97. This agrees with Philip Gleason's judgment that ethnocentrism was unacceptable but disagrees with his observation that "ethnicity was in fact compromised as a legitimate principle of group cohesiveness": see Gleason, "American Identity," 48.

Conclusion

1. McCallum and Bednarik, *Bednarik*, 31–33, quote on 31.

2. John F. Berko, "Thomas Bell (1903–1961): Slovak-American Novelist," *Slovak Studies* (Cleveland: Slovak Institute, 1975), 148. This is Berko's translation of an interview with Bell published in *Ľudovy denník*, 12 October 1946. June Granatir Alexander, "Thomas Bell," in *Making It in America: A Sourcebook on Eminent Ethnic Americans*, ed. Elliott Robert Barkan (Santa Barbara, Calif.: ABC-CLIO, 2001), 34–35.

3. Bell, *Out of This Furnace*, 410–11. Dobie was the third generation in a Slovak family, but, with a foreign-born father and an American-born mother, he was a second-generation American. For a description that describes him as a "third-generation Slovak," but given modern convention must be interpreted as meaning a third-generation American, see Gerstle, *American Crucible*, 168–69.

4. *St. Anne's Roman Catholic Church ... Golden Jubilee ... 1965* (Swissvale, Penn.: Krohmaly's Printing, 1965); NSS, *Dejiny a Pamätnica*, 196.

5. See, for example, Jacobson, *Special Sorrows.*

6. On intergroup tensions and conflict, see Ronald H. Bayor, *Neighbors in Conflict: The Irish, Germans, Jews, and Italians of New York City, 1929–1941* (Baltimore: Johns Hopkins University Press, 1978).

7. For this interpretation, see Gerstle, *American Crucible*, 168.

8. The weight of the evidence sustains Philip Gleason's argument that World War II accentuated "the ideological basis of American identity": Gleason, "American Identity," 48. It also upholds his observation that the wartime stress on ideology was "the accentuation of one element" in an already-existing "mix of beliefs, attachments, and loyalties": idem, "Americans All," 512. Gleason, though, does downplay the importance of ethnicity as a significant or energizing factor in World War II.

9. For recent scholarship on race, racialism, and "whiteness," see the sources cited in n. 13 of the introduction.

10. Roediger, *Colored White*, 138–68; Jacobson, *Whiteness.*

11. Thomas A. Guglielmo makes the same observation in *White on Arrival: Italians, Race, Color, and Power in Chicago, 1890–1945* (New York: Oxford University Press, 2003), 6.

12. Barrett and Roediger, "Inbetween Peoples," 3–44; see also, Roediger, *Colored White*, 138–68; Robert Orsi, "The Religious Boundaries of an Inbetween People: Street *Feste* and the Problem of the Dark-Skinned 'Other' in Italian Harlem, 1920–1990," *American Quarterly* 44 (September 1992): 313–47.

13. Roediger, *Colored White*, 166. For a different interpretation of contemporary usage, see Jacobson, *Whiteness*, 5–6, 9.

14. Guglielmo offers similar criticisms of "whiteness" studies, but his work appeared too recently to inform this study: see his *White on Arrival*, esp. 9–10.

15. For an excellent critique of "whiteness studies," see Peter Kolchin, "Whiteness Studies: The New History of Race in America," *JAH* 89 (June 2002): 154–73. He makes a similar point about blurring distinctions so that nationality-based antipathies are interpreted in terms of "whiteness." See also Guglielmo, *White on Arrival*, 10.

Index